IN THE INTERESTS OF JUSTICE

IN THE INTERESTS OF JUSTICE

REFORMING THE LEGAL PROFESSION

DEBORAH L. RHODE

OXFORD
UNIVERSITY PRESS

2000

150092

OXFORD
UNIVERSITY PRESS

Oxford   New York
Athens   Auckland   Bangkok   Bogotá   Buenos Aires   Calcutta   Cape Town   Chennai
Dar es Salaam   Delhi   Florence   Hong Kong   Istanbul   Karachi   Kuala Lumpur   Madrid
Melbourne   Mexico City   Mumbai   Nairobi   Paris   São Paulo   Shanghai   Singapore
Taipei   Tokyo   Toronto   Warsaw

and associated companies in
Berlin   Ibadan

Published by Oxford University Press, Inc.
198 Madison Avenue, New York, New York 10016

Oxford is a registered trademark of Oxford University Press

Library of Congress Cataloging-in-Publication Data
Rhode, Deborah L.
    In the interests of justice: reforming the legal profession / Deborah L. Rhode.
       p.   cm.
    Includes index.
    ISBN 0-19-512188-0 (cloth : alk. paper)
    1. Lawyers—United States. 2. Practice of law—United States. I.Title.

KF297 .R48 2000
340'.023'73—dc21
                                                                                      00-021530
9 8 7 6 5 4 3 2 1

Printed in the United States of America
on acid-free paper

For
LAWRENCE M. FRIEDMAN,
ROBERT W. GORDON,
and
WILLIAM H. SIMON

CONTENTS

THREE

FOUR

FIVE

ACKNOWLEDGMENTS

I n a book about justice, it is a daunting challenge to do justice to all those who have enriched and enabled this project. I owe more debts over more years than I can begin to acknowledge here. But some individuals contributed so directly and immeasurably to the final publication that they deserve some special recognition. My editors at Oxford, Thomas Le Bien and Dedi Felman, shaped the project at every stage with enormous insight and good judgment. Many colleagues provided crucial comments: Richard Abel, Barbara Babcock, Paul Brest, Pamela Karlan, Anthony Kronman, Robert Frank, David Luban, Judith Resnik and Paul Tremblay. Stanford librarians, especially Paul Lomio and Erika Wayne, and student research assistants, especially Ryan Fortson, Joshua Klein, and Shawn Vietor, gave tirelessly of their time and talents. My assistant, Mary Tye, suffered through seemingly endless drafts with endless patience, good humor, and good sense.

The book is dedicated to three colleagues who reviewed the entire manuscript and who made it better in more ways than I can ever adequately acknowledge: Lawrence Friedman, Robert Gordon, and William Simon. And had he been willing, this book, like all my work, would also have been dedicated to Ralph Cavanagh. His support and insight are what make everything else possible.

IN THE INTERESTS OF JUSTICE

CHAPTER 1

THE PROFESSION AND THE PUBLIC INTEREST

Lawyers belong to a profession permanently in decline. Or so it appears from the chronic laments by critics within and outside the bar. The profession, we are told, has lost its "fine sense of dignity and honor" and has become "contaminated with the spirit of commerce." That complaint came in 1895, but such sentiments were in ready supply a century earlier and later. Today's conventional wisdom is that the profession is "lost," "betrayed," and "in crisis." Such accounts typically feature wistful references to some hypothesized happier era, in which law was less a business than a calling. But if ever there was a true fall from grace, it must have occurred quite early in the profession's history. Over two thousand years ago, Seneca observed advocates acting as accessories to injustice, "smothered by their prosperity," and Plato condemned their "small and unrighteous souls."[1]

Given this historical context, it is tempting to discount the recent chorus of complaints about the profession as familiar variations on familiar themes. But while the novelty of recent critiques should not be overstated, their significance should not be undervalued. Discontent with legal practice is driven by structural factors that are increasingly difficult to challenge. Some of those factors are specific to the market for legal services, such as the bar's growth in size and competitiveness. Other causes reflect more general cultural trends that are reinforcing commercial priorities and eroding a sense of social obligation. All of these forces are widening the distance between professional ideals and professional practice.

Many lawyers are, in Auden's apt phrase, "trudging in tune to a tidy fortune," but they have lost their connection to the values of social justice that sent them to law in the first place. These problems of professionalism are compounded by problems in the justice system. For the vast majority of Americans, that system seems unwieldy, unintelligible, and unaffordable. The last two decades have reflected an increasing gap between rich and poor and a declining willingness to subsidize assistance for those who can least afford it. These inequalities in legal representation have magnified inequalities in adversarial processes. The result is aptly captured in a New Yorker cartoon picturing a well-heeled lawyer asking his client: "So, Mr. Pitikin, how much justice *can* you afford?"

Yet what is most disheartening about our current plight is the gap between the profession's and the public's perception of the problem and the failure of both groups to confront its underlying causes. Although lawyers and nonlawyers share some concerns, their central preoccupations and preferred solutions are vastly different. In one respect, however, they are quite similar. Neither the profession nor the public has been willing to address the structural sources of the problems they denounce or to invest the necessary resources in reform. The result has been symbolic crusades and policy paralysis.

This book seeks a clearer understanding of the challenges facing the legal profession. Discussion focuses on the conditions of practice, the advocate's role, the adversary system, the distribution of legal services, the regulation of lawyers' conduct, and the structure of legal education. On all of these issues, the public as well as the profession has a substantial stake. Given the centrality of law and lawyers in American life, the problems of legal practice become problems for us all. The central premise of this book is that the public's interest has played too little part in determining professional responsibilities. Too much regulation of lawyers has been designed by and for lawyers.

This is not to suggest that the system is purely self-serving. Without a doubt, the lawyers and judges involved in regulating the profession are committed to protecting the public. And as bar leaders are well aware, the public itself would not continue to delegate such regulatory authority if the profession pursued only its own interests. But no matter how well intentioned, lawyers regulating lawyers cannot escape the economic, psychological, and political constraints of their position. Nothing in the history of the

American bar indicates that attorneys are exempt from the natural human tendency to discount interests at odds with their own.

The self-regarding tendencies of self-regulating processes have been too long overlooked. Lawyers are the custodians of American political, social, and economic institutions, and their regulation should be a matter of broad social concern. Yet although lawyer bashing has been in ample supply, thoughtful critiques and constructive responses have not. This book aims to encourage more searching analysis by both the profession and the public about the points at which their interests diverge. To that end, this chapter surveys the problems facing lawyers from competing perspectives within and outside the bar.

The portrait that emerges is inevitably incomplete. This is a book with a reform agenda, and its focus is more on what is wrong with lawyers than on what is right. But that emphasis should not obscure a broader truth. The legal profession is also responsible for much that is best in American democratic processes. Lawyers have been architects of a governmental structure that is a model for much of the world. And they have been leaders in virtually all major movements for social justice in the nation's history. But these achievements are not grounds for complacency. Lawyers have also pursued their own and their clients' interests at the expense of broader public concerns. The challenges facing the American bar can only be met through fundamental changes in professional responsibility and regulation.

THE PROBLEM FROM THE PUBLIC'S PERSPECTIVE

"It's almost impossible to go too far when it comes to demonizing lawyers." That advice comes from the Lunz Research Companies in a recent guide for politicians—and not without reason. What the public doesn't like about lawyers could fill a lengthy book. And often has. Although the rank order of grievances shifts somewhat over time, certain continuities persist. Recent survey data, together with the critiques and caricatures that most often surface in popular culture, raise two primary concerns. The first involves character traits associated with lawyers. The second involves problems in the advocate's role and the adversary system for which lawyers are held at least partly responsible.[2]

Of all the traits that the public dislikes in attorneys, greed is at the top of the list. One classic definition presents a lawyer as "a learned gentleman who rescues your estate from your enemies and keeps it for himself." It is an old quip, but the perception remains widely shared. About three-fifths of

Americans describe attorneys as greedy, and between half and three-quarters believe that they charge excessive fees. There is even broader agreement that lawyers handle many matters that could be resolved as well and with less expense by nonlawyers.[3]

The public's other principal complaint about attorneys' character involves integrity. Only a fifth of those surveyed by the American Bar Association (ABA) felt that lawyers could be described as "honest and ethical." And in other studies, the ratings are even lower. Lawyers' ethics rank substantially below those of other occupations, including doctors, police officers, and business executives. Attorneys still edge out used car salesmen, but not by much.[4]

Other character issues involve arrogance, incivility, and inattention to client concerns. Less than a fifth of Americans in the ABA study felt that "caring and compassionate" described lawyers. Neglect of client interests is among the main sources of complaints to bar disciplinary authorities. Unsurprisingly, reports of callous or arrogant treatment are especially common in surveys of disempowered groups, such as indigent criminal defendants, but these criticisms are frequent even among influential business clients. Given these perceptions, it is also unsurprising that 90 to 95 percent of surveyed parents do not want their children to become lawyers.[5]

Of course, what the public dislikes about the legal profession is hard to disentangle from what it dislikes about the law, the legal system, and the lawyer's role within that system. Because the bar exercises so much power over legal institutions, it also is held accountable for their failures. One cluster of complaints focuses on attorneys' amoral advocacy—their willingness to defend causes and clients without regard to the ethical merits. Many individuals share the view of the nineteenth-century British critic Lord Macaulay, who questioned how a lawyer could "do for [money] what he would think it wicked and infamous to do for an empire." Two-thirds of surveyed Americans believe that attorneys are no longer "seekers of justice" and that they spend too much time finding technicalities to get criminals released.[6]

Attorneys similarly are blamed for perpetuating and profiting from an unnecessarily cumbersome system. Members of the bar, working as lobbyists, legislators, and judges, have created a structure that seems far too complex, expensive, and open to abuse. As newspaper columnist Art Buchwald once put it, "It isn't the bad lawyers who are screwing up the justice system in this country—it's the good lawyers. . . . If you have two competent lawyers on opposite sides, a trial that should take three days could easily last six months." Most Americans agree. Over three-quarters believe that litigation costs too much and takes too long and that the wealthy receive better treatment than everyone else.[7]

Lawyers are also held responsible for the overload of law in daily life. Over the last half century, legal regulation has become increasingly pervasive, and it is seldom a welcome guest. Everyone hears tales of disputes that are too big for courts, disputes that are too small, and disputes that should never have been disputes at all. Most Americans blame lawyers for filing too many lawsuits, and three-quarters believe that the United States has too many lawyers. Contemporary humor collections replay endless varieties on this theme. "Why does New Jersey have so many toxic waste dumps and California have so many lawyers? Because New Jersey got first choice."[8]

For the profession itself, these public perceptions have been a source of long-standing frustration. When asked to identify the most important problems facing the profession, lawyers consistently have put public image and credibility at the top of the list. Yet a majority of those surveyed believe that the public's negative perception of the profession is "due to ignorance and is fundamentally unjustified." Blame for this sorry state is widely distributed, but attorneys generally single out the media for a generous share. Portraits of vicious and venal lawyering are a Hollywood staple, and journalistic coverage seems similarly skewed. According to New York bar leaders, the fraud and felonies of a few "bad apples" get front page coverage while the profession's "countless other acts of quiet heroism go unnoticed and unpublicized." Lawyers reportedly are "their own worst salesmen. . . . They do not do a good job of blowing their trumpets about their own selfless activities." Many practitioners provide a "tremendous amount" of pro bono assistance and work "incredible hours" for reduced fees, sometimes "under minimum wages." A constant refrain among bar presidents is that "no other profession is as charitable with its time and money." There are no footnotes.[9]

There are, however, problems with the profession's response to public perceptions. Many portrayals by bar leaders are no less exaggerated than the media coverage they denounce. If, for example, long hours, low pay, and charitable contributions are the standards for comparison, the legal profession is unlikely to win a selflessness sweepstakes. Law is the second highest paid occupation, and surveyed lawyers' average pro bono contribution is estimated at under $85 per year. Most practitioners give no money and do no work for the poor or for public interest causes, and the average for the profession as a whole is estimated at less than thirty minutes a week per year. It is also doubtful that lawyers' excessive modesty is at the root of their public image problems. The legal profession is not known for resisting self-promotion. Lawyers spend well over $500 million annually in advertising their own services, and bar organizations devote substantial resources to public relations campaigns.[10]

The premise of such campaigns—that popular ignorance and a bad press are the central problems—is highly dubious. Indeed, the bar's own research suggests the contrary. The individuals most likely to have negative impressions of attorneys are those with the most knowledge and personal experience. Corporate clients are among lawyers' harshest critics. By contrast, those who know relatively little about the legal profession and the legal system, and who get their information primarily from television, have the most favorable impressions. Such perceptions stand to reason in light of other research indicating that the vast majority of television portrayals of lawyers are positive. The problem, in short, is less with the image of lawyers than with their practices. As then President Jerome Shestack observed, public relations campaigns are "not the answer. The cost is prohibitive, the outcome doubtful, and the idea professionally unapealing."[11]

Yet finding solutions is more difficult than the public or the profession typically acknowledges. A large part of popular dislike of lawyers stems from aspects of the legal system that are not primarily the fault of lawyers or that are not readily changed. Courts are overburdened and underfunded, and some discontent is inherent in even the best system of dispute resolution. The contexts in which people encounter the profession are often unpleasant: divorce, bankruptcies, personal injuries, or contractual disputes. This unpleasantness inevitably affects perceptions of lawyers who are profiting from others' miseries. Attorneys are also the bearers of unwelcome messages about the law, so they readily become scapegoats when the justice system fails to deliver justice as participants perceive it.

America's adversarial system compounds popular frustration. Litigation is rarely a win-win enterprise, and losers are apt to put some of the blame on lawyers. The targets of resentment are not, however, only—or even primarily—parties' own attorneys. Between two-thirds and three-quarters of surveyed individuals are satisfied with *their* lawyers. The public's major grievances involve perceived abuses by other people's lawyers and a system that fails to prevent those abuses. As one columnist notes, "Everyone would hate doctors, too, if every time you went in the hospital, your doctor was trying to take your appendix out, and the other guy's doctor was standing right there trying to put it back in."[12]

It is, however, by no means clear that the public would prefer a substantially different structure in which lawyers played a substantially different role. In fact, Americans are ambivalent. The vast majority believe that, despite the problems in the justice system, it is still the best in the world. And while most people are critical of the zealous representation that attorneys provide to accused criminals and other unpopular defendants, when individuals imagine themselves in litigation, a zealous champion is precisely what they have in mind. In other legal contexts, much of what Americans dislike about opposing counsel is what they value in their own. One of the most positive traits that the public associates with lawyers is that their first priority is loyalty to their clients. Yet one of the most negative traits is lawyers' willingness to manipulate the system on behalf of clients without regard to right or wrong. People hate a hired gun until they need one of their own.[13]

The public is similarly ambivalent about the tension between money and justice. Americans dislike the fact that the best legal representation typically goes to the highest bidder and that law is accessible only to those who can afford it. But Americans also dislike efforts to remedy those inequalities. Equal justice is what we inscribe over courthouse doors, not what we support in social policies. Our nation spends far less than other Western industrial societies on subsidized legal representation. Bar studies estimate that over four-fifths of the legal needs of low-income households and one-third of the needs of middle-income Americans remain unmet. As one Denver legal aid attorney observes, "The only thing less popular than a poor person these days is a poor person with a lawyer." We lament the inequalities in our justice system but fail to support policies that would address them. As a culture, we find it more convenient to fault the bar's greed than to acknowledge our own.[14]

Although part of the public's discontent with lawyers reflects misplaced or displaced frustrations, not all of its complaints should be so readily dismissed. As subsequent chapters make clear, many criticisms of professional conduct and regulatory processes have a strong basis in fact. On matters such as excessive fees, unresponsive disciplinary structures, and overbroad protections of the professional monopoly, the public is not ambivalent, and its concerns are not unwarranted. Even on issues like zealous advocacy, where popular opinion is more divided, the individuals who have the most contact with lawyers and knowledge about their practices are the least satisfied.[15]

On most important questions of professional regulation, the problem is not so much that the public is uninformed or undecided but rather that it is unorganized and uninvolved. For the vast majority of Americans, such issues are not a priority. Most people's direct contact with lawyers is limited. Routine users are usually organizational clients, which can deduct excessive legal costs as business expenses. Although egregious abuses or competitors' efforts can occasionally prod the public into action, nonlawyers seldom have sufficient incentives to organize around questions involving regulation of lawyers.

By contrast, the legal profession has every incentive to pursue regulatory concerns and to block initiatives that advance public interests at the expense of its own. Although such problems are by no means unique to this regulatory context, they are compounded by the bar's pivotal role in American policy making. Unless some substantial constituencies within the profession—lawyers, judges, or legislators—share a reform agenda, its prospects are highly limited. Yet the conditions for advancing such an agenda have seldom been better. Discontent within the profession is substantial. The challenge lies in refocusing that disaffection in more constructive directions and in identifying ways to bridge the gap between professional and public interests.

THE PROBLEM FROM THE PROFESSION'S PERSPECTIVE

Recent profiles of legal practice have all the makings of a medieval morality play. In most bar journal accounts, the tone is cheery and the text is worldly; the focus is on power and money, winners and losers, movers and shakers. But at appointed intervals come cautionary subtexts: worries about a decline in ethical values and the loss of professional soul. Prosperity has come at a price, and many lawyers seem to be "searching for their lost wigs."[16]

These competing themes reflect warring trends in contemporary legal practice. By many measures, lawyers have little cause for complaint. No profession offers a greater range of opportunities for financial security and public influence. In no other country do lawyers play such a significant role in social and economic policy. And in no other historical era has the legal profession been more diverse and more open to talent irrespective of race, gender, religion, and ethnicity. When asked directly about their current position, the vast majority of surveyed lawyers express satisfaction. Yet as chapter 2 notes, other evidence paints a gloomier picture. A majority of lawyers report that they would choose another career if they had the decision to make over, and three-quarters would not want their children to become lawyers. Only one-fifth of attorneys feel that the law has lived up to their expectations in contributing to the social good. Symptoms of professional malaise are also apparent in health-related difficulties. An estimated one-third of American attorneys suffer from depression or from alcohol or drug addiction, a rate that is two to three times higher than in the public generally.[17]

Although the primary sources of discontent vary somewhat across different areas of practice and demographic groups, common themes emerge. Lawyers are unhappy with the culture of the profession, the structure of their workplaces, and the performance of the justice system. At the most general level, the bar is concerned about the "decline of professionalism." That phrase captures a range of more specific complaints, such as increasing commercialism and competition and decreasing civility and collegiality. The perception of law as a craft and calling is under siege, and the consequence is an eroding sense of public service and cultural authority. About three-quarters of surveyed lawyers believe that practitioners are more "money conscious," half think they are less civil, and one-third report that they are more likely to lie than in the past. These perceptions partly reflect structural changes in the market for legal services. Increases in the number of lawyers have increased competition and diminished the force of informal reputational sanctions available in smaller professional communities. Price consciousness among corporate clients, together with the relaxation of bar restrictions on competitive practices within and across professions, have further intensified economic pressures. One result has been a strong emphasis on the bottom line, which squeezes the time available for pursuit of other professional values, such as mentoring and public service.[18]

A further consequence of increased competition has been increased instability in lawyer-client relationships and increased constraints on professional independence. Corporate clients more often shop for representation on particular matters, rather than build long-term relationships with firms that supply representation for most needs. As private practice becomes more competitive, specialized, and transactional, lawyers face more intense pressures to satisfy clients' short-term desires. Without a stable relationship of trust and confidence, it is risky for counsel to protest unreasonable demands or to deliver unwelcome messages about what legal rules or legal ethics require. Part of the dishonesty, incivility, and acrimony that lawyers find troubling in current practice seems driven by these profit dynamics. As Richard Posner points out, competitive markets are "no fun for most sellers." Law is not an exception, and fun is not the only casualty.[19]

Legal practice has become more competitive within as well as among law firms. A steady rise in costs, coupled with instability in demand, have led to greater insecurity in private practice. More public information about law firm salaries has intensified financial rivalries and lateral defections. The desire to attract and retain the most productive attorneys has kept compensation levels relatively high, but the profession pays the price in other ways.

Partnership means less and is harder to obtain. As the likelihood of promotion diminishes, the competition among young lawyers intensifies. Incoming associates are wined and dined, then worked to death. At senior levels, less productive partners may be squeezed out. Productive ones may be lured away. As working relations become more transient and more strained, fewer lawyers have a stake in investing in their professional culture. These trends are reflected and reinforced by the "eat what you kill" approach to law firm compensation. Partners who attract clients are at the top of the food chain. Lawyers with different priorities—mentoring, public service, quality of life—lack comparable leverage.

Indeed, for too many practitioners, "quality of life" is a nonissue. "What life?" Billable hour requirements have increased dramatically over the last two decades, and what has not changed is the number of hours in the day. Almost half of private practitioners now bill at least nineteen hundred hours per year, and to do so honestly they frequently need to work sixty-hour weeks. Especially in large firms, where hourly demands can be even higher, all work and no play is fast becoming the norm rather than the exception. What lawyers lose is not just leisure. They also lose the opportunities for pro bono service, civic involvement, and breadth of experience that build professional judgment and sustain a professional culture.[20]

The scope for crucial personal relationships is also narrowing. Almost half of American attorneys feel that they don't have enough time for their families. For employed women, who still spend about twice as much time on domestic responsibilities as employed men, the puritan ethic run amok poses special difficulties. Excessive hours are the leading cause of professional dissatisfaction among female practitioners. Recent reports on women's status in law firms describe, in deadening detail, the sweatshop schedules for many full-time attorneys and the glass ceilings for part-time practitioners. Those with the greatest family commitments often drift off the partnership track, leaving behind a decision-making structure insulated from their concerns. Such patterns help account for the persistent underrepresentation of women in positions of greatest professional status and reward.[21]

Other forces are at work as well. Some sixty recent reports on bias in the profession have chronicled persistent barriers to women and minorities. As chapter 2 notes, unconscious stereotypes and inadequate access to mentoring and business development networks compromise the profession's commitments to equal opportunity.

A further source of dissatisfaction involves the quality of work in private practice. Intellectual challenge is the main reason most attorneys choose law as a career, and for a substantial minority it falls well short of expectations. "Doing litigation" in the style to which junior attorneys have become accustomed often means endless cycles of scut work. As New York University professor Stephen Gillers observes, too many lawyers find too much of their practice "relentlessly repetitive, and strangely unconnected to a dimly recollected purpose in choosing law." This lack of larger purpose accounts for the greatest gap between expectations and experience among American lawyers and the widely shared perception that their work is not contributing to the social good.[22]

The reasons lawyers give for that failure partly overlap the ones the public gives. According to both groups, much of the problem involves a justice system that is unduly expensive and unwieldy, and ethical rules that are undemanding and underenforced. Most practitioners are unhappy with regulatory structures and with the incivility, hucksterism, and other misconduct that they seem powerless to prevent. All of these problems have left a growing number of lawyers disaffected or disengaged with their professional lives. Yale law professor Bruce Ackerman notes that although today's practitioners will spend most of their waking hours at work, "they will save their ultimate concerns for something else: family, friends, the bassoon, some little cottage in the Maine woods. Even if successful, this kind of life will . . . [leave] a vast professional hole—what *was* it that I spent most of my waking hours worrying about?"[23]

Although many lawyers are now asking that question, few seem willing to confront inconvenient answers. Most bar discussions of the decline of professionalism proceed with a highly selective historical memory. In this "golden age of legal nostalgia," heroic lawyer-statesmen ruled, if not the earth, at least the profession. Then came the Fall and our own Dark Age of crass commercialism, uncivil tactics, and amoral advocacy. When exactly this transformation took place remains unclear, because few commentators are interested in historical details. Those who are cast doubt on conventional assumptions. For example, although legal practice earlier in this century generally is painted in rosy hues, there is much to dislike about what then passed for professionalism. As Harvard professor Mary Ann Glendon notes, some of the bar's best and brightest made their reputations "using every tactic in the book (and many that were not) to help bust unions, consolidate monopolies, and obtain favorable treatment" from corrupt judges.[24]

Virtually every historical era that modern commentators applaud attracted its own share of critics with concerns similar to those heard today. In 1903, Supreme Court Justice Louis Brandeis warned lawyers that they were losing public respect because they were also losing their commitment to public service and their moral independence from clients. Several decades later, Supreme Court Justice Harlan Fiske Stone worried that the economic pressures of practice had transformed many attorneys into "obsequious servants of business, . . . tainted with the morals and the manners of the market place in its most antisocial manifestations." "More and more," Stone noted, "the amount of [a lawyer's] income has become the measure of his professional status." Even sweatshop hours, which are usually taken as a distinctively corrosive feature of contemporary practice, have long provoked concern. In 1928, Arthur Train published a novel featuring a Wall Street firm that "never slept," with partners who "arrive early, stay late, and die young."[25]

In some respects, however, current problems are more acute. Although commercialism and long hours are scarcely novel concerns, their meanings have changed, and not for the better. But on other issues of professionalism, such as lawyers' honesty or pro bono work, we lack evidence for the impressionistic assertions that bar commentary often presents as self-evident truths. "The spirit of public service is not what once it was," announces a New York Committee on the Profession. But we have no adequate records of what it used to be. Nor can we be sure whether many other commonly cited problems are getting worse or just more visible in a world with more lawyers and more publicity surrounding their conduct.[26]

Moreover, on at least some measures of professionalism, much is getting better. Increased competition also has encouraged increased efficiency and responsiveness to client concerns. The result for many consumers has been higher quality services at lower prices. Lawyers' greater self-consciousness about issues of professional responsibility is itself a sign of progress. So is the attention that these matters now receive in law schools. When I entered the profession some two decades ago, legal ethics was a recent, unwelcome, and scarcely visible intruder on the educational landscape. I took no course in professional responsibility, encountered no bar exam questions on the subject, and found only passing references in the legal literature. Lawyers today are at least grappling with problems that in earlier eras were not even acknowledged as problems.

The same is true with issues involving race, gender, and sexual orientation. Washington practitioner Sol Linowitz, in his recent account of the *Betrayed Profession*, recalls that his law school class in the 1950s had only two women. Neither he nor most of his male classmates questioned the skewed ratio at the time, although they did feel somewhat uncomfortable when their two female colleagues were around. And he now acknowledges with rueful candor, "It never occurred to us to wonder whether *they* felt uncomfortable." In today's climate, much progress remains to be made, but at least such questions are on the agenda. And as chapter 2 notes, they are attracting reforms from a wide spectrum of bar associations, judicial commissions, and organizations employing lawyers.[27]

We have moved in similar directions on access to legal services. Although, as earlier discussion indicated, lawyers' average pro bono contributions leave much to be desired, efforts to assist those most in need are substantially increasing. Until recently, little pro bono assistance went to systematically underrepresented interests. The vast majority of beneficiaries were family, friends, and organizations serving primarily middle- and upper-income groups, such as hospitals, museums, and Jaycees. No law schools required student pro bono activity, and few made substantial efforts to encourage voluntary involvement. By contrast, today's lawyers and law students are far more likely to engage in pro bono work targeted at poverty and public interest causes.[28]

There is, in short, little evidence for the common view that former Chief Justice Warren Burger expressed: that professionalism is in a "steady decline" or has reached a crisis of "epidemic proportions." The distance between professional ideals and professional practice has always been substantial, and in many respects the present is not demonstrably worse than the past. But neither are current conditions acceptable. And the bar as a whole is disturbingly passive and pessimistic in the face of its own problems. About two-thirds of surveyed attorneys predict that collegiality and civility will continue to decline. Yet few seem to believe that they could influence these trends. As lawyer/psychiatrist Benjamin Sells observes, "A majority of lawyers apparently have found ways to displace their responsibility for their own profession. Many lawyers seem never to have even entertained the idea that they could actually do something about how law is practiced." A more typical approach is for attorneys to "become focused primarily on their self-interests . . . and live their work lives with a kind of up and out fatalism."[29]

In short, the central problem facing the American legal profession is its own unwillingness to come to terms with what the problems are. At issue are competing values and concerns. Yet bar commentary on professionalism tends to paper over two central conflicts: the tensions between lawyers' economic and noneconomic interests, and the tensions between professional and public interests. Money is, of course, at the root of both conflicts. And while this fact is too obvious to overlook entirely, it is also a truth too uncomfortable to acknowledge fully. So various strategies of confession and avoidance have become common. For example, the American Bar Association's Commission on Professionalism asked, "Has our profession abandoned principle for profit, professionalism for commercialism?" "The answer," it turned out, "cannot be a simple yes or no." Like other bar commentators, the commission concluded that the pursuit of profit in an increasingly competitive market had compromised professional values. The solution is for lawyers to rise above their baser instincts. This approach, "just say no to greed," appears to have fallen somewhat short. Rather, as the California Commission on the Future of the Bar candidly acknowledged, lawyers have become habituated to "extraordinary incomes." In the process, luxuries have become necessities, wealth has become critical to self-esteem, and relative salaries have become a way of "keeping score."[30]

Yet that process is often self-defeating. As research summarized in chapter 2 indicates, people in general and lawyers in particular overvalue income as a way of achieving satisfaction. At lawyers' standard of living, the cliché is correct: Money doesn't buy happiness. Part of the reason is that some crucial factors affecting satisfaction are beyond individual control, such as biological predispositions, childhood experiences, disabling disease, or the death of loved ones. But the other principal circumstances affecting happiness are not directly related to income. They involve the quality of family relationships, the support of friends, a sense of performing key tasks effectively, and a feeling of control over one's fate. Of course, money may influence some of these factors. The ability to afford good child care, neighborhoods, and education affects family relationships and individuals' evaluation of their performance as parents. But most people overestimate how much money matters. They quickly adjust to higher earnings, and their expectations and desires increase accordingly. And the priority that many lawyers and law firms attach to salaries compromises other goals that are more central to satisfaction, such as time for friends and families and choice of work that is morally and intellectually satisfying.[31]

Lawyers also face a related trade-off that the professionalism debate fails to acknowledge. In the bar's idealized vision of professional life, lawyers can expect both moral independence and worldly rewards, such as power, wealth, and prominence. In actual practice, however, these interests frequently conflict. Historical and cross-cultural research suggests that in contexts where the legal profession has maintained greater independence from clients and has recognized greater ethical obligations to third-party and public interests than the contemporary American bar, attorneys have secured less income and influence than they now enjoy. Moral independence may bring lawyers an important measure of social esteem and self-respect, but it comes at a price.[32]

The rhetoric of professionalism tends to paper over this conflict by making a virtue out of expedience. Under prevailing views of professional responsibility, lawyers need not choose to exercise moral independence within their professional role. Rather, their preeminent obligation is loyalty to client interests. Over the last century, the bar's codes of conduct have progressively narrowed the ethical discretion that lawyers are expected to exercise once they have accepted representation. Except in limited circumstances, such as where a client seeks assistance in criminal or fraudulent conduct, lawyers are to maintain clients' confidences and to pursue their interests "zealously within the bounds of the law." In effect, an attorney's obligation is to defend, not judge, the client. Under this standard view, good ethics and good business are in happy coincidence.[33]

Yet such efforts to align moral commitments with financial interests are not entirely convincing. The conventional view, aptly summarized by the American College of Trial Lawyers, is that the most effective way to discover truth and preserve rights is through an adversarial process in which attorneys have "undivided fidelity to each client's interests as the client perceives them." But this faith in adversarial processes remains plausible only if all interests have adequate representation and comparable access to information and legal resources. Such conditions seldom prevail in the world that most lawyers encounter. And undivided fidelity to client objectives is often difficult to square with commonly accepted ethical principles. Familiar examples include contexts in which third parties' health, safety, or financial well-being is at risk. These contexts receive inadequate treatment both in the bar's ethical standards and in its discussions of professionalism. The result is a dispiriting disjuncture between current norms and traditional aspirations. The idealized vision of lawyers as morally independent "guardians of justice" is out of phase with prevailing practices.[34]

A final trade-off, similarly unacknowledged in professionalism debates, involves the tension between professional autonomy and public respect. As noted earlier, lawyers put public image at the top of the list of problems facing the profession. Many practitioners' self-esteem is tied to their view of law as an "honorable" and honored profession. Yet despite concerns about their poor public reputation, most lawyers resist efforts to address its sources. They particularly resist seeing any connection between public respect and public accountability or any tension between public accounta-

bility and professional autonomy. Rather, the assumption frequently repeated in ethical codes and bar discussions is that self-regulation serves the common good by helping to "maintain the legal profession's independence from
government domination."[35]

Almost never do bar leaders acknowledge the possibility that self-interest
might occasionally skew lawyers' judgments on matters of professional regulation. To the contrary, as the New York City Bar's Committee on the
Profession confidently asserted, "While superficially there may appear to be a
tension between professional responsibility and self-interest, in fact, broadly
speaking, there is none." Such assertions say less about the bar's potential for
self-interest than its capacity for self-deception. No occupational group, however well intentioned, can make unbiased assessments of the public interest
on issues that place its own status and income directly at risk. As virtually
every expert observes, the greater a profession's control over its own regulation, the greater the risks of tunnel vision. Eliot Freidson, one of the nation's
leading experts on professions, notes that any self-governing occupation
"quite naturally forms a perspective of its own, a perspective all the more distorted and narrow by its source in a status answerable to no one but itself."[36]

The American legal profession is no exception. Standards of conduct
have been drafted, approved, and administered by bodies composed almost
entirely of attorneys. Nonlawyers have had no representation in the adop-
tion of those standards by courts and bar associations and have obtained
only token representation on disciplinary bodies. These lay members typically are chosen by the profession and rarely have the backgrounds,
resources, or ties to consumer organizations that could create a significant
check on professional self-interest.[37]

Given this structure, it is scarcely surprising that studies of bar regulatory processes uniformly find serious flaws in their responsiveness to ordinary consumer grievances. As chapter 6 notes, less than 2 percent of complaints to bar disciplinary agencies result in public sanctions. Yet although
the vast majority of surveyed attorneys concede that the current disciplinary
process is inadequate, comparable numbers reject changes in its structure.
The bar's unwillingness to confront trade-offs in its regulatory objectives
undermines its professionalism agenda. As long as lawyers resist public
accountability, they are unlikely to win public confidence.[38]

If lawyers are seriously committed to fostering professionalism, they
first must confront the structural reforms it requires. The bar needs a vision
beyond the wistful nostalgia and wishful exhortation that dominates current
debates.

RECASTING THE PROBLEM,
RETHINKING THE RESPONSES

Over the last decade, the professionalism problem has launched a cottage industry of efforts: commissions, conferences, courses, centers, creeds, and codes. Despite these efforts, chronic ethical dilemmas remain unresolved. Part of the problem involves the lack of consensus about what the problems are or what trade-offs should be made among competing professional and public interests. Only at the most abstract level do lawyers rally around the same vision. Today's profession has become too diverse and specialized, and its leadership too weak and divided, to enforce any unifying vision of professional ideals. The result, as a study by American Bar Foundation researchers notes, is that the professionalism campaign has remained at a level of "comforting generality, with vague invocations of 'shared' values that really aren't shared, a symbolic and nostalgic crusade . . . which has little to do with everyday working visions of American lawyers." Few of these efforts seem likely to matter much. Almost none focus on reforms that could matter in bar ethical standards and regulatory processes. Rather, the bar has lurched from project to project, leaving in its wake an overload of soggy lamentations, war-weary clichés, and mixed metaphors far worse than the one just constructed. Unsurprisingly, an increasing number of veterans have joined the call for a "professionalism nonproliferation treaty."[39]

Any serious response to the dilemmas confronting the American legal profession must begin from different premises. That alternative vision, developed more fully in the chapters that follow, reflects several guiding principles. These involve the ethical responsibilities of lawyers, access to legal services, and bar regulatory structures.

The first of these principles calls for lawyers to accept personal moral responsibility for the consequences of their professional acts. To satisfy this principle, lawyers' conduct needs consistent, disinterested, and generalizable foundations. The rationale for professional actions cannot depend on a retreat into role that denies the need for reflection at precisely the moment when reflection is most needed. In effect, this principle demands greater practical content for professional values. If lawyers see themselves as officers of justice, they must accept greater obligations to *pursue* justice. No longer should ethical analysis be short-circuited through appeals to some idealized vision of the adversary process.

Rather, as chapters 3 and 4 argue, attorneys need to consider the consequences of their advocacy in a realistic social context where not all interests are adequately represented and not all unjust conduct is adequately regulated. The fact that clients have a legal right to pursue a certain objective does not mean that they have a moral right to do so or that justice necessarily will be served by zealously representing their interests. Some conduct that is inconsistent with social values remains legal either because prohibitions are too difficult or costly to enforce or because policy makers lack sufficient information or independence from special interests. Client objectives must be tempered by other important concerns. Lawyers have a responsibility to prevent unnecessary harm to third parties, to promote a just and efficient legal system, and to respect core values such as honesty, fairness, and good faith on which that system depends. At a minimum, that responsibility requires attorneys to counsel clients about the full range of ethical considerations that bear on particular decisions and to avoid assisting actions that compromise accepted moral values.[40]

This reformulation of role does not contemplate that attorneys are accountable for all aspects of their clients' conduct. Under conventional ethical theories, moral responsibility depends on a range of factors, including an individual's degree of information, involvement, and capacity to affect action, as well as the action's likely consequences and connections to broader moral principles. So, for example, protecting free speech for unpopular causes or fair trials for criminal defendants may justify zealous representation despite other possible costs. But the rationale for advocacy in such cases should not serve as some all-purpose paradigm for cases involving no such principles. Nor should lawyers defer all responsibility for just outcomes to a process that is demonstrably incapable of achieving them. Lawyers will, of course, often differ over what constitutes "justice" and how to weigh the values at issue. But their actions also must satisfy commonly accepted ethical principles, not just the minimal standards set forth in bar ethical codes. Nor should the general importance of encouraging client trust and protecting confidentiality trump all competing values.

A second guiding principle calls for equitable access to legal services and adequate choices in the services available. One of the public's central concerns about lawyers and legal processes involves their expense and inaccessibility. To address that concern, more efforts should focus on reducing the need for legal assistance, lowering the costs of services, and expanding the range of alternatives available. As chapter 5 notes, one cluster of strategies should emphasize reforms that would enable individuals to handle more of their own problems directly. Procedural simplification and assistance for pro se litigants are obvious examples. A related set of initiatives should focus on competition, accessibility, and consumer choice in the market for legal services. Qualified nonlawyers should be licensed to offer routine legal assistance for matters like uncontested divorces. And they should be permitted, under appropriate regulations, to join lawyers as partners in multidisciplinary firms. Consumers should have access to consolidated "one stop shopping" alternatives in which attorneys collaborate with other professionals such as accountants and family therapists.[41]

Further efforts should also center on increasing the availability of subsidized services. Other industrialized nations provide more accessible justice systems through some combination of insurance coverage and progressive subsidies for basic legal needs. A comparable system in this country might enjoy broader public support and prove less vulnerable to restrictions than current programs serving only the poor. More pro bono work by the private bar is another step in the right direction. Organizations employing lawyers need to place higher value on public service in practice, not just in principle, and to reward such work in promotion and compensation decisions.[42]

Americans also should have greater access to mediation and alternative dispute resolution programs. A growing number of jurisdictions are moving toward "multidoor courthouses" that allocate different types of cases to appropriate procedures based on the nature of the controversy, the relationship between the parties, and their procedural priorities, such as speed, cost, or opportunities for direct participation. We need more development of such alternatives and more systematic information about their effectiveness.[43]

To make these changes plausible, a final guiding principle demands public accountability for professional regulation. Acting under their inherent power to regulate the practice of law, courts have overvalued professional independence and have delegated too much of their own oversight responsibility to the organized bar. The result has been a system that fails to address legitimate public concerns, particularly those involving the cost, quality, and accessibility of legal services, the protection of societal interests, and the sanctions for lawyer misconduct. All too often, bar ethical codes and enforcement committees have resolved conflicts between professional and public interests in favor of those doing the resolving.

To be sure, lawyers need some measure of independence from governmental control if they are to check governmental abuses. But prevailing regulatory frameworks overvalue autonomy at the expense of accountability. As chapter 6 notes, other countries with independent legal professions have oversight structures that permit more responsiveness to consumer concerns. And experts on occupational licensure generally agree that some external checks are necessary to prod professionals into living up to their own aspirations. Lawyers can no longer assume, in the face of mounting evidence to the contrary, that today's self-regulatory structures serve societal interests. Bar disciplinary authorities generally have neither the resources nor jurisdiction to pursue the most common client grievances, such as "mere" negligence or fee disputes. Nor have these authorities generally proved willing to impose serious sanctions except in the most egregious cases of fraud or criminal conduct. These failures of bar-controlled oversight structures have prompted a growing range of other responses, including civil liability suits and administrative agency regulations. But significant gaps remain. The challenge is to build a more coherent oversight system that balances the need for public accountability and professional autonomy.[44]

It is also time to reconsider whether an occupation as large and varied as the American bar is well served by a unified regulatory structure. This is an era of "postmodern professionalism," with increasing diversity along lines of personal background, substantive specialty, and practice setting. Although commissions on professionalism have long insisted that "more unites than separates" attorneys, such claims seem closer to aspirations than descriptions. The concerns of a small-town divorce lawyer in a solo practice bear little resemblance to those of an urban federal prosecutor or a Wall Street associate specializing in corporate mergers. Attorneys from different backgrounds and practice contexts need different preparation and sources of guidance. Our current one-size-fits-all model of legal education and professional regulation badly needs revision.[45]

Effective training for an increasingly diverse profession requires corresponding diversity in educational structures. As chapter 7 notes, a more flexible accreditation system could enable some law schools to continue providing a generalist degree program, together with advanced interdisciplinary instruction for students and practicing lawyers in particular substantive areas. Other schools could offer shorter, less expensive options that would prepare paralegals to provide routine low-cost services in limited fields.

Changes in professional regulatory structures are equally critical. Bar ethical codes are not an adequate source of guidance. In a profession that is sharply divided and scarcely disinterested, such codes end up reflecting too high a level of abstraction and too low a common denominator of conduct. In order to achieve consensus, bar standards must satisfy a group that is varied in social background, practice settings, and ideological views, but largely united in its desire to maximize members' income and minimize their risks of disciplinary or malpractice sanctions. The resulting ethical codes offer an unsatisfying mix of vague directives (charge "reasonable" fees), moral exhortation (volunteer pro bono service), and minimal prohibitions (refuse to assist criminal conduct).[46]

A true commitment to professionalism will require more specific and more demanding standards. Some promising efforts have been made to develop such standards by groups like the American Academy of Matrimonial Lawyers and an ABA Tax Section Committee. If more specialized bar associations adopted such codes and certified lawyers who complied, the consequence could be a more efficient market in reputation and a more effective reward structure for ethical performance. And if more demanding rules were reinforced by courts, bar agencies, and workplace policies, the result might be improved practices throughout the profession. More public and private sector employers could assist this process by adopting internal policies, oversight structures, and training programs designed to encourage ethical conduct. As chapter 6 notes, courts or legislatures could also require such initiatives for all organizations above a certain size or for those whose lawyers have engaged in sanctionable misconduct. For example, trial judges, bar committees, or administrative agencies like the SEC could require that attorneys who violate ethical standards submit a regulatory plan to ensure future compliance.[47]

Reform efforts should also focus on other workplace conditions that undermine professional values. A growing number of employers and professional associations have developed successful policies concerning part-time schedules, mentoring, diversity, and extended family leaves. But many have not, and some employers tolerate a wide gap between formal policies and actual practices. Fewer than 5 percent of lawyers work reduced hours, and most others believe, with good reason, that taking part-time status would limit their opportunities for advancement. The inadequacy of policies on family and diversity issues are leading causes of job dissatisfaction, stress, depression, and attrition. These take a toll on client representation as well as on employers' bottom lines. Lawyers have long been leaders in the national struggle for equal opportunity. The challenge remaining is for them to confront the barriers in their own profession.[48]

The term *profession* has its origins in the Latin root "to profess" and in the European tradition of requiring members to declare their commitment to shared ideals. The American bar has maintained the form but lost the substance of that tradition. Entering lawyers may still profess to serve justice as officers of the court, but that declaration has little moral content in contemporary practice. Efforts to revive a richer sense of professionalism have foundered on the lack of consensus about what that concept should require and how to reconcile it with more worldly interests.

In this context, it makes sense to view professionalism not as a fixed ideal but rather as an ongoing struggle. The challenge is to work toward understandings of professional responsibility that are both more and less demanding. They must ask for more than current codes and enforcement structures, but they must offer a vision that also seems plausible in practice. Recent debates on professionalism have suffered from overly idealistic goals and overly limited responses.

That mismatch is by no means inevitable. On matters of public interest not involving their own regulation, lawyers have been crucial in bridging the gap between ideals and institutions. By turning similar energies inward, the bar may give more substantial content to its highest aspirations.

CHAPTER 2

LAWYERS AND THEIR DISCONTENT

For American lawyers, these are the best of times and the worst of times. No profession offers a surer path to affluence and influence. Yet no profession creates a wider gap between the expectations it raises and the experiences it provides. Recent changes in the conditions of practice have left many attorneys in a state of wistful resignation. Competition and commercialization are accelerating, while collegiality and civility are heading in the opposite direction. The consensus is that professionalism is in decline and that the stresses of practice are likely to increase. Yet most lawyers seem to have no sense that they can alter those trends or reshape their collective future.[1]

This chapter aims to provide a clearer sense of where the profession is headed and what it would take to shift course. The basic message is one that practitioners seem reluctant to hear. In today's economic environment, certain values are in conflict. And lawyers, both individually and collectively, need to confront some hard trade-offs. Doing good and doing well do not always push in similar directions. And equal opportunity for women and minorities will not be possible without significant changes in workplace priorities. Rather than lament the loss of some romanticized past, the bar must forthrightly face the challenges of its future.

To that end, the discussion below surveys the causes and consequences of recent trends in legal practice. The aim is to identify the sources of lawyers' discontent, the dynamics of race and gender bias in the profession, and the social costs of current institutional arrangements. The structure of legal workplaces carries a substantial, if not always visible, price for the public as well as the profession. Many of the concerns addressed throughout this book are at least partly traceable to that structure. Adversarial excesses, anticompetitive rules, fee-related abuses, and inequitable distributions of legal services are often rooted in the economic dynamics of practice. Lawyers play a central role in American life, and the failure to address their problems creates problems for everyone else.

Discussion here focuses primarily on lawyers in private practice. About three-quarters of the nation's nine hundred thousand attorneys work in such settings. A majority are in firms; slightly under half, about a third of the profession, are in solo practice. Most of the remainder work in private industry (about 10 percent) or in government (about 10 percent). A small number are judges (about 3 percent), academics (about 1 percent), or legal aid, public defenders, or public interest lawyers (about 1 percent). The analysis that follows places special attention on law firms both because they are where most attorneys practice, and because they tend to set standards for the profession generally. The point is to gain a clearer understanding of the effects of practice structures on lawyers themselves and on their own stake in altering current trends. For the American bar, Ogden Nash had it right: "Progress may have been all right once, but it has gone on too long."[2]

THE DYNAMICS OF DISCONTENT

"Miserable with the Legal Life;" "Running from the Law;" "Counsel for the Depressed and the Stressed;" by press accounts, all is not well in the American legal profession. Such accounts are, however, highly selective. The press and the public are disproportionately drawn to tales of woe. The news, after all, needs to be new—or at least somehow engaging. And who wants to hear about happy, well-paid lawyers? In fact, there are lots of them, although there are also indications of significant discontent and dysfunction. The picture is complicated by differences in how researchers assess dissatisfaction—in what and whom they ask. Lawyers are a highly diverse group, and discontent varies across demographic groups and practice settings. Surveys on career satisfaction have yielded mixed results, and their portraits are surprisingly incomplete. However, recent research, both on workplace satisfaction in general and on legal practice in particular, yields important insights about what makes for a meaningful professional life and why law too often fails to provide it.[3]

When asked directly about job satisfaction, most attorneys, like most Americans, are generally positive. In a large-scale ABA survey of young lawyers, about three-quarters were somewhat or very satisfied with their current positions. A study by the American Bar Foundation (ABF) similarly found that 85 percent of Chicago practitioners were satisfied, the same percentage as American workers generally. But other evidence points in more disturbing directions. In the ABA survey, less than one-fifth of lawyers felt that the profession had met their expectations to contribute to the social good. A RAND Institute study of California practitioners found that half would choose a different career. And smaller, less systematic surveys reveal higher levels of dissatisfaction than the ABA or ABF studies. Virtually all of this research finds that the vast majority of attorneys, typically around three-quarters, would not want their children to become attorneys.[4]

In accounting for these mixed results, researchers note that direct questions about job satisfaction tend to yield overly positive accounts. That is particularly true in studies like those involving Chicago lawyers, which rely on oral interviews. Most people are reluctant to admit to a stranger, and often even to themselves, that they are unhappy in their current circumstances. It is difficult to acknowledge that they have made the wrong choices or have not taken steps to improve their situation. More revealing measures of satisfaction typically come from less direct questions, such as whether or when lawyers plan to leave their jobs, whether they would do so if they had a good alternative, or whether they would make the same career choice again for themselves or for their children. On these measures, lawyer discontent is substantial. And, of course, studies that survey only practicing attorneys exclude those most likely to be dissatisfied: those who have left the law for an alternative career.[5]

Moreover, as chapter 1 noted, professional life is taking a substantial toll on many lawyers, regardless of their reported sense of satisfaction. Attorneys are four times more likely to be depressed than the public at large, and they have the highest depression rate of any occupational group. About a fifth of lawyers have a substance abuse problem, twice the rate of Americans generally. Two-thirds to three-quarters of lawyers report high levels of stress, and one-third acknowledge that it is damaging their physical and emotional well-being.[6]

Of course, not all sources of lawyers' discontent and dysfunction are attributable or distinctive to legal practice. Some are rooted in broader social trends. Increases in competition, commercialization, and pressure are common to many workplaces. Racial and gender bias are problems widely shared. Erosions in civility, collegiality, and a sense of social responsibility extend well beyond professional or even national boundaries. The British legal profession reports greater dissatisfaction than the American bar. Part of lawyers' discontent may also reflect personal rather than occupational characteristics. Some evidence suggests that law attracts individuals with personality traits that are disproportionately likely to result in disaffection and dysfunction. Highly competitive and perfectionist workers will be frustrated in many environments; so will idealists who find that their best efforts fail to achieve the social progress they expected. It is impossible to know how much dissatisfaction is the result of legal practice and how much reflects self-selection among practitioners.[7]

Yet while practice structures may not be the sole cause of lawyer discontent, they are an essential part of the solution. To identify appropriate reforms, we need a clearer understanding of the specific sources of workplace dissatisfaction. Since information concerning lawyers is incomplete, it makes sense also to review research on workers in general. Two points emerge clearly from this review: individuals' satisfaction with their work life is determined more by internal than external rewards, and workers are surprisingly poor judges of what is most likely to increase their own happiness.

The people who are most satisfied with their lives are those who are most satisfied with themselves. A sense of personal effectiveness—of having met life's challenges—is the best predictor of long-term happiness. Such self-esteem depends far less on external rewards than conventional wisdom suggests. Above a minimal subsistence level, income explains less than 2 percent of the variation in satisfaction levels. Most studies find equally little correlation between job status and job enjoyment. People's greatest fulfillment generally comes from opportunities to develop skills in contexts where they feel in control and competent. The star-studded achievements that many lawyers strive for—large salaries, courtroom triumphs, or professional honors—may yield little enduring satisfaction. Such rare moments have a less positive effect than the accumulation of much smaller but repeated satisfactions. Paradoxically enough, grand achievements can even work against long-term satisfaction by skewing expectations, encouraging grossly excessive work, and diluting the pleasure of more modest but attainable goals. Psychologist David Myers notes, "Better to have our best experiences be something we experience fairly often" than to sacrifice daily sources of pleasure in pursuit of occasional but elusive brass rings." Satisfaction is less a matter of getting what you want than of wanting what you have.[8]

Expectations also shape experience in other respects. Part of lawyers' dissatisfaction is rooted in the disjuncture between the anticipated rewards and the daily realities of legal practice. Too many students enter law school by default. As Mary Ann Glendon has noted, a legal degree has become "'the degree of choice for those who would rather not make any irrevocable choices, who could use some time, some room, some psychic slack.' At the end of the day, for many of these halfhearted lawyers, the vaunted flexibility of their degrees is not flexible enough." Many students launch their legal careers with little understanding of what lawyers actually do and how the demands of practice are likely to affect their lives. Much of their information comes from film and television portrayals, which take considerable dramatic license. Law in prime time offers wealth, excitement, and heroic opportunities at every turn. Law in real time is something else again.[9]

Law schools have little reason to correct this romanticized view. Their institutional self-interest lies in recruiting students and encouraging the belief that legal work is financially rewarding, intellectually challenging, and at the frontier of social justice. Faced with stable or shrinking applicant pools and escalating costs, most schools are reluctant to advertise the unbecoming aspects of life in law. The less said the better on topics like the drudgery of document preparation, the hustling for clients, the hassles of billing, the burdens of debt, and the shortages of public interest placements. Those who enter the profession expecting to save the world on Wall Street salaries or to reenact courtroom dramas on a daily basis are bound to feel betrayed. William Keates's *Proceed with Caution,* a disaffected profile of law firm life, notes that most students envision themselves "using the legal system to right social wrongs." In fact, many end up "fighting to make rich clients richer," in a practice more boring, more demanding, and less financially rewarding than they had anticipated. Graduates with undistinguished credentials face significant risks of unemployment or underemployment, and increasing numbers end up in practice settings like franchise law firms with long hours, low pay, and tedious routines. As a recent account of the escalating loan obligations among young attorneys indicates, these practitioners are registering increasing regrets about choosing a profession in which "they can't reconcile their debt with their dreams."[10]

If lawyers' dissatisfaction partly reflects the gap between expectation and experience, the question then becomes how best to address it. As chapter 7 notes, law students and applicants clearly deserve a more realistic picture of legal life. But practicing attorneys also deserve a greater opportunity to realize some of the aspirations that led them to law in the first instance.

At least part of what lawyers find dispiriting and disillusioning is not inherent in the practice of law. To that end, the following discussion seeks a clearer understanding of which problems are largely unavoidable conditions of practice, and which are attributable to choices that lawyers make, individually and collectively, implicitly and explicitly. With that understanding, practitioners might assert more control over the forces that they now simply lament.

THE STRUCTURE OF PRACTICE

Some of lawyers' disaffection is an inevitable by-product of legal practice, given the circumstances in which they and their clients tangle with the law. Individuals who are not ordinarily difficult to deal with may become so as clients. Divorces, bankruptcies, personal injuries, and other civil or criminal litigation seldom bring out the best in human nature. Moreover, as Walter Bachman points out in *Law v. Life,* some clients have ended up as clients because their behavior deviates from any acceptable standard; they are irresponsible or deceitful in personal dealings, and their relations with lawyers are no exception. For solo and small firm practitioners with narrow profit margins, unpaid fees are a chronic difficulty. Even attorneys who have attempted to avoid these difficulties by taking salaried legal aid, public defender, or public interest work find that "not all clients are as attractive as their causes." And for lawyers in other practice settings, not all causes are particularly attractive.[11]

Although about three-quarters of surveyed clients are satisfied with their own attorney, those who are not can create significant difficulties. Lawyers often become scapegoats for problems not of their own making. They bear unwelcome messages about what the law requires and what adversaries can extract, and certain legal contexts invite unpleasantness. Clients in family disputes can be unstable, unyielding, and irrational in their demands on counsel as well as on each other. In business settings, lawyers often look like deal breakers, or a drain on time and money that could be more profitably spent. Individuals represented by legal aid or court-appointed lawyers may be understandably unhappy about having to rely on someone whom they do not know and did not choose. Other clients may be equally displeased about paying through the nose for legal tussles that they do not want and cannot escape.[12]

Other unappealing aspects of legal practice reflect forces that lawyers can do little to control. In many fields of law, increasing complexity has encouraged increasing specialization. Lawyers know more and more about less and less, and their intellectual horizons have correspondingly narrowed. The problem cuts across many practice areas. Generalists in solo or small firm practice may find it difficult to maintain competence in multiple fields, while specialists in large firms may feel stifled by restricted subject matter. Associates doing scut work on complex transactions, partners trapped in narrow "niche" fields, or solo practitioners and franchise firm attorneys handling heavy routine caseloads all may find too much of their work dispiritingly dull or relentlessly repetitious.[13]

While innovative technology has eliminated some of the most tedious tasks, it has imposed new burdens and constraints. In many high-volume practices, lawyers' services need to fit within limited time frames and standardized programs, which narrows opportunities for intellectual challenge and personal problem solving. As more information becomes immediately accessible on-line, more information needs to be reviewed. At any moment, some court may be reversing, distinguishing, or extending a relevant precedent. As the pace of communication accelerates, the pressures of practice intensify. Legal life lurches from deadline to deadline, and in some fields, unpredictable and oppressive demands are disturbingly predictable. With E-mail, beepers, cell phones, and faxes, lawyers can be perpetually on call, and instant responses can be expected. The pressures are particularly intense for solo practitioners, who lack colleagues to provide backup assistance, but attorneys in any setting can become tethered to transportable worksites. Stories of lawyers in hospital delivery rooms drafting documents while timing contractions are disturbingly common.[14]

The result has been a kind of a civilian arms race with escalating personal and financial costs. Although lawyers as a group would benefit if schedules were less extended and frenetic, many practitioners are unwilling to risk a unilateral withdrawal from the competition. And lawyers who have opted out of the competitive struggle in private practice may face similar pressures in different settings. Attorneys serving low-income clients and public interest causes cope with staggering caseloads and grossly inadequate resources. The stress of cutting so many corners in the face of so many critical needs takes a substantial toll.[15]

Other difficulties relate to increases in the size of the profession. Over the past three decades, the number of attorneys has more than doubled. That growth is partly attributable to increased demand for legal services among consumers, but it also reflects increased demand for law schools among academic administrators. Because legal education is relatively cheap

and prestigious to provide, and because students are able to finance high
tuitions, law schools have been attractive start-up ventures. Their growth in
size and numbers has produced more graduates who cannot find the positions they want, particularly in public service.[16]

The bar's increase in size has coincided with other forces to intensify
competition. Supreme Court decisions on advertising and solicitation of
clients have reduced anticompetitive restraints. Consumer demand also has
limited the bar's ability to preempt competition by nonlawyers for certain
law-related services such as real estate closings, tax and financial planning,
and divorces. Accounting firms have made especially threatening inroads on
the legal profession's traditional turf. Globalization has added to the appeal
of those firms and brought more foreign competitors to American financial
centers. Moreover, corporate clients, who are facing increased pressures in
their own markets, have responded by curtailing legal costs. Businesses have
moved more routine work in-house, more actively supervised billing practices, and parceled out more projects based on short-term competitive considerations rather than long-term lawyer-client relationships.[17]

From the consumer's perspective, these developments have had some
positive effects in reducing prices and promoting efficiency. For lawyers,
however, many of the consequences have been less favorable. The bar's
increase in size has brought decreases in collegiality and in the informal reputational sanctions that traditionally helped control unprofessional behavior. The more time that lawyers need to spend on marketing their craft, the
less time they have available for practicing and improving it and for pursuing more fulfilling interests, such as family and pro bono activities. The
more price-conscious the client, the more difficult it becomes to bill for
training junior lawyers and providing the mentors necessary for their professional growth and satisfaction. The decline of long-term client relationships has also compromised lawyers' abilities to provide informed and candid counseling. Practitioners scrambling for business have difficulty refusing cases or resisting pressures to cut ethical corners. The trend in private
practice is often described as "leaner and meaner." It is scarcely surprising
that many lawyers find this trend disturbing; it would be even more disturbing if they did not.[18]

What is, however, surprising and unsettling is how reluctant attorneys
have been to address conditions of practice over which they have control.
Much of what drives dissatisfaction is a function of the profession's own priorities. And in private practice, where discontent is most intense and most
avoidable, the preoccupation with profit is at the root of the problem.

THE PRIORITY OF PROFIT

The mood of contemporary private practice is aptly captured in a *New Yorker* cartoon featuring a limousine conversation in which a well-heeled professional explains to his colleague: "I may be overcompensated, but I'm not overcompensated enough."[19]

Over the past half century, lawyers' income has increased substantially in comparison with the population at large. The median income for attorneys is now over five times that of other full-time employees, and the legal profession has become the second highest paying occupation. Yet while wealth has been rising, satisfaction has not, and there is little relationship between income and fulfillment across different fields of practice. Discontent is greatest among well-paid large firm associates and least pronounced among relatively low-earning academics, public interest, and public sector employees.[20]

Lawyers' experience reflects the more general point noted in chapter 1: above a minimum level, money is not an effective route to happiness. Americans' income, controlled for inflation, is twice what it was in the late 1950s, but fewer report being very happy, and more objective evidence concerning mental health difficulties also suggests a decline in well-being. Researchers consistently find that differences in income above subsistence levels bear relatively little relationship to differences in satisfaction. Yet despite such evidence, the desire for wealth has intensified both among lawyers and the public generally. Although this is not the occasion for a comprehensive analysis of materialism and its discontents, neither is it possible to understand the conditions of legal practice without some reference to broader cultural trends.[21]

Like other Western industrialized societies, the United States is experiencing an erosion in civic and community values that could serve as counterweight to market priorities. Being well-off financially is now the most important life goal of American college students. Three-quarters rate it as essential or very important, a figure that has doubled over the past quarter century. What counts as well-off has also escalated. As economist Juliet Schor notes in *The Overspent American,* the standard of living among the wealthy is more widely watched and envied. The more money that individuals earn, the more they believe is necessary. Among those in lawyers' income range, over two-thirds think that they need an increase of 50 to 100 percent in earnings in order to achieve satisfaction. Almost three-quarters of surveyed attorneys do not feel financially secure and are not sure that they ever will.[22]

The desire for increased affluence reflects a variety of causes apart from objective needs, although those needs clearly play a significant role. Many lawyers enter the profession with large educational debts. Some are planning or supporting families, and they live in areas with high housing costs and poor public schools and services. Parents working long hours find that quality child care seldom comes cheap. To provide what most attorneys generally consider an adequate lifestyle under those circumstances requires a substantial income. However, what constitutes adequate is a subjective matter, and lawyers' felt needs are skewed upwards for several reasons.

One explanation involves frames of reference and standards of comparison. Relative income affects well-being because it also affects expectations and status. For attorneys in private practice who work with and for corporate managers, investment bankers, start up entrepreneurs and other highly paid professionals, a desire for similar rewards can be hard to resist, especially if these individuals have similar credentials and shorter hours. The more direct exposure lawyers have to luxury lifestyles, the more natural and necessary they seem. And desires, once satisfied, beget more desires. The eighteenth-century French philosopher Diderot described this pattern in his now famous autobiographical account of how the acquisition of an expensive scarlet dressing robe left him dissatisfied with its shabby surroundings. Gradually, all of his study's threadbare furnishings came to need replacement to conform to the robe's "imperious . . . elegant tone." Similarly, for contemporary lawyers, upscale business entertaining calls for upscale dining and clothing, upscale housing invites upscale furnishings, and all require upscale incomes.[23]

Yet expensive purchases often do not yield enduring satisfactions. Once their novelty wears off, new sources of pleasure are required. Desires, expectations, and standards of comparison tend to increase as rapidly as they are satisfied. Individuals earning $200,000 are not significantly happier than those earning half that much. Nor does high pay translate into satisfaction with pay, as comparative surveys of law firm salaries and disaffection levels make clear. Moreover, for many lawyers, the work required to generate large incomes creates a heightened sense of deprivation that fuels heightened consumer demands. Attorneys working sweatshop hours feel entitled to goods and services that will make their lives easier and their leisure time more satisfying. This pattern of compensatory consumption can then become self-perpetuating. As accounts like Keates's *Proceed with Caution* make clear, lawyers frequently use the "substantial income from their jobs in an attempt to fill the voids created by their jobs." Part of the reason many professionals accept grueling schedules is to afford "extras" that they have little time to enjoy. Yet after lawyers become accustomed to this lifestyle, they often find it hard to give up in exchange for more satisfying working conditions.[24]

A desire for relative status and "positional goods" pushes in a similar and equally self-defeating direction. For many individuals, including lawyers, money is a way of keeping score, and spending money is a way to signal achievement and social status. The increasingly public nature of personal salaries has made the scoring competition easier to play and harder to win. As Steven Brill, the former editor of the *American Lawyer,* has noted, once legal periodicals began comparing law firm salaries, "suddenly all it took for a happy partner making $250,000 to become a malcontent was to read that at the firm on the next block a classmate was pulling down $300,000." With on-line chat rooms like "Greedy Associates," changes in law firm compensation packages become instantly known and subject to competition. "I am lawyer, hear me whine" is a distressingly dominant refrain in legal life. And the stakes are no longer just salaries but everything from free yoga classes and pet insurance, to in-house massages. Of course, as Brill and other commentators have pointed out, public disclosures of compensation structures have had some positive effects in discouraging misrepresentations about earnings and in exposing unjustified salary disparities. But the publicity has also launched an arms race for relative status with almost no winners and many losers. There is, in fact, no room at the top. "Addictive ambition" fuels desires not readily satisfied. Attorneys who look hard enough can always find someone getting something more. And the purchases that signal status today may look inadequate tomorrow. Well-paid professionals can always find another category in which to compete: trips, cars, fashion, charity, even children's parties. The market is inexhaustibly obliging.[25]

Not only do individual lawyers tend to overvalue income as a means to fulfillment. Many organizations employing lawyers have difficulty giving higher priority to anything else. Since money is at the top of almost everyone's scale, it is easier to reach consensus on financial rewards than on other values such as shorter hours or substantial pro bono commitments. Firms that sacrifice compensation for other workplace satisfactions also risk losing talented members and recruits who prefer greater earnings and have ample options. Once high pay scales are established, they can readily become self-perpetuating; downward mobility is painful, and generous earnings attract those who are looking for large incomes. The working conditions necessary to sustain such incomes then help create the sense of deprivation and entitlement that fuels desires for further material rewards. Even attorneys who initially entered law school with modest financial aspirations often become trapped in these reward cycles. If they cannot afford to do the kind of public interest work that they would really like, they want at least to be very well paid for what they are doing.[26]

The priority of profit has, in turn, encouraged practice structures that carry other costs. Although many lawyers would like the control over their hours and cases that comes with solo or small firm practice, they are often unwilling to assume the accompanying financial risks and sacrifices. Once lawyers have gained some expertise, they usually can earn more by retailing the labor of subordinates than by relying on their own. Private practice is increasingly moving into law firms with pyramid structures. Partners at the top profit from their skills, experience, reputation, and relationships by supervising and marketing the work of associates. Under this arrangement, junior lawyers allow firms to profit from their labor in exchange for training and opportunities to compete for partnership. A central objective is to provide all participants with incentives to avoid "shirking," "grabbing," or "leaving"—evading work, hoarding business, or departing with clients in tow.[27]

Whatever their effectiveness in accomplishing this objective, profit-driven pyramids come at a price. Part of that price involves the increase in size or ceiling on advancement that such structures encourage. Growth is inevitable unless promotions occur only when a partner departs. In firms committed to remaining small, associates may be left in lingering limbo, with no ground rules about the timing or chances of advancement. Since such a system makes it hard to recruit and retain associates, many firms promote some critical mass beyond the vacancies left by partners' departure. This growth pattern is encouraged by the cultural tendency to view size as a measure of status and to assume that the largest firms are also the leading firms. The result is that an increasing number of lawyers, about a third of those in private firms, are in firms with over fifty lawyers, and a growing number are in midsize firms or branch offices of nationally franchised firms.[28]

Yet with increases in size come increases in bureaucratization, impersonality, and pressure to generate business for additional attorneys. The larger the organization, the harder it becomes to sustain a sense of collegiality, institutional loyalty, and collective responsibility. These difficulties are compounded when firms seek increased business by expanding their geographic reach or fields of expertise through branch offices and mergers. Associates in these large firms often report a sense of anonymity and alienation, particularly when management decisions are made at a distance or a partner they have never met assigns tedious work in a case they have never heard of.

Whatever their size, firms that cannot generate sufficient business to support their growth must generally resort to painful downsizing strategies. Rather than reduce partner salaries or publicly admit their economic difficulties, many firms pass off their pruning as merit decisions. Lawyers dismissed under such circumstances pay a substantial and undeserved price.[29]

Profit-driven priorities have had other unhappy consequences. To maximize partners' income and control, many firms have reduced the percentage of associates who obtain partnership status, and have pushed out even senior colleagues who are not "fully employed." When demand declines for a particular specialty, able attorneys may be asked to leave before they have a chance to retool. Insecurity and competition have increased at all levels in firms of all sizes. Where chances for advancement dwindle, associates experience La Rochefoucauld's insight that it is not enough to succeed; others have to fail. Among partners, the premium placed on attracting business has encouraged "eat what you kill" compensation structures that exacerbate internal rivalries and undermine teamwork. Hoarding business and squabbling over who made the kill are increasingly common and have led to more lateral departures. At large firms, only half of surveyed partners feel supported by other partners.[30]

A preoccupation with profit also drives the escalation in billable hours that so adversely affects most lawyers in private practice. Close to half of these lawyers bill at least nineteen hundred hours per year, and a substantial number, particularly at large firms, meet much higher quotas. Only about two-thirds of the time spent in the office can honestly be billed to clients; the remainder is taken up by personal and organizational needs such as dealing with internal firm matters and keeping current in areas of specialization. As a consequence, lawyers often work sixty hours or more per week. Unsurprisingly, most lawyers feel that they do not have enough time for themselves, and close to half feel that they lack sufficient time for their families.[31]

Although law firms often blame sweatshop hours on client demands, other factors are clearly at work. Extended hours and total availability may be important to some clients under some circumstances, but such expectations cannot account for the routinely oppressive schedules typical of large firms. Clients do not get efficient services from bleary, burned-out lawyers. If concerns other than profit maximization were priorities, firms generally could staff projects to provide quality service under more reasonable conditions. The problem, as chapter 6 indicates, is that the predominant hourly billing system pegs profits more to the quantity of time spent than to the efficiency of its use, and profits have become the dominant concern. High hourly demands also serve economic interests in indirect ways, by screening out individuals with competing values. Those most often excluded are lawyers with substantial family commitments, generally women. But this consequence is often dismissed as a necessary, although regrettable, by-product of a competitive practice culture.[32]

Although many lawyers acknowledge these problems, they generally manage to place responsibility anywhere and everywhere else. Law firm partners blame mercenary and unrealistic associates, while associates blame mercenary and unfeeling partners. In fact, there is plenty of blame to go around. According to an *American Lawyer* overview of law firm economics, "It's hard to find any partner who thinks that first year salaries make any economic sense." The irrationality of current compensation structures began, rationally enough, when competition for the ablest new associates pushed starting salaries well above what hourly billing rates justified. These raises have forced compensation increases for other attorneys as well, a problem compounded by salary wars with accounting firms and internet companies. Because competitive pressures have prevented comparable increases in billing rates, the choice has been either to decrease partner profits or to raise associates' workload. Predictably, most partners have opted for the latter choice. And they have blamed the oppressive schedules that result on associates who seem to prefer high salaries to more humane working conditions. Managing partners often report experiences similar to the one that Walt Bachman describes in *Law v. Life*. When his firm attempted to freeze both hours and starting salaries, applicants flocked to other firms. Many of these young associates were predictably miserable when they got there. Law, like life, rarely offers a free lunch. In partners' view, junior attorneys can't have it both ways—high salaries and low hours—so they need to think more carefully about which way they want it.[33]

From associates' perspective, the trade-off looks somewhat different. Most leave law school with high debt burdens and little, if any, experience of what life is like when billing at two thousand hours. Many entering associates do not yet have demanding family commitments, and the allure of creature comforts after years of genteel poverty often is irresistible. In their view, the way for employers to avoid unmanageable workloads is to reduce income at the top, not at the bottom, of the hierarchy. Why should so many senior attorneys get so much more money than juniors for essentially similar work? The difficulty, of course, is that firms which allow incomes to fall below market rates run the same risks of desertion at the upper levels that they do at the entry levels. Profitable partners who feel undercompensated have become increasingly willing to move, often taking clients and promising associates with them. Firm managers also worry that if their workplaces begin to value quality of life over profitability, they will end up with a disproportionate share of shirkers. Particularly at the associate level, a willingness to work long hours often functions as a proxy for commitment and is highly valued in promotion decisions. The result is a prisoners' dilemma. Attorneys often end up with far more demanding schedules than they would like, but find themselves within organizations that offer no alternative.[34]

A preoccupation with the bottom line has squeezed out other values that are central to a satisfying professional life. It has preempted time not only for families but also for community involvement and cultural pursuits. In the process, it has stunted opportunities for lawyers to develop the broad-gauged experience that qualifies them for counseling and leadership roles. And it has foreclosed opportunities for the pro bono legal work that lawyers traditionally have ranked among their most satisfying professional experiences.

Nowhere is the gap between professional ideals and professional practice more apparent than on issues of public service. Few lawyers come close to satisfying the American Bar Association's Model Rules, which provide that "a lawyer should aspire to render at least fifty hours of pro bono publico legal services per year," primarily to "persons of limited means or to organizations assisting such persons." In fact, about half of attorneys perform no pro bono work and the average contribution is less than half an hour a week. Much of the uncompensated assistance that lawyers do provide goes not to low-income clients but to family, friends, clients who fail to pay their fees, and middle-class organizations like hospitals and schools that might become paying clients. Involvement in public interest and poverty law programs remains minimal at many of the nation's leading law firms and in-house corporate counsel's offices. Only about a third of the nation's five hundred largest firms have agreed to participate in the ABA Pro Bono Challenge, which requires a minimum annual contribution of 3 percent of the firm's total billable hours. Attorneys at these firms often would like to pursue such work but are deterred by policies that fail to count pro bono activity toward billable hour requirements or to value it in promotion and compensation decisions.[35]

This absence of support is shortsighted in several respects. Particularly for young attorneys, public service can provide valuable training, trial experience, and contacts that are hard to come by in early years of practice. And for lawyers at all stages of their careers, such work can give purpose and meaning to professional lives. Pro bono contributions have been responsible for many of the nation's landmark public interest cases and have helped millions of low-income families meet basic needs. The lawyers involved have generally found such representation to be a crucial way of expressing their professional identity and moral commitments. Attorneys who lack the time or support for such experiences often feel short-changed. As previously noted, the greatest source of disappointment among surveyed lawyers is the sense that they are not "contributing to the social good." Moreover, for many lawyers, pro bono poverty work provides their only exposure to how the justice system functions—or fails to function—for the have nots. The failure to provide more support for public service activities represents a significant lost opportunity for the profession as well as the public.[36]

A final casualty of the dominant profit orientation has been mentoring relationships. Experienced lawyers who are under growing pressure to generate business and billable hours often have inadequate time or incentive to train junior colleagues, most of whom will never become partners. This lack of mentoring frustrates many associates and accelerates their departures. The cycle can then become self-perpetuating and ultimately self-defeating. Over 40 percent of associates leave within three years, frequently before their firms have had time to recover their initial investment in recruiting and training. Moreover, the attorneys most likely to fall by the wayside are those whose race, gender, ethnicity, or sexual orientation imposes additional barriers to mentoring relationships. As the following discussion makes clear, this selective attrition process compounds other biases and compromises commitments to diversity and equal opportunity.[37]

MYTHS OF MERITOCRACY

"Don't have any. Don't want any." That was one employer's response to a mid-1990s Los Angeles bar survey about gay and lesbian attorneys. For most of this nation's history, that also was the prevailing view toward women and racial and ethnic minorities. Over the last several decades, all of these attitudes have changed dramatically. Women's representation grew from 3 percent of new entrants to the bar in the 1960s to 45 percent by the late 1990s; minorities increased from 1 to 20 percent. Whether or not the proportion of gays and lesbians has changed remains unclear, given their traditionally closeted status, but the number who are able to be open about their sexual orientation has grown significantly.[38]

However, as bar commissions repeatedly acknowledge, while progress has been substantial, the agenda remains "unfinished." Women and minorities remain overrepresented at the bottom and underrepresented at the top of professional status and reward structures. For example, women constitute only about 13 percent of full partners in law firms, 10 percent of law school deans, 10 percent of top in-house legal positions at *Fortune* 500 companies, and 5 percent of large firm managing partners. Minorities account for 9 percent of law school deans, 3 percent of law firm partners, and 2 percent of *Fortune* 500 general counsel. Salaries are substantially lower for women, minority men, and openly gay and lesbian attorneys than for other lawyers with comparable qualifications and positions. Women are half as likely to achieve partnership as similarly situated men. And the limited data available on minority, gay, and lesbian lawyers also document significant disparities in retention and promotion.[39]

The bar's response has been a mix of confession and avoidance. Commissions have been created, reports issued, policies developed, and educational programs implemented. Concerns about diversity are on the profession's reform agenda, and that itself represents significant progress. But ironically enough, this progress has created its own obstacles to further change. A widespread perception is that barriers are coming down, women and minorities are moving up, and equal opportunity has been substantially achieved. Whatever racial or gender differences remain are attributed to different choices and capabilities. To many lawyers, bias either is not a significant issue or whatever happens in their own workplaces is not an example. As attorneys in a Texas bar survey put it, "The so-called gender gap is vastly overblown. If people who enter the arena will concentrate on the job and get the chip off their shoulders . . . they should do fine in today's society." "Women should grow up and stop whining." "Of all the problems we have as lawyers . . . discrimination is low on the list of important ones."[40]

This "no-problem" problem has itself become a central problem. Over the last two decades, some sixty surveys have been completed on bias in the profession, and they consistently find substantial race and gender disparities in opportunities as well as in perceptions of opportunities. Between two-thirds and three-quarters of women report experiencing gender bias, while only one-quarter to one-third of men report observing it. In the ABA's most recent survey, about two-thirds of blacks, but only about 10 percent of whites, believe that minorities are treated less fairly in hiring and promotion processes. A study by the National Association for Law Placement revealed similar race and gender gaps concerning selections for partnership. Significant progress will require a clearer understanding of these differing perceptions of the problem and the challenges involved in addressing it.[41]

A place to start is with competing definitions of discrimination. To many attorneys, discrimination implies overt intentional prejudice. The professional workplaces they inhabit produce few clear examples. Lawyers with conscious racial and gender biases generally have the sense not to share them openly. Less egregious conduct may pass unnoticed among those who do not need to notice because it does not affect *their* lives. And much of what they do see—demeaning assumptions, inadvertent slights, petty harassment—will seem like isolated instances, not institutionalized patterns. But the legal landscape looks different to attorneys who are on the receiving end of repeated forms of bias, however unintended. The black woman partner of a Chicago firm sees patterns when she is mistaken for a stenographer at *every* deposition she attends. For lawyers with these experiences, the problem has less to do with intentional discrimination than with unconscious stereotypes, unacknowledged preferences, and workplace policies that are neutral in form but not in practice.[42]

Both psychological research and empirical surveys underscore the lingering influence of gender and racial stereotypes. Women and minorities do not enjoy the same presumption of competence as their white male colleagues. Traditionally disfavored groups find that their mistakes are more readily noticed and their achievements more often attributed to luck or special treatment. For African American and Hispanic attorneys, long-standing myths of intellectual inferiority, coupled with lower average grades and test scores, make these stereotypes particularly difficult to overcome. As diversity expert Jacob Herring notes, "Minorities are regarded as representative of their entire race when they fail, but are considered the exception when they succeed." The mismatch between characteristics traditionally associated with women and those typically associated with professional success leave female lawyers in a persistent double bind. They are faulted for being too passive or too pushy, too feminine or not feminine enough. What is assertive in a man is abrasive in a woman.[43]

Women with children face another double standard and another double bind. Working mothers are held to higher standards than working fathers and are often criticized for being insufficiently committed, as either parents or professionals. Those who seem willing to sacrifice family needs to workplace demands appear lacking as mothers. Those who want extended leaves or reduced schedules appear lacking as lawyers. These mixed messages leave many women with the uncomfortable sense that whatever they are doing, they should be doing something else. Lawyers who ignore those cues may be reminded by irate colleagues, although seldom with the candor of one Washington, D.C., lawyer: "You can hardly handle one child. What are you doing going for another?" Several women in a recent study by the

Boston Bar Association reported receiving "friendly advice" that was never given to men: having more than one child would be "death to [their] career." The problem is compounded by workplace structures that resist part-time work. Less than 3 percent of firm lawyers take reduced schedules, and most surveyed women believe, with considerable justification, that accepting such status would seriously compromise their careers.[44]

Of course, the difficulty of reconciling work and family demands is not exclusively a "women's issue." Workplaces that are reluctant to accommodate mothers often have even less tolerance for fathers. As one associate in the Boston bar study put it, "it is okay for men to say they would like to spend more time with their kids, but it is not okay for them to do it, except once in a while." A common attitude among male partners is that "I have a family and I didn't get time off. Why should you?" Ironically enough, some lawyers interpret these attitudes as evidence that gender bias is not a problem. After all, women are more likely than men to receive "special treatment" concerning family leaves and flexible schedules. But that interpretation misses a central part of the problem. Penalizing men with family commitments also penalizes women. It discourages male attorneys from assuming an equal share of household work and reinforces traditional gender roles. Employed women end up with about 70 percent of family responsibilities and pay a professional price.[45]

The force of traditional stereotypes is compounded by other cognitive biases. People are more likely to notice and recall information that confirms their prior assumptions than information that contradicts them. Many lawyers assume that a working mother is unlikely to be fully committed to her career, and they more easily remember the times when she left early than the times when she stayed late. Attorneys who assume that their minority colleagues are beneficiaries of affirmative action, not meritocratic selection, will recall their errors more readily than their insights. A related problem is that people share what psychologists label a "just world" bias. They want to believe that individuals generally get what they deserve and deserve what they get. Perceptions of performance are often unconsciously shifted to match observed outcomes. If women and minorities are underrepresented in positions of greatest prominence, the most psychologically convenient explanation is that they lack the necessary qualifications or commitment.[46]

However, a more adequate explanation would acknowledge that careers can also be waylaid by adverse stereotypes and inadequate access to mentoring and client networks. As a wide array of research demonstrates, people feel more comfortable with those who are like them in important respects, and they are more likely to assist those with similar backgrounds.

Women, minority men, gay, and lesbian attorneys frequently report being left out of the loop of advice, collaboration, and business development.[47]

For each of these groups, the dynamics of exclusion are somewhat different, but the adverse consequences are much the same. Women with substantial family commitments and high billable hour requirements lack time for informal socializing. Men worried about inappropriate appearances or unintended sexual harassment also are reluctant to initiate invitations. Lawyers of color often find that differences in socioeconomic or cultural backgrounds impose an additional obstacle. Many of these lawyers report being pressured to specialize in areas where their racial identity is thought particularly useful, or they find themselves included on matters only to provide a token presence. For example, black associates have been assigned to defend race discrimination cases, or they have been invited to meetings with potential minority clients where their only real function is to "sit there and be black." Gay and lesbian attorneys have been excluded from contexts not only where colleagues feel uncomfortable but also where they worry that others, such as judges or clients, might feel uncomfortable. Over time, these policies can become self-perpetuating. Senior lawyers do not want to invest time mentoring those who are likely to leave. Women and minorities who do not receive mentoring and do not perceive equal opportunities generally do in fact leave. Their disproportionate attrition then reduces the pool of mentors and role models for lawyers of similar backgrounds and perpetuates the expectations that perpetuate the problem.[48]

The problem is compounded by the disincentives to raise it. A common response is to shoot the messenger. Women who express concerns learn that they are "overreacting" or exercising "bad judgment." Most lawyers are not comfortable with complaints about discrimination, and they prefer not to work with people who make them uncomfortable. Gay and lesbian attorneys who would "rather have a career than a lawsuit" similarly learn to let even explicit homophobia pass unchallenged, particularly since formal complaints are seldom effective. In one New York bar association survey, less than 4 percent of reported incidents of discrimination based on sexual orientation resulted in any remedial action. The result is to prevent candid discussions of diversity-related issues. Targets of bias are reluctant to appear confrontational, and decision makers are reluctant to air performance-related concerns that could make them appear biased. Moreover, because most employment decisions are subjective and confidential, clear proof of bias is hard to come by. Discrimination claims involving lawyers are expensive to litigate in both personal and financial terms. Plaintiffs risk having all their deficiencies publicly aired, and the rare individual who wins in court may lose in life. As one Chicago practitioner put it, an attorney who sues for discrimination "may never eat lunch in this town again."[49]

Paul Barrett's recent profile of *The Good Black* provides a case history of these dynamics. Lawrence Mungen, an African American graduate of Harvard College and Harvard Law School, attempted to fit the model that Barrett's title invokes. As a senior associate, he joined the Washington, D.C., branch office of a Chicago law firm, Katten, Muchen, and Zavis, and attempted to "play by the rules." After being hired to do complex bankruptcy work in an office that generated too little of it, he fell through the cracks and landed off the partnership track. But until late in the process, he failed to complain or to raise other race-related concerns. He did not want to be typecast as the "angry black," and he declined to support or mentor any of the small number of other minority lawyers at the firm. When his difficulty in obtaining work became clear, some partners made a few well-meaning but ineffectual responses. They slashed his billing rate, which enabled him to take over some routine matters, but also undermined his reputation as someone capable of demanding, partnership-caliber work. Although the senior partners eventually offered to relocate him to another office, they did not promise opportunities that would lead to promotion. He sued for race discrimination and alleged multiple examples, such as the firm's failure to provide formal evaluations, informal mentoring, invitations to client meetings, or help with business development. A largely black District of Columbia jury found in his favor, but a divided appellate panel reversed. Unable to find another comparable position, Mungen made do with temporary, low-level assignments at other firms and, by the end of the book, was contemplating an alternative career.[50]

As many commentators have noted, the case was a kind of "racial Rorschach test" in which observers saw what they expected to see. To lawyers in the firm and sympathizers outside it, including the appellate court, this was a morality play in which no good deed went unpunished. From their perspective, Mungen was treated no worse than white associates and in some respects considerably better. The slights and oversights that he alleged at trial were "business as usual mismanagement." And the extra efforts that the firm made to keep Mungen were evidence of a commitment to equal opportunity. By contrast, critics, including Barrett, saw this as a textbook case of "a reckless indifferent affirmative action." From their vantage, the firm's efforts were too little too late. Unsurprisingly, these competing perceptions usually divide along racial lines and typify attitudes within the profession generally.

In a national ABA survey, only 8 percent of blacks, but 41 percent of whites, believed that firms had a genuine commitment to diversity.[51]

Much, of course, depends on what counts as commitment. Katten's management, like that at many firms, undoubtedly did want minority lawyers to succeed. Even from a purely pragmatic standpoint, it helps in recruitment and business development if a firm includes more than the single black lawyer that Katten's Washington office had during Mungen's employment. But while many attorneys want to achieve greater diversity, they do not necessarily want to rethink the structures that get in the way. According to many surveyed lawyers, their firms pay "lip service" to the value of diversity but do not make it a priority or pursue affirmative efforts to achieve it. The reluctance to support "special treatment" is widely shared. The ABA's survey found that only 42 percent of white lawyers, compared with 92 percent of blacks, favored affirmative action. To opponents, reliance on race, ethnicity, or gender perpetuates a kind of preferential treatment that society should be seeking to eradicate. In critics' view, such treatment implies that women and men of color require special advantages, which reinforces the very assumptions of inferiority that we should be trying to counteract.[52]

Yet while these lawyers are correct that affirmative action carries a price, the question is always "Compared to what?" The costs of inaction are also substantial. Only by ensuring a critical mass of minorities and women in top positions can we secure a workplace that is fair in fact as well as form. Although the stigma associated with diversity initiatives can present substantial problems, critics mistake its most fundamental causes and plausible solutions. Assumptions of inferiority predated affirmative action and would persist without it. The absence of women and men of color in key legal roles is also stigmatizing. Moreover, we are unlikely to reduce racial or gender prejudices if we ignore their continuing effects or treat all forms of preferential treatment as equally objectionable. Disfavoring women and minorities stigmatizes and subordinates the entire group. Disfavoring white males does not. In some contexts, "special" treatment may be essential to counteract special obstacles.

Contrary to critics' assertions, the measures necessary for diversity do not compete with quality but rather enhance it. Adequate representation of lawyers with different backgrounds and experiences is critical for success in an increasingly diverse marketplace. Moreover, as the following discussion indicates, many strategies that promote equal opportunity for women and minorities can improve the quality of life for all attorneys. Better management of human resources is an issue on which the entire profession has a stake.

ALTERNATIVE STRUCTURES

In a celebrated essay, "The Importance of What We Care About," philosopher Harry Frankfurt underscored an obvious but often overlooked truth. Individuals are most fulfilled when they are engaged in work that they find meaningful and when they have reflected, at the deepest level, about what work meets that definition. It is, Frankfurt emphasized, worth "caring about what we care about" and refusing to settle, at least in the long term, for workplaces that fall short. Lawyers, both individually and collectively, need to ask hard questions along the lines that Frankfurt proposed. Although some gap is inevitable between idealized aspirations and daily realities, it by no means follows that current conditions of practice are the best we can achieve. Increased competition may be a given, but lawyers can change what they are competing over. The legal profession has much more control over workplace priorities than most occupations. The vast majority of lawyers work in organizations owned or run by lawyers. They can choose to place greater emphasis on values other than profit, and they can create structures that permit such choices. Law schools, law firms, bar associations, and other legal institutions also can help increase understanding of the conditions that are central to professional satisfaction.[53]

A place to start is with educating attorneys who hold managerial positions. Despite the outpouring of complaints about the decline of the profession into a business, many lawyers have failed to incorporate effective business management strategies in structuring their professional workplaces. As experts often note, the state of human resources initiatives in most law offices is nothing short of "Dickensian." Law schools offer few if any courses on such subjects or on other marketing, technological, and financial aspects of running a practice. Seldom do managing attorneys receive formal training in personnel issues, and seldom have they made adequate use of research on employment satisfaction. In general, that research identifies several conditions that are most likely to yield professional fulfillment: tasks that individuals view as challenging and valuable; some measure of responsibility and control over their work; sufficient time for personal, family, and public service commitments; and supportive collegial environments. Lawyers, particularly those with managerial responsibilities, need more systematic information about how well their own practice settings satisfy these conditions. However, the preceding discussion suggests certain general directions for reform.[54]

One obvious goal should be increasing opportunities for public service. Pro bono work is an effective way of enabling attorneys to gain skills and recognition in pursuit of causes that they find meaningful. Legal workplaces need to provide more support for such involvement: pro bono assistance should count toward meeting billable hour requirements and should carry positive weight in performance evaluations. Bar associations could encourage such policies by requiring all lawyers to contribute a specified amount of time, such as fifty hours per year, or the financial equivalent, to pro bono service primarily for persons of limited means.

Such proposals have previously been rejected on both ethical and pragmatic grounds. One concern involves the fairness of requiring lawyers, but not other professionals, to provide charitable assistance; another involves the enforceability and efficiency of having inexperienced or unmotivated attorneys dabbling in poverty law. Such concerns are not without force, but it is also the case that lawyers have special privileges imposing special obligations. American attorneys have obtained a much more extensive and exclusive right to provide essential services than lawyers in other nations or members of other occupations. The bar has closely guarded that prerogative, and its success in restricting lay competition has helped to price services out of the reach of many consumers. Under these circumstances, it is not unreasonable to expect lawyers to make some modest pro bono contributions in exchange for their privileged status. Concerns about efficiency can be mitigated by allowing attorneys to substitute financial contributions for direct service and by providing the kind of brief but effective training and backup assistance that voluntary bar programs already have developed. Even if public service requirements could not be fully enforced, they would at least push in socially useful directions. For many impoverished clients, some assistance, however inexperienced, is preferable to what they have now, which is none. And for many lawyers, who would like to participate in pro bono programs but are in unsupportive working environments, bar requirements could provide the necessary leverage for change.[55]

Another priority for reform should be better accommodation of work and family commitments. Lawyers should have opportunities to choose extended leaves or reduced schedules without paying a permanent professional price. As the NALP survey put it, "up or out" should be "dead and gone." Both individuals and organizations can benefit from more flexible structures. Establishing adequate part-time and family leave policies, as well as more humane and flexible working schedules, would be steps in the right direction. The greater challenge, however, is to ensure that lawyers who take advantage of these options are not relegated to second-class status and penalized in assignment and promotion decisions. Commitment should be measured less in terms of the quantity of hours billed and more in terms of the quality of work performed.[56]

Other strategies should focus directly on diversity and equal opportunity. Many legal employers still need policies that prohibit discrimination on the basis of sexual orientation, that extend benefits to domestic partners, that promote effective recruitment, and that create adequate channels for raising diversity-related concerns. Many workplaces also lack formal mentoring programs that ensure adequate support for women and minorities. Too few employers have realistic goals for hiring and retaining underrepresented groups, and fewer still hold supervising attorneys accountable for meeting those targets. Ensuring that a critical mass of women and minorities occupy decision-making positions is often crucial for securing these other strategies for change. To assist that process, an increasing number of organizations have made effective use of diversity training and consultants. In other legal workplaces, however, these strategies have functioned more as a substitute than as a catalyst for change. As one disillusioned associate noted, firms "can put on programs until the cows come home," but significant progress will require lawyers to act on the recommendations they hear."[57]

Bar associations also must do more to assist those efforts. One obvious strategy is to follow the lead of organizations that have developed model policies, training materials, and continuing legal education programs on diversity issues. Greater support should be available for diversity goals and timetables and for Minority Counsel Programs, in which participating firms and in-house counsel departments pledge to increase their representation and use of minority lawyers and their referrals of business to minority-owned firms. More effort should also focus on evaluating the effectiveness of these initiatives. Anecdotal reviews of some programs are mixed, and systematic research is necessary to identify strategies that are most useful.[58]

The bar also can work in partnership with law schools and public interest organizations to address issues concerning the quality of professional life. For example, more attention should focus on helping solo and small firm practitioners develop financially viable ways to meet the needs of underserved communities. Such initiatives are beginning to emerge through cooperative networks providing advice, referrals, mentoring, and technological assistance. Additional strategies along these lines are crucial, as are law school and continuing legal education courses concerning quality of life and managerial issues. Collaborative efforts could also be made to develop best practice standards to evaluate legal employers on dimensions such as diversity, ethical practices, mentoring, family accommodations, and pro bono programs. Survey data could be used to assess not just formal policies but actual experiences. Legal employers are now ranked primarily in terms of size, profitability, and income. They need more incentives to compete on other levels.[59]

Changes in legal practice along the lines identified here will, of course, require broader changes in the legal culture. Lawyers will need to rethink their priorities as well as their policies. But widespread dissatisfaction with some aspects of practice makes reassessment seem plausible. A number of years ago at a Stanford symposium on corporate law firms, a distinguished group of managing partners were invited to begin that reexamination. "Why," they were asked, "didn't more firms give lawyers a choice to meet family or pro bono commitments by opting for saner schedules and lower salaries?" "Because," one senior partner explained impatiently, "reduced workloads cost money. Getting additional lawyers up to speed, accommodating those with restricted availability, and paying extra overhead are expensive. And who is going to pay for all that?" The answer, which appeared to come somewhat as a shock, was "You will." At least in the short term. But over the long run, the investment can pay off from gains in morale, recruitment, and retention. Moreover, especially at major law firms, where partners' salaries are over ten times those of the average American worker, it does not seem unreasonable to expect some modest short-term financial sacrifice that will promote more satisfying professional lives.

Oscar Wilde once observed that in this world there are only "two great tragedies. One is not getting what one wants, the other is getting it." Most lawyers want not only a comfortable lifestyle but also a supportive practice environment and socially useful work. Ironically enough, attorneys' success in achieving the first objective has limited their ability to achieve the others. The result may not be a tragedy, but neither is it all that lawyers should aspire to achieve.

CHAPTER 3

THE ADVOCATE'S ROLE IN THE ADVERSARY SYSTEM

M y first legal case was almost my last. It brought home Dostoevski's definition of an advocate as "a conscience for hire." And it made me wonder about putting mine on the market.

The insight came when I was interning at the Washington, D.C., public defender's office after my first year in law school. Two of the office's juvenile clients had stomped an elderly "wino" to death, just for the fun of it. They confessed to my supervising attorney and to the arresting officer; indeed, they appeared somewhat proud of their accomplishment. However, the police committed a number of constitutional and procedural violations in obtaining the confession and other inculpating evidence. My supervisor was able to get the case dismissed on what the public would consider a "technicality." He also was proud of his accomplishment. The clients were jubilant and unrepentant. I had no doubt that the office would see them again. Nor did I doubt that I was utterly unsuited to be a criminal defense lawyer. I wasn't sure I was ready to be a lawyer at all.

Now, with the benefit of a quarter century's hindsight, I think both my supervisor and I were right. He was providing an essential and ethically defensible safeguard for constitutional values. And I was right to feel morally troubled by the consequences. I had assisted a process that sent the wrong messages to guilty clients: some lives are cheap; a gifted lawyer can get you off.

This is one of the "hard cases" in legal ethics. Its moral tensions arise from deeply rooted conflicts in America's commitments to both individual rights and social responsibilities. This conflict plays out in many law-related contexts, and legal ethics is no exception. When lawyers straddle these cultural contradictions, the public both demands and condemns their divided loyalties. Defense of disempowered clients and unpopular causes earns lawyers their greatest respect but also their sharpest criticism. The clash between lawyers' responsibilities as officers of the court and advocates of client interests creates the most fundamental dilemmas of legal ethics. All too often, the bar has resolved this conflict by permitting overrepresentation of those who can afford it and underrepresentation of everyone else. The result is to privilege the profession's interests at the expense of the public's.

What compounds the problem is the bar's frequent denial that there is in fact a problem. Many attorneys see no significant conflict between professional priorities and social responsibilities. As the American Trial Lawyers' Foundation Code of Conduct puts it, "Lawyers serve the public interest by undivided fidelity to each client's interests as the client perceives them." This assumption has obvious advantages for lawyers, whose financial success and professional status generally depend on satisfying the individuals who retain them. Bar ethics codes make a virtue out of expedience.[1]

Yet what is professionally convenient is not always socially desirable. In many contexts, the moral justifications for zealous advocacy are unconvincing. The following discussion explores the social costs of current practices. That focus should not, however, serve either to overstate the frequency of ethical dilemmas or to understate the diversity in lawyers' responses. Most routine legal work does not pose significant moral issues. And when such issues do arise, lawyers with different values in different practice settings react differently. But attorneys' ethical decision making is also shaped by codified rules, collegial expectations, and economic pressures that are widely shared and deeply disturbing.

Taken together, these practice structures have reinforced a professional role that compromises public interests. Overzealous representation of powerful clients has exposed innocent third parties to substantial health, safety, and financial risks. And inadequate representation of poor and unsophisticated clients has left them similarly vulnerable. Neither of these problems is readily solved. But a better understanding of their underlying causes may push us toward more promising responses.

Any socially defensible conception of the advocate's role will require more ethically demanding professional codes and institutionalized practices. In essence, lawyers need to accept moral responsibility for the consequences of their professional actions. That responsibility requires advocates to consider all the societal interests at issue in particular practice settings. Loyalty to clients is a crucial concern, but it needs to be balanced against other values involving truth, justice, and prevention of unnecessary harm. Ethical obligations will inevitably depend on context. The degree of partisanship appropriate for criminal proceedings is not necessarily justifiable for civil litigation.

Under this contextual moral framework, lawyers will, of course, sometimes disagree about how to accommodate competing values. But at least they will need to confront the hard questions and to accept public responsibility for their professional choices.

THE EVOLUTION OF THE ADVOCATE'S ROLE

American lawyers generally assume that the current advocate's role reflects some fixed, time-honored understanding. In fact, until this century, the governing principles were largely informal, frequently imprecise, and highly incomplete. Competing visions of professional obligations were apparent in the first major treatises on legal ethics. Writing in the 1830s, law professor David Hoffman argued that "[i]t would be dishonorable folly" for advocates to argue for unmeritorious positions that would result in bad law. Pennsylvania judge George Sharswood was more ambivalent. His influential 1869 treatise maintained that the advocate was "not morally responsible for . . . maintaining an unjust cause." Lawyers should not "usurp the functions of both judge and jury." Yet somewhat inconsistently, Sharswood also claimed that attorneys should refuse to assist plaintiffs "aiming to perpetrate a wrong" through means that were technically legal.[2]

These competing conceptions of the lawyer's role still figure in contemporary debates over legal ethics. However, the view of lawyers as morally neutral advocates who defend, not judge, their clients has gradually become more dominant. A variety of forces have contributed to this trend, including the increased commercialism and competitiveness of legal practice and the absence of a widely shared vision of the public interest. For most private practitioners, social obligations are increasingly removed from daily practice; they are accommodated instead in separate public interest career paths or in minimal pro bono contributions.

Contemporary ethical codes reflect and reinforce these principles of moral neutrality and client loyalty. The American Bar Association's Model

Rules of Professional Conduct, which about two-thirds of the states have adopted, require that lawyers abide by clients' decisions concerning the "objectives of representation" and emphasize that legal assistance "does not constitute an endorsement of the client's political, economic, social, or moral views or activities." Comparable provisions appear in the ABA's Model Code of Professional Conduct, which preceded the Model Rules and is still in force in about a fifth of the states.[3]

Bar ethics provisions do include some important qualifications to partisan principles. Neither the Model Rules nor the Code requires lawyers to accept a client or cause that they find unjust, or to engage in offensive but legal tactics. Lawyers may not knowingly assist criminal or fraudulent conduct, and they may limit representation from the outset or withdraw under certain circumstances, such as where the client insists on "repugnant or imprudent" actions and the matter is not pending before a tribunal. However, if lawyers are not able to withdraw from representation, then the client's decision on substantive matters must prevail. Attorneys also must keep client confidences except in a narrow category of circumstances, such as where necessary to prevent criminal conduct that is likely to result in imminent death, substantial bodily harm, or serious financial injury. Even in these contexts, the code provisions applicable in most states do not *require* disclosure of confidences; the attorney has discretion to remain silent despite life-threatening consequences for innocent third parties. And bar ethics rules in many jurisdictions prevent lawyers from divulging noncriminal but fraudulent client conduct, whatever the consequences to others.[4]

The bar generally defends such rules, and the advocacy model that they reflect, on both ethical and pragmatic grounds. The ethical claims build on broader understandings of role morality that have generated significant dispute. Theorists use the concept of role to describe the cultural expectations and obligations that arise in particular social contexts. According to sociologists such as Erving Goffman, the self does not exist outside of roles; we are always playing some part, such as parent, friend, employee, or advocate. On similar reasoning, some philosophers maintain that ethical decision making requires consideration of the functions appropriate to particular roles. Lawyers who maintain that their job is to defend, not judge, a client are asserting a claim of role-differentiated morality. Their implicit assumption is that zealous advocacy is appropriate even when it results in injustice in a particular case, because the advocacy role promotes justice in most cases.[5]

Yet this reflexive retreat into role begs the most relevant questions. Is morally neutral advocacy really the best way of achieving justice? Or would society benefit from an alternative conception of role that permitted greater sensitivity to nonclient and other societal interests? As law professor and philosopher David Luban points out, an appeal to role is ultimately no more than a "shorthand method of appealing to the moral reasons [justifying] . . . that role. And these may be, must be, balanced against the moral reasons for breaking [or changing] the role." Few lawyers, however, seem interested in striking such a balance. The reasons have more to do with pragmatic than moral considerations. Prevailing concepts of the advocate's role effectively serve professional interests even as they compromise public values.[6]

THE PREMISES OF PARTISANSHIP

The standard ethical justifications for the advocate's role rest on two major premises. The first assumption, drawing on utilitarian reasoning, is that an adversarial clash between opposing advocates is the best way of discovering truth. The second assumption, based on individual rights, is that morally neutral partisanship is the most effective means of protecting human freedom and dignity. Both claims unravel at several key points.

The truth-based rationale for the advocate's role assumes that the "right" result is most likely to occur through competitive presentations of relevant law and facts. As a report by the Joint Conference of the American Bar Association and the Association of American Law Schools emphasized, only when a decision maker "has had the benefit of intelligent and vigorous advocacy on both sides" can society have confidence in the decision. This faith in partisan processes is part of a broader worldview that underpins America's basic social and economic institutions. Robert Kutak, chair of the ABA commission that drafted the Model Rules of Professional Conduct, observed that our commitment to the advocate's role in an adversarial framework reflects "the same deep-seated values we place on competition" in other contexts.[7]

A second defense of neutral partisanship involves the protection of rights and the relationships necessary to safeguard those rights. Here again, the priority we give to personal liberties is rooted in more general cultural commitments. In a highly legalistic society, preservation of personal dignity and autonomy requires preservation of access to law. According to bar leaders, individual freedom would be severely compromised if the profession began screening cases on the basis of their moral merit. The result would be an "oligarchy of lawyers," in which "saints [would] have a monopoly on lawsuits," and lawyers would have a monopoly on determining who qualified for sainthood. The legal profession has no special claim to right-eousness and no public accountability for their views of justice. By what right should they "play God" by foreclosing legal assistance or imposing "their own views about the path of virtue upon their clients"?[8]

If advocates assumed such authority, bar leaders further claim that eth-ical professionals would refuse to assist those clients most in need of ethical counseling. And if advocates were held morally accountable for their clients' conduct, less legal representation would be available for those most vulner-able to popular prejudice and governmental repression. Our history pro-vides ample illustrations of the social and economic penalties directed at attorneys with unpopular clients. It was difficult enough to find lawyers for accused communists in the McCarthy era and for political activists in the early southern civil rights campaign. Those difficulties would have been far greater without the principle that legal representation is not an endorsement of client conduct.[9]

These rights-based justifications of neutral partisanship assume special force in criminal cases. Individuals whose lives, liberty, and reputation are at risk deserve an advocate without competing loyalties to the state. Ensuring effective representation serves not only to avoid unjust outcomes but also to affirm community values and to express our respect for individ-ual rights. Guilt or innocence should be determined in open court with due process of law, not in the privacy of an attorney's office. The consequences of an alternative model are readily apparent in many totalitarian countries. Where defense lawyers' role is to "serve justice," rather than their clients, what passes for "justice" does not commend itself for export. Often the roles of counsel for the defendant and the state are functionally identical and the price is paid in innocent lives. A case in point involves China's celebrated prosecution of the Gang of Four following the Cultural Revolution of the 1960s. The attorney appointed to defend Mao Tse Tung's widow chose not to honor his client's request to assert her innocence or to conduct any inves-tigations, present any witnesses, or challenge the government's case. According to the lawyer, such advocacy was unnecessary because "the police and the prosecutors worked on the case a very long time and the evidence they found which wasn't true they threw away."[10]

This country has had similar experiences when the crime has been espe-cially heinous or the accused has been a member of a particularly unpopu-lar group. To take only the most obvious example, for most of this nation's history, southern blacks accused of an offense against a white victim stood little chance of anything approximating zealous advocacy or a fair trial. Despite substantial progress, racial and ethnic bias in legal proceedings remains common, as most Americans and virtually every bar task force agree. The risk of abuse is significant in other contexts as well. Perjury, fabrication of evidence, and suppression of exculpatory material by law enforcement officials remain pervasive problems. Such abuses were present in some two-thirds of the sixty-odd cases involving defendants facing the death penalty who recently have been exonerated by DNA evidence. And conduct by the Office of Independent Counsel in investigating the Clinton-Lewinsky affair offers a sobering reminder of the risks of prosecutorial excess. Without the prospect of defense counsel willing to challenge law enforcement conduct, government officials have inadequate incentives to respect constitutional rights or to investigate facts thoroughly. Providing uncompromised advocacy for defendants who are guilty is the best way of protecting those who are not.[11]

Although these rationales for zealous advocacy have considerable force, they fall short of justifying current partisanship principles. A threshold weakness is the bar's overreliance on criminal defense as an all-purpose paradigm for the lawyer's role. Only a small amount of legal work involves either criminal proceedings or civil matters that raise similar concerns of individual freedom and governmental power. An advocacy role designed to ensure the presumption of innocence and deter prosecutorial abuse is not necessarily transferable to other legal landscapes. Bar rhetoric that casts the lawyer as a "champion against a hostile world" seems out of touch with most daily practice. The vast majority of legal work assists corporate and wealthy individual clients in a system that is scarcely hostile to their interests. When a Wall Street firm representing a *Fortune* 500 corporation squares off against understaffed regulators or a victim of unsafe products, the balance of power is not what bar metaphors imply.[12]

A similar problem arises with traditional truth-based justifications for neutral partisanship. Their underlying premise, that accurate results will emerge from competitive partisan presentations before disinterested tribunals, depends on factual assumptions that seldom hold in daily practice. Most legal representation never receives oversight from an impartial decision maker. Many disputes never reach the point of formal legal complaint, and of those that do, over 90 percent settle before trial. Moreover, even cases that end up in court seldom resemble the bar's idealized model of adversarial processes. That model presupposes adversaries with roughly equal incentives, resources, capabilities, and access to relevant information. But those conditions are more the exception than the rule in a society that tolerates vast disparities in wealth, high litigation costs, and grossly inadequate access to legal assistance. As a majority of surveyed judges agreed, a mismatch in attorneys' skills can distort outcomes; a mismatch in client resources compounds the problem. In law, as in life, the haves generally come out ahead.[13]

Conventional defenses of neutral partisanship fail to address these structural inequalities. According to the preamble of the ABA Model Rules, "When an opposing party is well represented, a lawyer can be a zealous advocate on behalf of a client and at the same time assume that justice is being done." If the opposing party is not well represented, the Rules offer no such assurance. Bar leaders typically respond that "the solution to this problem is not to impose on counsel the burden of representing interests other than those of his client, but rather to take appropriate steps to insure that all interests are effectively represented." How that representation can realistically be achieved and financed is a matter diplomatically overlooked.[14]

Other truth-based defenses of neutral partisanship rest on equally unrealistic assumptions. The claim that adversarial clashes yield factually accurate results is not self-evident. The vast majority of countries do not have an adversarial system; they rely primarily on judges or investigating magistrates, not partisan advocates, to develop a case. Nor do lawyers generally rely on adversarial methods outside of the courtroom; they do not hire competitive investigators. Further problems arise with the bar's related claim that whatever "truth" emerges from adversarial processes constitutes a just outcome. This assumption confuses procedural and substantive fairness. Even if both parties are "well represented," the result may be inequitable because the underlying law or the trial process is flawed. Wealth, power, and prejudice skew both legislative and legal decision making. Public policy makers may lack access to relevant information, single-interest groups may exercise undue influence, and formal rules may be under- or over-inclusive because the costs of fine-tuning are too great. Judges and jurors may have other difficulties in reaching just results, given their lack of access to confidential facts and unrehearsed witnesses.[15]

For similar reasons, the bar's traditional rights-based justifications offer inadequate support for prevailing adversarial practices. Such justifications implicitly assume that clients are entitled to assistance in whatever the law permits. This assumption confuses legal and moral rights. Some conduct that is socially indefensible may remain lawful because adequate prohibitions appear unenforceable or because decision-making bodies are too uninformed or compromised by special interests to impose effective regulation. As chapter 4 suggests, an ethic of undivided client loyalty in these contexts has encouraged lawyers' assistance in some of the most socially costly enterprises in recent memory: the distribution of asbestos and Dalkon Shields, the suppression of health information about cigarettes, and the financially irresponsible ventures of savings and loan associations.[16]

Defenders of neutral partisanship typically respond that protection of client rights is ethically justifiable despite such consequences because individual liberty and autonomy are of paramount value in a free society. Moral philosophers generally make no such mistake. As David Luban notes, this standard justification for zealous advocacy blurs an important distinction between the "desirability of people acting autonomously and the desirability of their autonomous acts." It is, for example, morally desirable for clients to make their own decisions about whether to attempt to defeat a needy opponent's valid claim through a legal technicality; it is not morally desirable for them actually to do so. Autonomy does not have intrinsic value; its importance derives from the values it fosters, such as individual initiative and responsibility. If a particular client objective does little to promote those values, or does so only at much greater cost to third parties, then the ethical justification for zealous advocacy is less convincing.[17]

Lawyers manage to avoid this conclusion only by selectively suspending the moral principle they claim to respect. Under the bar's ethical codes and prevailing practices, the legal rights and personal autonomy of clients assume overriding importance; the rights and autonomy of third parties barely figure. As a practical matter, this difference in treatment makes perfect sense. Clients are, after all, the ones footing the bill for advocates' services. But from a moral standpoint, such selective concern is impossible to justify. Particularly when the client is an organization, values of individual autonomy often cut against the bar's traditional priorities. A corporation's "right" to maximize profits through unsafe but imperfectly regulated methods can hardly take ethical precedence over a consumer's or employee's right to be free from reasonably avoidable risks. And contrary to bar leaders' claims, an attorney's refusal to assist legal but morally dubious conduct does not necessarily compromise individual autonomy or impose a professional oligarchy. Unless the lawyer is the last in town, his or her refusal to provide representation will not foreclose client choices. It may simply prompt reevaluation of their ethical consequences or impose the financial and psychological costs of finding alternative counsel.

It is, of course, true that lawyers have no special expertise in evaluating those consequences. But attorneys at least will have a more disinterested perspective than their clients. Moreover, the bar's moral humility is highly selective. When clients' conduct is at issue, advocates readily become agnostics. Lawyers insist that they are not "presumptuous enough to pass judgment" on what constitutes the "public interest" or to cast themselves as "unique guardians of the public good." Yet when an ethical standard regulating attorneys' own conduct is at issue, they generally have no similar difficulty in determining where the public interest lies. Indeed, the organized bar has sought exclusive authority to pass judgment on many ethical questions, such as whether protecting client confidences should trump other social values, or whether lawyers should have obligations to prevent foreseeable injuries to third parties.[18]

The real question is not "by what right" do lawyers "impose" their moral views but by what right should they evade a fundamental moral responsibility of all individuals: to accept accountability for the consequences of their actions. Of course, reasonable people often disagree about whether particular conduct is justifiable. They also disagree about whether it is possible to reach any "right" answer in moral disputes. But even if a lawyer believes that objectively valid moral decisions are impossible, it does not follow that all views are equally valid. Some positions are more coherent, free of bias or self-interest, and supported by reliable evidence. Lawyers can, and should, act on the basis of their own principled convictions, even when they recognize that others could in good faith hold different views.

As most legal ethics experts agree, the moral justification for current adversarial principles is ultimately unconvincing. But the practical appeal is often irresistible, particularly when coupled with a regulatory framework that permits lawyers to avoid advocacy that appears personally distasteful or financially imprudent.

PROFESSIONAL INTERESTS AND PARTISAN PRACTICES

Whatever their inadequacies in serving the public interest, prevailing adversarial practices have been reasonably effective in serving professional interests. They permit all the justice that money can buy for a client who can afford it, and they impose few responsibilities on those who cannot. Although bar justifications for zealous advocacy trade heavily on lawyers' commitment to protect poor and unpopular clients, that commitment often breaks down in practice.

Despite some significant and heroic exceptions, the mainstream American bar generally has avoided social pariahs with shallow pockets. To cite only the most obvious examples, almost all prominent practitioners declined to accept accused communists during the McCarthy era; the profession, in Felix Frankfurter's phrase, gave a "miserable account of itself." The southern bar's record on race cases was no better throughout most of this century, and the list of less celebrated recent illustrations is easily extended. Radical student organizations, far-right political groups, gay rights activists, and criminal defendants like the Oklahoma City bombers all have faced difficulties finding local counsel. Many lawyers also decline any pro bono matter that might undercut the position of a paying client. Others are reluctant to accept or vigorously pursue cases that might offend potential sources of business. The reasons for this reluctance are understandable. Counsel for unpopular causes have long paid a substantial price, and the costs have been imposed by other attorneys as well as the public. Lawyers for perceived radicals and suspects of particularly heinous crimes have been vulnerable to multiple forms of harassment, including loss of clients and referral networks, bar disciplinary proceedings, contempt prosecutions, and death threats.[19]

In response to this history, bar ethical codes steer an expedient course. They attempt to minimize the penalties for partisanship by emphasizing that representation of unpopular clients does not imply endorsement of their actions but, rather, is consistent with the highest standards of the profession. Yet at the same time, these codes acknowledge attorneys' right to decline or withdraw from representation that they consider morally repugnant. Although bar aspirational standards remind lawyers of their responsibility to provide pro bono service, which includes a "fair share of . . . indigent or unpopular clients," that responsibility is widely evaded in practice. Less than half of American lawyers contribute any pro bono assistance to underserved groups, and little of their charitable work involves ostracized causes. In effect, the bar's rhetorical commitments to the unpopular have functioned most often to justify representing the disreputable wealthy, not the discreditable indigent.[20]

The practical advantages of this approach are obvious. As legal theorist Karl Llewellyn noted a half century ago, the prudent strategy for professional success is for lawyers "to choose the convenient ethic at the convenient time." When rich clients have unattractive cases, then the governing principle can be that every individual deserves due process. When some "starved pinched fellow" needs such assistance, then lawyers' own moral repugnance can come to the rescue. To most attorneys, this double standard is perhaps regrettable but scarcely indefensible. After all, lawyers need to make a living, and why should they be subject to demands not imposed on other professionals? Doctors, for example, receive far less criticism for failing to serve unmet needs among poor and unpopular patients, although the social costs of that refusal are considerable.[21]

Yet these arguments, while not without basis, somewhat miss the point. From an ethical standpoint, both lawyers and doctors can be faulted, particularly since their failures to address public needs are coupled with attempts to block services by competing low-cost providers. And what is distinctively problematic about the bar's performance is its insistence on dressing up professional expedience as professional ethics. All too often, lawyers invoke their obligations to the poor and oppressed as rationalizations for defending clients who are anything but, such as tobacco companies in their opposition to health warnings, disclosure obligations, and marketing restrictions.[22]

In some respects, the American advocate's role offers the worst of both worlds. The bar's insistence that lawyers are free to refuse "repugnant" matters, but are not accountable for the ones they accept, compromises both competing principles. That compromise is by no means inevitable. For example, the legal profession in Great Britain is subject to a "cab rank principle"—barristers, like taxis, must accept work on a "first come first served" basis. Although many practitioners find ways to evade this obligation, it at least establishes a more demanding principle concerning unpopular causes than the standards governing the American bar.[23]

A related problem with adversarial premises is how frequently they yield when competing professional interests are at stake. Zealous advocacy often fails to materialize for clients who lack sufficient information or financial resources to demand it. This is not to imply that attorneys are motivated solely by self-interest or that they routinely and consciously compromise client interests. Rather, the problem is more subtle and arises from complex trade-offs between personal and professional responsibilities. If clients cannot afford or even identify what effective representation requires, their needs may be eclipsed by attorneys' own concerns. A wide array of research reveals how zealous advocacy gives way before lawyers' interests in maximizing income, meeting caseload pressures, and preserving their relationships with other participants in the legal system. In law, as in other contexts, individuals with conflicting personal and professional concerns often unconsciously reduce the conflict by redefining their professional role.[24]

The pressure to cut corners is especially intense in criminal cases, where a wide gap persists between popular perceptions and daily realities. Most Americans are convinced that the legal system coddles criminals. Defense lawyers appear ready to exploit every technicality, however guilty or dangerous their clients. The trials featured in news and entertainment media reinforce this perception. In the courtrooms that the public sees, zealous advocacy is the norm. O. J. Simpson's lawyers left no stone unturned. But they were charging by the stone. Most defense counsel cannot. And it matters. For the vast majority of defendants in American halls of justice, "the only justice is the halls." Outside the courtroom, overburdened and underprepared lawyers strike hasty plea bargains for indigent clients with no realistic alternatives. Missing are all the adversarial safeguards that, in other contexts, the bar presents as essential to informed decision making. The reasons for this lapse in partisan protections is obvious. As a federal oversight commission candidly noted, most criminal defense lawyers face an "inherent conflict between remaining financially solvent and providing vigorous advocacy."[25]

About two-thirds of felony defendants are poor enough to qualify for court-appointed counsel. Fee arrangements for these attorneys take three main forms. Some jurisdictions rely on competitive bids; lawyers agree to provide representation for a specified percentage of the courts' total criminal caseload for a fixed annual amount, irrespective of the number or complexity of cases. Such systems discourage zealous advocacy by selecting attorneys who are able to turn over high volumes of clients at low cost. Caseloads can range as high as 3500 misdemeanors and 900 felonies annually, and some attorneys haven't taken a case to trial in years.[26]

Similar disincentives for effective representation occur in jurisdictions that assign private practitioners to handle matters on a case-by-case basis. These lawyers receive minimal flat fees or hourly rates, coupled with a ceiling on total compensation. Limits of $1,000 are common for felony cases, and some states allow less than half that amount. Low ceilings apply even for defendants facing the death penalty, and attorneys subject to such compensation caps have ended up with hourly rates below $2. In states like Virginia with $300 ceilings on felony cases, kids selling sodas on the beach on a summer weekend do better than court-appointed counsel. For most court-appointed lawyers, thorough preparation is a quick route to financial ruin. Analogous problems often arise in the remaining jurisdictions, which rely on public defender offices. Although the quality of representation in some of these offices is quite high, others operate with crushing caseloads and grossly inadequate resources. Efforts to increase these resources and raise statutory fees meet strong resistance from a public anxious to get tough on criminals, not to subsidize their defense. The chair of a Missouri appropriations committee expressed common attitudes with uncommon candor in announcing publicly that he "did not care whether indigent criminal defendants were represented or not."[27]

Defendants who hire their own counsel do not necessarily fare better. Most of these individuals are just over the poverty line and cannot afford substantial legal expenses. Their lawyers typically charge a flat fee, payable in advance, which creates obvious incentives to plea bargain. Only defendants who can meet steep charges, usually in white-collar or organized crime cases, have ready access to the highly skilled advocacy that the public sees in movies or publicized trials. Where defendants lack such resources, counsel face substantial pressure to curtail their advocacy. A quick plea spares lawyers the strain and potential humiliation of an unsuccessful trial. Such bargains also preserve good working relationships with judges and prosecutors, who face their own often overwhelming caseload demands. In this system, zealous advocacy is the exception, not the rule, and it is generally better to be rich and guilty than poor and innocent.[28]

Neither market forces nor bar regulatory systems effectively counteract these structural incentives. Most defendants lack sufficient information to second-guess lawyers' plea recommendations; rarely do they have access to knowledge about prosecutorial, juror, and judicial behavior in comparable cases. Even if clients doubt the adequacy of their appointed counsel, they can do little about it. Indigent defendants have no right to select their attorneys, and court-appointed lawyers do not depend for their livelihood on the satisfaction of clients. Indeed, a reputation for zeal on behalf of the accused is unlikely to work to counsel's advantage among the judges who control appointments. Courts coping with already unmanageable caseloads often resist appointing "obstructionist" lawyers who routinely raise technical defenses or demand lengthy trials.[29]

Other oversight structures similarly fail to ensure effective advocacy. In theory, inadequate representation could trigger malpractice remedies. In fact, such remedies are almost never forthcoming, because convicted criminals are unsympathetic plaintiffs and prevailing doctrine denies recovery unless they can overturn their conviction or prove their innocence. Bar disciplinary authorities do not impose sanctions for "mere" negligence against criminal defense attorneys. And only in the most egregious cases will courts reverse convictions for ineffective assistance of counsel. Courts have declined to find inadequate representation where attorneys were drunk, on drugs, or parking their car during key parts of the prosecution's case. And defendants have been executed despite their lawyers' lack of any prior trial experience, ignorance of all relevant death penalty precedents, or failure to present any mitigating evidence. One systematic survey found that over 99 percent of ineffective assistance claims were unsuccessful.[30]

The extent of judicial tolerance is well illustrated by a series of sleepy lawyer cases. In one Texas death penalty trial, defense counsel fell asleep several times during witnesses' testimony that he found "boring," and he spent only about five hours in preparing for trial. In rejecting claims of inadequate representation, a Texas appellate court reasoned that the decision to sleep might have been a "strategic" ploy to gain sympathy from the jury. And a federal judge reviewing that decision concluded, "The Constitution says that everyone is entitled to an attorney of their choice. But the Constitution does not say that the lawyer has to be awake." Other courts agree. Instances of courtroom napping are sufficiently common that an entire jurisprudence has developed to determine how much dozing is constitutionally permissible. Some courts even apply a three-step analysis: did counsel sleep for repeated and prolonged periods; was counsel actually unconscious; and were crucial defense interests at stake while counsel was asleep?[31]

Other lapses in lawyers' advocacy and judicial oversight are also depressingly frequent. As Stephen Bright, director of the Southern Center for Human Rights, notes, too many poor defendants have appointed lawyers who have never tried a criminal case before or never should again. In recent studies, the leading cause of reversals on appeal was errors by defense counsel, between half and four-fifths of counsel entered pleas without interviewing any prosecution witnesses, and four-fifths did so without filing any defense motions. The rationalizations for such inadequate efforts were well illustrated by another Texas case in which a defendant managed to win release after seven years in prison. His claim of ineffective representation prevailed largely because of exceptional candor by his former court-appointed attorney. In that lawyer's view, his professional role did not require "going out to sleazy bars to look for witnesses," particularly since he assumed that his client was guilty.[32]

This is not to imply that most court-appointed lawyers willingly or consciously compromise their clients' interests. Rather, they are caught within a structure that fails to provide the necessary resources, standards, or oversight to ensure effective representation. And while financial and caseload pressures are especially acute in indigent criminal defense, they are by no means unique to that context. Related problems can arise whenever client resources or financial stakes are too limited to underwrite adequate representation or when zealous advocacy will antagonize individuals whose support is critical to lawyers' self-interest. For example, studies of attorneys working in small towns or handling modest consumer and insurance claims find that these practitioners frequently curtail their representation. They are reluctant to provoke ill will among opponents likely to supply future work, refer other business, or cooperate on more significant cases. Similar difficulties confront other particularly vulnerable clients. Research on legal aid programs and divorce cases finds that many individual needs are inadequately met. "Cooling the client out" is a common technique: parties' expectations are revised downward to accommodate overworked or undercompensated attorneys.[33]

Certain fee arrangements also discourage unqualified advocacy. As chapter 6 indicates, class action litigation can present conflicts between clients' interest in maximizing their recovery and attorneys' interest in maximizing the return on their time. Since individual class members often lack sufficient information, incentives, or resources to monitor their counsel's performance, the result may be settlements that provide more generously for the lawyers than for the clients. Similar problems arise in contingent fee litigation, where attorneys' fees represent a specified percentage of a successful claim, usually about a third. Here again, clients' interest in gaining the highest possible recovery often competes with lawyers' desire to maximize returns on their efforts. A quick modest settlement before substantial trial preparation may benefit attorneys at the expense of their clients. Although courts have authority to set aside unreasonable contingent or class action fees, most judges lack the time and information to do so except in egregious cases.[34]

Taken as a whole, the bar's current combination of advocacy principles and enforcement practices works reasonably well for lawyers. Where clients can afford zealous advocacy, attorneys can claim a moral high ground in supplying it. Where clients cannot, lapses in bar regulatory structures provide the necessary accommodation for their lawyers' interests. The prevailing advocate's role offers psychological advantages as well, by representing lawyers with a conveniently simplified moral universe. Troubling consequences of client conduct need not arise, and the awkwardness of accountability is easily evaded. Clients can claim that their decisions are approved by counsel, and counsel can claim that the authority to decide rests with clients. If injustice occurs, the blame lies anywhere and everywhere else.[35]

THE PRICE OF PARTISANSHIP

Yet these financial and psychological comforts come at a price. The avoidance of ethical responsibility is ultimately corrosive for lawyers, clients, and the legal framework on which they depend. For many practitioners, the neutral partisan role undermines the very commitments that led them to become lawyers. As chapter 1 indicated, a primary source of career dissatisfaction among surveyed attorneys involves the sense that they have not been able to pursue justice. That discontent may partly reflect the problem that many philosophers like Gerald Postema and Richard Wasserstrom describe. The submersion of self into a role too often leaves the advocate alienated from his own moral convictions. When professional action becomes detached from ordinary moral experience, the lawyer's ethical sensitivity erodes. The agnosticism that neutral partisanship encourages can readily spill over into other areas of life and undercut a lawyer's sense of moral identity.[36]

This erosion of ethical values ill serves clients as well. One of lawyers' most crucial contributions involves helping individuals live up to their best instincts and deepest moral values. That role requires advocates who are willing to pass judgment and to identify ways of harmonizing client and public interests. Even highly profit-driven businesses often need and want counselors who can provide a "corporate conscience." In that capacity, lawyers can help clients evaluate short-term economic objectives in light of long-term concerns that include maintaining a reputation for social responsibility and managerial integrity.[37]

Attorneys representing individuals under stress can help them look beyond the anger and anxieties that may skew judgment in legal disputes. For example, many couples in divorce proceedings are poorly served by agnostic advocates, who view themselves as "bombers" or "technicians," unconcerned with the ethical dimensions of their actions. The result often is a war of attrition in which clients as well as children become casualties. Zealous partisanship in these contexts can undercut chances for durable financial agreements and cooperative parenting relationships that ultimately would benefit all concerned.[38]

Neither lawyers' nor clients' long-term interests are served by eroding the institutional frameworks on which an effective rule of law depends. Taken to its logical extreme, a professional role that gives primary allegiance to client concerns can undermine the legal order. Yale law professor Robert Gordon gives an example: "[T]ake any simple case of compliance counseling; suppose the legal rule is clear, yet the chance of detecting violations low, the penalties small in relation to the gains from noncompliance, or the terrorizing of regulators into settlement by a deluge of paper predictably easy. The mass of lawyers who advise and then assist with noncompliance in such a situation could, in the vigorous pursuit of their clients' interests, effectively nullify the laws." In many contexts, loophole lawyering encourages a race to the bottom that, in turn, stimulates demand for an increasingly intrusive regulatory structure. This expanded oversight ultimately narrows the scope of client autonomy that zealous advocacy is designed to preserve. A profession truly committed to individual rights must assume responsibility for a legal framework that can maintain them.[39]

The bar has similar responsibilities concerning core cultural values. Norms like good faith, honesty, and fair dealing are essential for efficient markets and effective regulatory systems. These values depend on some shared restraint in the pursuit of short-term client interests. Legal processes present frequent opportunities for obstruction, obfuscation, and overreaching. An advocacy role that imposes few practical constraints on such behavior erodes expectations of trust and cooperation. These expectations are common goods on which clients as a group ultimately depend. In the short term, free riders can profit by violating norms that others respect. But these values cannot survive if deviance becomes a routine and acceptable part of the advocate's repertoire. Over the long run, a single-minded pursuit of clients' individual self-interests is likely to prove self-defeating for clients as a group.

These points have not entirely escaped professional notice. The organized bar's formal pronouncements on professionalism acknowledge responsibilities that transcend and sometimes trump the neutral partisanship role. According to a prominent Conference Report by the American Bar Association and the American Law Institute, lawyers' primary obligation runs not to clients but to the "procedures and institutions of the law." Yet this recognition surfaces mainly on ceremonial occasions, when, as Gordon notes, attorneys feel entitled to rise on "wings of rhetorical inspiration far above the realities of daily practice." Seldom do these lofty aspirations drift downward, at least where well-heeled clients' immediate interests dictate otherwise. Significant progress will require a reformulation of the advocate's role that can survive translation in lawyers' actual working relationships.[40]

AN ALTERNATIVE FRAMEWORK

An alternative framework for the advocate's role needs to be ethically justifiable in principle and consistently reinforced in practice. At its most basic level, such a framework would require lawyers to accept personal responsibility for the moral consequences of their professional actions. Attorneys should make decisions as advocates in the same way that morally reflective individuals make any ethical decision. Lawyers' conduct should be justifiable under consistent, disinterested, and generalizable principles. These moral principles can, of course, recognize the distinctive needs of lawyers' occupational role. Ethically responsible decision making always takes into account the context and capacity in which a person acts. The extent of attorneys' responsibilities for client conduct will depend on their knowledge, involvement, and influence as well as on the significance of values at stake.

However, unlike the bar's prevailing approach, this alternative framework would require lawyers to assess their obligations in light of all the societal interests at issue in particular practice contexts. An advocate could not simply retreat into some fixed conception of role that denies personal accountability for public consequences or that unduly privileges clients' and lawyers' own interests. Client trust and confidentiality are entitled to weight, but they must be balanced against other equally important concerns. Lawyers also have responsibilities to prevent unnecessary harm to third parties, to promote a just and effective legal system, and to respect core values such as honesty, fairness, and good faith on which that system depends. In accommodating those responsibilities, lawyers should, of course, be guided by relevant legal authority and bar regulatory codes. Respect for law is a fundamental value, particularly among those sworn to uphold it. Adherence to generally accepted rules also serves as a check against the decision maker's own bias or self-interest. But attorneys may confront cases in which the applicable rules are so indeterminate or inadequate that reference to broader moral principles is necessary.

Most ethical dilemmas arise in areas where the governing standards already leave significant room for discretion. Individual attorneys can decide whether to accept or withdraw from representation and whether to pursue certain tactics. In resolving such questions, lawyers need to consider the social context of their choices. They cannot simply rely on some idealized model of adversarial and legislative processes. Rather, lawyers must assess their actions against a realistic backdrop, in which wealth, power, and information are unequally distributed, not all interests are adequately represented, and most matters will never reach a neutral tribunal. The less confidence that attorneys have in the justice system's capacity to deliver justice in a particular case, the greater their own responsibility to attempt some corrective.

Such demands that lawyers accept accountability for the consequences of their professional actions provoke three major objections. The first involves ambiguity. According to many lawyers, terms like "justice," "fairness," and "good faith" are too vague to serve as the basis for moral condemnation or disciplinary action. This objection is highly selective. When acting in legislative, judicial, or administrative capacities, lawyers frequently assume that others should be liable for failing to meet such standards. The legal system routinely requires judges, juries, and prosecutors to pursue "justice" or to determine "fairness," and it imposes sanctions on businesses that fail to act in "good faith." Lawyers charge substantial fees for interpreting such requirements. The interpretative process is no different when lawyers' own actions are involved.[41]

The bar's second objection to heightened responsibility is that even if attorneys are able to determine what standards like justice or fairness require, it is not their role to do so. As Clarence Darrow put it, "My job is not to judge a man . . . [but to] defend him." Often this argument proceeds without further elaboration, as if its force were self-evident. But the claim that "it is not my role" begs the question at issue, which is what that role *should* be. After all, attorneys have considerable autonomy, individually and collectively, to determine the appropriate scope of their professional obligations. And, as the legacy of war crimes tribunals makes clear, "it was just my job" is not a morally adequate defense.[42]

In rejecting demands for greater ethical obligations, lawyers often lapse into humility: they disclaim any "special" expertise to determine what justice requires. Yet as noted earlier, such modesty is highly selective and ultimately beside the point. The bar frequently claims expert knowledge about where justice lies when regulations governing its own conduct are at stake. In any case, the rationale for greater accountability is not that lawyers have special moral expertise but rather that they deserve no special moral exemption. Lawyers should consider the justness of their actions not because they have distinctive ethical capacities but because they have the same ethical responsibilities as everybody else.[43]

In resisting such responsibilities, attorneys often claim that they lack the formal structure of accountability that would justify passing judgment. For lawyers to impose their moral views on clients threatens the legitimacy of a system committed at least in principle to equal access to justice. The merits of a client's cause should be determined by judges or juries with due process safeguards, not by individual attorneys with no procedural protections. Yet as a practical matter, the vast majority of legal representation lacks such safeguards. Little of lawyers' transactional, counseling, or even litigation-related work ever reaches a judge or jury. In many legal contexts, if lawyers decline to pass judgment, no one else will be available to do so. When mechanisms of formal institutional accountability are absent, the need for informal, internalized standards of moral accountability becomes particularly compelling.

A final objection to such accountability is pragmatic. All of the economic and psychological pressures that make neutral partisanship attractive also make the alternative seem unrealistic. The most obvious difficulty is, of course, money. Former judge Marvin Frankel put it bluntly: "Why should the client pay for loyalties divided between himself and [justice]?" If the client is not interested in moral advice, many observers also doubt that it will prove effective. And if lawyers resign rather than participate in actions that appear unjust, the result could be counterproductive. Yale law professor Geoffrey Hazard voices a widely shared concern that resignation will result in replacement by a less "high minded" successor, who will insulate the client from future conscientious advice.[44]

Such concerns are not without force, but neither are they as compelling as many practitioners assume. It is by no means clear how often a moral stand by lawyers will force them to resign and make way for someone worse. When attorneys are prepared to refuse assistance for ethical reasons, they raise the stakes for clients, both psychologically and economically. In some cases, the costs of finding and educating a new lawyer will be sufficient to prompt clients to rethink their objectives rather than replace their attorney. In other contexts, where resignation would clearly have little impact on client decision making, lawyers are entitled to consider that fact in weighing their responsibilities. An ethically reflective and contextualized decision will take into account not only the magnitude and likelihood of harms resulting from client conduct but also the attorney's capacity to affect them and the personal costs of attempting to do so. In some circumstances, lawyers' limited leverage and access to information, together with the adverse effects of jeopardizing a client relationship, will justify suspension of judgment. But where the ethical stakes are substantial, lawyers have an obligation to refuse assistance whatever the other consequences. We do not normally absolve individuals of moral responsibility on the ground that their successor could be worse.

Frankel's question—Why should clients pay for divided loyalties?—is usually taken as rhetorical. But the answer is by no means self-evident. Clients should pay because clients as a group ultimately benefit; constraints

on partisanship reinforce their better instincts and maintain a well-func-
tioning legal system. Individual clients also benefit from lawyers whose
reputation for candor and fair dealing leads to greater trust and cooperation from opponents and regulatory authorities. A decent relationship with
opposing counsel can often keep disputes from escalating and promote
equitable settlements. Equally to the point, clients typically *will* pay for
divided allegiance when that is the only realistic choice available. A more
ethically demanding role for lawyers would not reduce the need for legal
services.

Of course, increasing attorneys' social responsibilities might encourage
some clients to withhold damaging information. And some lawyers might
reap short-term profits by resisting moral accountability. But such responses also would carry a cost. Clients would lose access to well-informed
advice. And lawyers would lose the psychic and actual income that comes
from maintaining a sense of personal integrity and social responsibility.
Attorneys' status, self-esteem, and credibility in the legal community partly depend on adherence to established understandings of the advocate's
role. Redefining that professional role is likely to have some effect on
adversarial practices, particularly if the changes are reinforced by bar ethical codes and civil liability standards.

The extent of that effect, however, should not be overstated.
Reconstruction of the advocate's role will not address the financial and
resource constraints that make effective representation for some clients so
difficult to realize in practice. Moreover, for obvious reasons, lawyers prefer
practice settings that minimize conflicts between moral convictions and
client objectives. Economic and psychological pressures also encourage
attorneys to perceive issues in ways that avoid such conflicts. As social science research indicates, assigning individuals to defend a position greatly
increases the likelihood that they will come to believe in it. These processes
of self-selection and psychological adaptation may help explain why a
majority of surveyed lawyers report that they have never needed to turn
down a case for ethical reasons. Yet at least part of the reason that these practitioners experience so little moral difficulty is that they have internalized a
role that represses it. That process is not inevitable. Many attorneys choose
law as a profession in part because of its connections to broader issues of
social justice. Most of these individuals are disappointed by the absence of
such connections in daily practice, as the bar's own surveys make clear. A
redefinition of the advocate's role is one way of reestablishing the linkage
between personal values and professional responsibilities.[45]

HARD CASES

The ultimate test of any alternative ideology of advocacy is its capacity to resolve hard cases. This is not the only test; the most difficult dilemmas of legal ethics are not routine intruders in daily practice. But these dilemmas can provide useful case studies: They clarify how general principles of moral responsibility would apply in concrete legal settings. Of course, any framework that builds on general principles while remaining sensitive to social context will leave room for argument about appropriate results. What makes an ethical dilemma a dilemma is the clash of competing values. Individual lawyers may have good faith disagreements about how these conflicts should be resolved. The advantage of the contextual framework proposed here is not that it promises bright-line answers but, rather, that it promotes ethically reflective analysis and commitments.

Hard cases for advocates generally fall into one of two categories. The first involves justifiable means to achieve unjust ends. The second involves unjust means to achieve justifiable ends. Long-standing disputes have centered on the first situation, in which lawyers rely on morally defensible rules to serve morally indefensible goals. The two leading nineteenth-century experts on legal ethics disagreed about whether lawyers should invoke the time limits in a statute of limitations to defeat a just claim and about whether they should use "artifice" and "ingenuity" to prevent conviction of the guilty. Contemporary ethics experts similarly differ over attorneys' reliance on technical defenses or misleading arguments to achieve substantively unmerited outcomes. That argument gained renewed prominence during the impeachment proceedings against President Clinton. Many commentators denounced the president's lawyers for their "legalistic," "hairsplitting" defenses of Clinton's patently wrongful conduct.[46]

Debates about such tactics cannot be resolved in the abstract. Under generally accepted ethical principles, context is critical. For example, in civil matters, these principles generally counsel against the use of legal rules to frustrate just claims unless this strategy would serve the purposes underlying those rules. So, for example, a statute of limitations is designed to prevent stale claims; it protects individuals who otherwise would be unable to defend themselves because memories fade, documents are lost, or witnesses cannot be located. But in cases where a client has suffered no significant prejudice from delay, attorneys should not seek dismissal of a substantively justifiable claim.[47]

They should, however, normally inform the client about options that are legally available though morally problematic. The American Bar

Association's Model Rules of Professional Conduct require lawyers to provide such information—and with good reason. When legal tactics can affect outcomes, the decision to forego them should rest with clients. They are, after all, the ones who have to live with the result and, as noted earlier, their right to make autonomous choices is a value worthy of respect. But the choices that clients make are not always ones that attorneys should assist. Lawyers also have a right and a responsibility to determine whether their support is ethically justifiable.[48]

However, where the context involves criminal proceedings, the stakes are somewhat different, and so, accordingly, are lawyers' obligations. As the earlier discussion made clear, such proceedings are distinctive in two respects: in their potential for governmental abuse and in their effect on individuals' lives, liberty, and reputation. Those special characteristics justify special safeguards, including the presumption of innocence, the freedom from self-incrimination, and the guarantee of legal representation. That last right would be of little value if it did not respect the others. If lawyers were entitled to suspend their advocacy when clients appeared guilty or disclosed inculpating information, then a system of procedural safeguards could not be effectively enforced.

Although most Americans support that system in the abstract, their commitment often fades in practice, at least where seemingly guilty and dangerous offenders are involved. To many observers, the rights of these accused criminals should not take precedence over the rights of innocent victims. Why should confessed rapists or serial child molesters receive the benefit of every conceivable tactic, however misleading? From this perspective, accused offenders should be entitled to require the prosecution to prove its case. But they should not be entitled to defense tactics that obstruct, obscure, or play to racial prejudices. According to then Independent Counsel Kenneth Starr, the legal profession has a "duty not to impede the search for truth." Law professor Harry Subin similarly notes, "It is one thing to attack a weak government case by pointing out its weakness. It is another . . . to attack a strong government case by confusing the jury with falsehoods." To William Simon, unqualified advocacy appears appropriate only when the values justifying such partisanship are at issue in a particular case. For Simon, these cases would include proceedings where the defendant may be innocent, where law enforcement officials may have violated constitutional rights, or where racial bias may have tainted the government's case.[49]

Yet while these restraints on advocacy seem reasonable in theory, they are likely to prove deeply problematic in practice. The rationale for such restraints implies that the primary ethical problem in criminal defense is excessive partisanship—that too many guilty defendants go free as a result of too much zealous advocacy. But as the research summarized earlier suggests, the most common problem in criminal cases is under- rather than overrepresentation. Inadequate investigation is extremely common. Acquittal is extremely rare; about 98 percent of felony defendants plead guilty or are convicted at trial. Proposals to curtail advocacy for criminal defendants could push in precisely the wrong direction; they risk reinforcing the practical pressures that already work against effective assistance of counsel.[50]

To make lawyers' responsibilities depend on clients' apparent guilt or dangerousness would present unacceptable risks of injustice. Predictions of future violence, even when made by trained mental health professionals, are inaccurate in about two-thirds of cases: untrained attorneys would scarcely do better. As Stanford law professor Barbara Allen Babcock notes, factual guilt is not the same as legal guilt. Clients who have engaged in punishable activities often can claim legitimate defenses or mitigating circumstances. Zealous representation of those who are guilty also protects those who are not. The prospect of vigorous challenge by defense counsel creates incentives for law enforcement officers to do their jobs effectively and to respect individual rights. Cases involving the most brutal offenses are the ones that prosecutors most want to win. Not surprisingly, these also are the cases where government abuses are most likely and the need for scrutiny by defense counsel is most intense.[51]

The recent impeachment proceedings underscore the risks of unchecked prosecutorial power. Although there is much to dislike about Clinton's conduct and his choice of legal strategies, there is also much to dislike and more to fear about the investigation. The lawyers who defended Clinton there could justifiably insist that "legalities" be observed. Perjury and obstruction of justice are technical charges that justify technical defenses. And the president's lawyers played a crucial role in exposing prosecutorial misconduct far more serious than the misstatements about consensual sex that launched the Independent Counsel's Lewinsky inquiry. Such adversarial abuses included coercive and harassing treatment of witnesses, leaks of highly prejudicial information, interference with parties' rights to counsel, threats to prosecute their family members for technical, unrelated crimes, and disclosure of needlessly graphic and humiliating sexual histories. Without some measure of legal accountability, the risks of prosecutorial excess are all too apparent. Our cultural commitment to individual rights presupposes a legal profession equally committed to their defense. Lawyers who insist that prosecutors abide by technicalities are maintaining, not subverting, the rule of law.[52]

Of course, as ethics experts note, zealous advocacy in the few cases that go to trial or attract public attention provides inadequate protection for the vast majority that do not. For example, William Simon would prefer increasing the resources for criminal defense and ensuring greater oversight of counsel's performance, particularly in plea bargaining contexts. Such reforms are highly desirable in theory but unlikely to prove adequate in practice. This nation has never been willing to subsidize representation for criminal defendants at anything close to adequate levels. Nor have most judges been willing to monitor their assistance. Courts could and should do more. They could, for example, require statements from court-appointed counsel detailing their work, and decline to accept pleas or proceed to trial until adequate preparation has occurred. More judges could also follow the lead of some jurisdictions and require states to provide adequate resources for public defenders and realistic statutory fee schedules for private counsel. And the organized bar could devote more of its lobbying and pro bono efforts to improving indigent defense. But given the difficulties in enforcing effective assistance of counsel, an ethic of zealous advocacy remains crucial. As it is, that ethic often fades in practice. But in criminal cases, we have too much to lose from compromising its moral force.[53]

Of course, that commitment to partisanship has its limits. Lawyers have the same basic obligations as any citizens to refrain from conduct that, if generalized, would undermine the justice system. Knowing use of perjury or facilitation of future criminal conduct are obvious examples. To be sure, reasonable people can differ about whether they have sufficient facts to be sure about their clients' honesty or intentions in particular cases. But lawyers do sometimes "know," in any common sense use of the term, that their client is lying or engaging in illegal activity. It is, as Geoffrey Hazard has noted, one thing to represent a defendant charged with a criminal offense and "quite another to be on retainer to the Mafia."[54]

For similar reasons, it is one thing to defend groups like the American Nazi Party or the Ku Klux Klan on a civil liberties issue and quite another to serve as in-house counsel for all their legal needs. Yet this distinction is not always apparent to the public, as is clear from several celebrated cases over the past two decades. One involved the American Civil Liberties Union's representation of Nazis seeking to parade through a predominantly Jewish suburb of Chicago. Many ACLU members resigned in protest. In their view, such exercises of First Amendment principles caused enormous and unnecessary pain to the Holocaust survivors and families of genocide victims living in the area. The Nazis could march elsewhere, and the ACLU could find "a better class" of clients. Given the scarcity of organizational resources, why should the ACLU "defend the free speech rights of would-be tyrants [who would] . . . crush free speech rights the moment they get power"?[55]

An analogous controversy involved an ACLU cooperating attorney's defense of the grand dragon of the Texas Ku Klux Klan. The Klan was challenging efforts by the Texas Commission on Human Rights to compel disclosure of Klan membership lists. The attorney, Anthony Griffin, was an African American who also served as the general counsel of the Port Arthur branch of the NAACP. The controversy arose after the Klan began a systematic campaign to harass and intimidate blacks who had received public housing in all-white projects in the predominantly white city of Vidor, Texas. This desegregation effort followed a federal court's finding of blatant discrimination by public housing officials. In defending his representation, Griffin pointed to important First Amendment precedents from the 1960s civil rights struggle. Some involved organizations like the NAACP, which had successfully resisted hostile efforts by southern prosecutors to obtain membership lists. In Griffin's view, civil rights organizations had a strong stake in preventing disclosure of members who might be subject to harassment or intimidation.[56]

Yet many NAACP members remained unconvinced, and Griffin lost his position with the Port Arthur branch. From their perspective, the Klan was distinguishable from the civil rights organizations involved in earlier membership cases; it had a demonstrated history of violence and intimidation that the other groups did not share. Some NAACP members also believed that the Klan's defense by an African American lawyer was likely to enhance its credibility and increase the risks to potential victims.

These arguments are not without force, but conventional moral principles can also justify the decisions of ACLU attorneys. Principles of free expression and association protect no one if they do not protect everyone. Our commitment to these principles is tested at the extreme; we compromise their legitimacy if we deny their application to the groups we despise. For that reason, it makes sense for the ACLU to spend scarce resources in representing clients whom other lawyers reject. The "better class" of First

Amendment cases have no comparable difficulty finding advocates. And
the institutional credibility of civil liberties organizations depends upon a
willingness to defend their enemies on civil liberties issues. ACLU lawyers
who fight for the Nazis' right to march or the Klan members' right to privacy occupy different moral ground than lawyers who defend these organizations on any matter, who are uncommitted to First Amendment principles, and who argue against those principles when it serves their clients'
interests.[57]

A final category of hard cases involves the classic dilemma of "dirty
hands": the use of unjust means for just ends. This dilemma is by no means
unique to law. As Machiavelli long ago recognized, it presents one of the
central challenges of political life. But lawyers confront the problem in distinctive form when, as officers of the law, they perceive strong moral reasons
to subvert it.

One frequently debated example involves divorce practice before no-
fault legislation. Until the late 1960s and early 1970s, many states permitted divorces only under very narrow circumstances. In New York, where
adultery remained the sole ground until 1966, trial records revealed countless reenactments of the same courtroom charade. With attorneys' assistance, paid investigators would testify that they had discovered an unfaith-
ful spouse in a compromising position. As hearings on this practice noted,
lawyers had a standard script. The "other woman" inevitably appeared in a
"sheer pink robe. It was never blue. Always pink. And [the husband was]
always in his shorts when they found him." The attorneys responsible for
these recycled narratives clearly lacked dramatic imagination. It is less clear
whether they also lacked ethical justifications. Many clients had strong
equitable, if not legal, grounds for divorce. Many were victims of domestic
violence, cruelty, or desertion. Their marriages were over, and the law's
unwillingness to recognize that fact could only compound their personal
miseries and economic hardships.[58]

Contemporary dilemmas of dirty hands arise in many contexts where
a client's position seems morally but not legally justified. Poverty law practice presents especially wrenching cases. Many impoverished clients have
compelling claims for assistance that the law fails to acknowledge. For
example, the typical welfare grant to poor families provides grossly inadequate income, averaging well under three-quarters of the poverty level. To
meet basic subsistence needs, indigent clients typically have no alternative
but to supplement their governmental support with unreported income.
Recent surveys suggest that almost all welfare mothers are in these circum-

stances. Lawyers who become aware of awkward financial facts confront difficulties of their own.[59]

One of my own first cases, as a law student working for a legal aid office, involved precisely this situation. It appeared obvious from our client's circumstances that she had undisclosed income that would have made her technically ineligible for benefits. But without that support she would have lost the chance to finish an educational program that could help her escape poverty and achieve long-term financial independence. Then, as now, she seemed to be precisely the kind of recipient whom the statutory scheme was designed to help. Our office had to decide whether to provide assistance that might help her maintain benefits to which she probably was not entitled.

Such cases prompt three basic responses from legal ethics experts. At one end of the spectrum are those who believe that lawyers have responsibilities to pursue substantive justice and that such responsibilities may sometimes authorize noncompliance with formal legal requirements. In defending this position, William Simon analogizes to the decisions of judges or juries when they nullify a law. Our system accepts their refusal to enforce an outmoded statute or to convict a guilty defendant when necessary to avoid serious injustice. In Simon's view, we should grant lawyers similar discretion to disregard legal rules that appear plainly wrong and that compromise fundamental values. Under his analysis, rules that irrationally withhold minimal welfare support might justify such noncompliance. At the other end of the spectrum are ethics experts who deny that the equities for clients should define the responsibilities for attorneys. According to Harvard law professor Andrew Kaufman, "Being on the wrong side of the entitlement line does not seem to me to give the welfare mother any moral claim to the lawyer's assistance." Geoffrey Hazard similarly argues that the appropriateness of lawyers' strategies in divorce cases should not "turn on the underlying merits." From these commentators' perspective, respect for formal rules is essential for effective legal processes. If these rules result in substantial injustice, a lawyer should work publicly for their reform, not subvert them privately for particular clients.[60]

An intermediate position, and the one most compatible with the contextual ethical framework proposed here, seeks ways of advancing justice without violating formal prohibitions. Lawyers taking this position may pursue a result that is morally but not substantively justified as long as they refrain from illegal conduct such as knowing presentation of perjury or preparation of fraudulent documents. So, for example, in the era of restrictive fault-based divorce statutes, some lawyers found evasive strategies that were not technically unlawful. In jurisdictions that recognized physical cruelty as a ground for divorce, attorneys provided advice about the minimum evidence necessary to meet this requirement. Where courts demanded two physical assaults separated by a cooling-off period, some inventive lawyers orchestrated compliance. They witnessed one spouse gently slap the other twice, with a civilized lunch break in between. Many poverty lawyers have developed strategies of selective ignorance. In my first welfare case, it was quickly apparent that a little knowledge was a dangerous thing, and more would have been worse. My supervising attorney managed to avoid "knowingly" assisting a client's misrepresentation by avoiding information that would have clearly revealed it.

Such strategies are an imperfect solution, but we live in an imperfect world. An approach that can tolerate occasional evasions but not violations of the law is more likely to satisfy conventional ethical principles than any proposed alternative. Permitting lawyers to disregard legal requirements entirely would set a troubling precedent based on a troubling analogy. We can accept nullification by judges and juries because their noncompliance is public and subject to some limited review. Parties unhappy with their decisions can file appeals or seek other legal remedies. When that strategy is unavailable or unsuccessful, the visibility of nullification may prompt reform. Lawyers' decisions lack such accountability. And in some contexts, attorneys' covert defiance may both erode respect for the justice system and reduce the pressures for constructive change. New York might have gotten a more realistic divorce statute sooner if more lawyers had worked for political reform and fewer had tolerated perjury. Moreover, a framework in which legitimate ends justify illegitimate means poses considerable temptations for abuse. Given the economic and psychological pressures of practice, attorneys may too often convince themselves that fundamental values and irrational rules permit covert noncompliance. If the bar's history is any guide, the clients most likely to benefit from such decision making would not be the poor and oppressed.

Yet the converse position, which makes equities entirely irrelevant to ethical judgments, is equally unsatisfying. Reform efforts are not always realistic alternatives. To suggest that poverty lawyers could rectify injustices in welfare rules through political initiatives is to ignore the forces that gave rise to those rules in the first instance. Such suggestions also overlook the statutory prohibitions on political activity and welfare reform litigation by government-funded legal aid lawyers. Even if the prospects for legislative change were less daunting, they would offer no answer for clients with pressing economic survival needs and compelling moral claims. In these circumstances, conventional ethical principles can justify partisan practices that would be indefensible in other contexts. An impoverished mother struggling to escape welfare stands on different ethical footing than a wealthy executive attempting to escape taxes.[61]

The point of this contextual moral framework is not, however, to create a double standard of advocacy: one rule for the haves and another for the have nots. Our current system too often entrenches such double standards, and it would be neither realistic nor desirable to attempt simply to change the beneficiaries. Rather, the aim of this alternative framework is for lawyers to make the merits matter and to assess them from a moral as well as a legal vantage. Not all poor clients would be entitled to unqualified advocacy. But neither would factors like poverty be irrelevant if they affect the justice of a particular claim. Of course, in a profession as large and diverse as the American bar, different lawyers will make different judgments about what is in fact just. Although such judgments should be defensible under accepted ethical principles, their application will necessarily reflect individuals' own experiences and commitments. As William Kunstler once put it in explaining why he would defend the World Trade Center bombers but not the Ku Klux Klan, "Everyone has a right to a lawyer, that's true. But they don't have a right to me." Not all ethically reflective advocates would agree with his priorities or with the balance that Anthony Griffin struck between associational privacy and racial equality in the Klan membership case. Nor would all reasonable attorneys make the same trade-offs between procedural legitimacy and human needs in the divorce and welfare contexts. But the framework proposed here does not demand that lawyers reach the same results in hard cases. It demands rather that lawyers recognize that such cases *are* hard and that they call for contextual moral judgments.[62]

This alternative understanding of the advocate's role is not the first effort to inspire a greater sense of ethical responsibility among practicing attorneys. But it does attempt to avoid a common liability of the bar's professionalism initiatives: realistic proposals seem uninspiring, and inspiring ones seem unrealistic. The contextual ethical framework proposed here makes demands that are both aspirational and plausible. They require concern for what is just as well as what is expedient. However, they are rooted not in some utopian vision but in attorneys' own considered moral judgments. The full effects of such an approach are difficult to predict. But at the very least it should reduce the gap between lawyers' personal ideals and professional practices.

If more advocates feel responsible for the consequences of their efforts, more clients could end up with the kind of wisdom that Abraham Lincoln once shared with someone seeking his legal assistance:

> Yes, we can doubtless gain your case for you; we can . . . distress a widowed mother and her six fatherless children and thereby get you six hundred dollars to which you seem to have a legal claim, but which rightfully belongs, it appears to me, as much to the woman and her children as it does to you. You must remember that some things legally right are not morally right. We shall not take your case, but will give you a little advice for which we will charge you nothing. You seem to be a sprightly, energetic man; we would advise you to try your hand at making six hundred dollars in some other way.[63]

CHAPTER 4

AMERICA'S SPORTING THEORY OF JUSTICE

I n medieval England, before the evolution of adversarial procedures, a common form of adjudication was trial by ordeal. In theory, the process rested on faith that divine intervention would ensure a just result. In practice, the risks of litigation were substantial. For example, one common ordeal involved weighting defendants down with stones and throwing them into the water. Those who sank often perished before they could be rescued; those who managed not to sink were judged guilty and subjected to criminal penalties.[1]

For many participants, litigation remains an ordeal, although of a different sort. We no longer place all our faith in divine will, but neither have we found a wholly satisfactory replacement. Our substitute is what legal theorist Roscoe Pound described as a "sporting theory of justice." Its premise is that truth will prevail in the clash of zealous adversaries. Its practice gives us pause. To courthouse veterans, many juries look like twelve people deciding who has the better lawyer. And as the public well realizes, it generally is money, not justice, that determines the allocation of legal talent.[2]

Even where legal skills are more or less equally balanced, disparities in information and resources can still be decisive. Not all parties can afford what Oscar Wilde once labeled "the best evidence money can buy." Moreover, unlike early English trials by ordeal, which at least were merci-

fully brief, today's versions can drag on interminably. As one seasoned litigator notes, "An incompetent attorney can delay a trial for years. . . . A competent attorney can delay one even longer."[3]

At least in private, most lawyers acknowledge these flaws. But the bar's
official position has long been that the adversary system is the best means
available to pursue truth and protect rights. Chapter 3 explored the limitations of these traditional defenses of the advocate's role. This chapter
explores similar problems in adversarial practices, problems such as civility,
confidentiality, and relations with witnesses. On all these issues, the basic
problem is much the same. Our current system overvalues lawyers' and
clients' interests at the expense of the public's.

This mismatch of professional priorities and societal values presents a
central challenge of legal ethics. How can we make concerns like truth, fairness, and cost-effectiveness assume greater importance where the short-term
advantages for attorneys and their clients lie elsewhere? To that question
there are no simple or uncontested answers. But we certainly can identify
more promising candidates than those that the organized bar has supported. Its recent focus on professionalism campaigns and voluntary civility
codes is reminiscent of a classic vaudeville act. There, a drunk searches fruit-
lessly for his lost wallet near a lamppost. When someone passing by asks
whether he is sure that is where he lost his money, the man responds, "No,
but that's where the light is." The American bar is equally unlikely to find
effective solutions for adversarial abuses in the most convenient locations.
Aspirational codes and professionalism programs may be positive steps. But
they are no substitute for what is required: fundamental changes in ethical
rules, enforcement structures, and economic incentives.

PROCEDURAL PATHOLOGIES AND PRESCRIPTIONS

Over the past decade, the organized bar's central focus of concern regarding
adversarial practices has been incivility. About 90 percent of state and local
bar leaders identify uncivil behavior as a problem, and over a hundred bar
organizations have adopted voluntary codes to address it. No other issue
involving adversarial practices has attracted comparable consensus or reform
efforts. Yet underlying this apparent agreement are deeper, contested questions about the definition, seriousness, and causes of the problem, as well as
the strategies most likely to prevent it.[4]

For the legal profession, as for the culture more generally, *civility* has
become a catchall term for a range of concerns about a fraying social fabric.

About 90 percent of surveyed Americans think that incivility is a problem among the general public, and lawyers rank high among the perceived offenders. Yet what exactly the problem is evokes less agreement. Bar codes, commissions, and courses have targeted a broad spectrum of behavior, including everything from courtroom apparel to clear violations of existing rules against frivolous claims. For example, Virginia wants attorneys to maintain a "neat and tasteful appearance" and to shake hands with opposing counsel. Most civility efforts, however, focus on conduct that does not technically violate existing requirements or that constitutes violations that are difficult or expensive to prove.[5]

Examples of such conduct are not in short supply. Techniques for evading, exhausting, or exploiting an adversary include the following:

- Abuse of pretrial discovery such as refusals to stipulate to uncontested facts; creation of "document debris" by prolonged questioning on peripheral matters; or reliance on boilerplate inquiries to opposing parties with hundreds of questions of dubious relevance and (so that "no one will mistake the attorney's virility") labeling these the "First Set of Interrogatories";

- "Antics with semantics," such as those that President Clinton perfected: quibbling over the meaning of "is," redefining the meaning of "alone," or contorting the meaning of "sex;"

- Unreasonable scheduling practices, such as arranging depositions in order to impose maximum inconvenience and expense; refusing reasonable requests for extensions; and delivering documents under time constraints that will prevent adequate responses or that will force opposing counsel to work over holidays, weekends, and vacations;

- Abusive conduct toward opposing counsel, such as obscene language, and sexually or racially demeaning comments;

- Objectionable questioning techniques, such as probing for peripheral but humiliating disclosures, objecting to reasonable inquiries, or inappropriately coaching witnesses and instructing them not to answer;

- "Sharp practices," such as exploitation of an adversary's inadvertent error in order to obtain a default judgment;

- Evasive strategies designed to make "discovery" anything but, such as asserting the attorney-client privilege without an adequate basis; per-

manently "misplacing" or reshuffling documents to prevent an opponent from locating relevant materials; coding data in defective or misleading fashion; relocating "smoking pistol" information in an "irrelevant mess in the middle of [a] warehouse and invit[ing] the adversary
to visit for a spell."[6]

The frequency of such conduct is difficult to gauge, and recent research
suggests considerable variation in levels of abuse. Much depends on the type
of litigation and geographic location. Most serious discovery abuse arises in
a relatively small percentage of high stakes cases, particularly in large legal
communities that lack informal sanctions and significant judicial oversight.
In these cases, the general rule is "disclose as little as possible as late as possible," and the average litigant is "over-discovered . . . over-charged, over-
exposed, and over-wrought." However, in many other cases, adversaries
engage in more modest forms of incivility and distortion that undermine
the dispute resolution process.[7]

These problems have multiple causes. Withholding or obstructing
access to prejudicial information can protect clients from legal liability or
adverse publicity. Delaying tactics can enable them to continue engaging in
profitable activities of dubious legality or to buy time for nonlegal strategies
such as political or public relations initiatives. By turning litigation into an
expensive war of attrition, parties may also be able to force a favorable settlement or to discourage other potential adversaries from filing suit. As one
attorney for R. J. Reynolds tobacco company indiscreetly noted in a memo
to the files, "The aggressive posture we have taken regarding . . . discovery
in general continues to make these cases extremely burdensome and expensive for plaintiffs' lawyers. . . . To paraphrase General Patton, the way we
won these cases was not by spending all of [R. J. Reynolds'] money but by
making that other son of a bitch spend all of his." Such hardball tactics
often breed hardball responses. In many contexts, legal combat easily esca-
lates beyond what the stakes justify.

Lawyers' own incentives also contribute to adversarial abuses.
Prolonging pretrial maneuvers to force settlements can avoid the possibility
of defeat and the accompanying loss of reputation. Attorneys attempting to
maximize billable hours have an obvious interest in "meter-running," a
strategy that litigators frequently report experiencing but almost never
admit pursuing. Particularly in high stakes cases, lawyers understandably
tend to be risk averse. Overpreparation has obvious advantages if the client
has deep enough pockets. This strategy often holds particular appeal for

junior attorneys. Many law firm associates lack effective mentoring and face strong pressure to meet billable hour quotas, to cover all bases, and to avoid second-guessing the tactical choices of supervising attorneys. These pressures help account for some of the most celebrated cases of litigation abuse, such as the Berkey-Kodak antitrust lawsuit. There, a senior partner lied under oath that certain documents had been inadvertently destroyed, and an associate who knew otherwise remained silent. Although this perjury eventually came to light, in most cases it does not. If a supervising attorney plays hardball, subordinates may perceive it as the only game in town.[8]

Finally, some lawyers and clients find that retaliation has its own rewards. Two wrongs don't make a right, but they may seem the next best thing when locking horns with an abusive opponent. Some attorneys appear to believe that procedural niceties need not be observed if they are on the side of the angels; much prosecutorial excess seems rooted in such self-righteousness. When defense counsel feels entitled to respond in kind, the cycle becomes self-perpetuating. The bar's increased size has also made other responses less effective. In large communities, informal reputational sanctions have diminished force. "Drive-by" incivility, in which lawyers deliver a "cheap shot and move on," is more common when they do not expect to encounter each other again. Some clients want scorched earth tactics, and some attorneys market themselves accordingly. As one participant in an ABA seminar on civility acknowledged, at her firm, "We pride ourselves on being assholes. It's part of the firm culture."[9]

Yet that kind of culture carries a cost for all concerned. In the short run, combative approaches often do more to escalate than to resolve disputes. Adversarial abuses can provoke retaliation and undercut constructive settlement efforts. In the long term, such conduct can compromise a lawyer's reputation for integrity and reasonableness. The result is likely to be less credibility and fewer referrals from courts and opponents, as well as more unpleasant working environments. Working with uncivil attorneys can be as alienating as working against them. Relations with clients also may suffer. Many individuals want lawyers who can avoid, not amplify, conflict. Minimizing the risks or costs of litigation is of particular value where the parties are likely to have some continuing relationship, where their reputations matter, or where significant third party interests are at stake.[10]

Nowhere are those concerns more apparent than in family law. The breakup of a marriage rarely brings out the finest aspects of the human spirit, and vengeful spouses have found no lack of professional accomplices. To some family lawyers, fairness and civility are beside the point. Maurice

Franks asks his male clients: "Has it occurred to you that in divorce action, children can be a valuable commodity?" Raoul Felder, part of New York's legendary "matrimonial mafia," announces with pride that he is a "technician," not a "moralist." He is "not concerned with whether my client is right or wrong. My client is always right." Roy Cohn put the point more bluntly: in divorce, "You're at war. Only one side wins." Yet what constitutes winning is more complicated than these lawyers acknowledge. Unqualified partisanship rarely produces unqualified victories. The more common results include humiliating disclosures, concealment of assets, and child custody claims that become bargaining chips for vindictive and unstable settlements. Ethically responsible attorneys need to consider clients' long-term interests as well as their short-term desires. And, as the American Academy of Matrimonial Lawyers notes, those interests are not well served by making children "pawns in the adversarial process" or by extorting lopsided settlements that prevent cooperative relations after the divorce. Rather, as experts emphasize, a collaborative problem-solving approach generally works better than legalized combat in minimizing the miseries of family disputes.[11]

Moreover, the price of partisanship extends beyond the parties to the dispute. In many business contexts, excessive legal expenses are passed on to consumers and subsidized by the public through government funding for the courts and tax deductions for litigation costs. Some companies also use legal expenses to silence critics. SLAPPs (strategic lawsuits against public participation) have been filed against environmental, consumer, and neighborhood groups for allegedly false claims about corporate practices. Although such suits almost never succeed in court, they often succeed outside it by muzzling critics who cannot afford the costs of protracted proceedings. Moreover, even in other contexts, where the parties are more evenly matched, adversarial abuses can yield unjustified outcomes, which cause broader social costs.[12]

A case in point involves an early 1990s products liability lawsuit against Fisons Corporation, a large pharmaceutical manufacturer. The litigation featured sharp practices by defense counsel that are exceptional only in the public visibility they received. At issue was a generic drug, theophylline, which Fisons had marketed for treating asthma. During the early 1980s, increasing reports of the drug's hazards for children with viral infections prompted the company to warn a selected group of doctors of those risks and to recommend an alternative, cromolyn-based Fisons drug, Intal. An internal office memorandum also detailed the dangers and recommended that the company cease its promotion efforts of theophylline and instead encourage the use of cromolyn. Fisons did not follow that recommendation. In 1986, a two-year-old with a viral infection suffered severe brain damage while taking theophylline. Her parents sued the company and the child's physician, who had not received a warning letter. He settled with the family and sought to recover that judgment from Fisons, based on its failure to disclose the relevant risks. Lawyers from Bogle and Gates, a prominent Seattle firm, defended the company on the ground that it had insufficient knowledge of the drug's danger to warrant such disclosures.

During pretrial discovery proceedings, the physician's lawyer sought copies of any letters that Fisons had sent to doctors concerning theophylline's risks for children, as well as any documents regarding cromolyn products. Defense counsel responded that they would produce letters regarding only theophylline, and they objected to requests concerning cromolyn drugs as "irrelevant," "overbroad," and "harassing." In support of that objection, counsel claimed that the material they were releasing included all documents reasonably related to the physician's case. Based on that claim, the court granted Fisons' request to narrow the discovery order. Defense counsel then produced thousands of documents, but not the warning letter or internal memo; these were in a file for Intal not subject to discovery. None of the material available to the plaintiff indicated that Fisons employees were aware of theophylline's risks before the child's illness.

After four years of discovery finally ended, and the case was verging on trial, attorneys for Fisons discovered the warning letter and internal memo. However, they decided not to produce copies for opposing counsel. Their reasoning was that the documents did not explicitly refer to the brand-name drug taken by the child, that they were intended to promote a cromolyn-based drug, and that they therefore fell outside the revised scope of discovery. Under normal circumstances, the lawsuit would have ended there. Without these smoking guns, the case undoubtedly would have been dismissed for lack of evidence. Instead, an anonymous whistle-blower sent the letter to the physician's lawyer. He then succeeded in obtaining full discovery of relevant documents, including the internal memo. After a trial on the merits, a lower court awarded the physician several million dollars, but refused to sanction defense counsel for their nondisclosure. On appeal, the Washington Supreme Court reversed the sanctions decision. In its view, defense attorneys were obligated to make good on their representation that all relevant documents had been produced; any questions about the scope of the revised discovery order should have been taken to the trial court. After that decision, Fisons and Bogle and Gates settled for a $325,000 fine.[13]

What makes this case so instructive is not the outcome, which is quite atypical. Evasive discovery rarely comes to light and rarely results in significant sanctions. Rather, what makes the case notable was the defense team of fourteen leading ethics experts, who all testified that the firm's conduct was not in fact notable or deserving of sanctions. Two of these experts had been presidents of the Washington state bar, and one had served as the reporter for the American Bar Association's Model Rules of Professional Conduct. All fourteen maintained that defense counsel's conduct was "typical" as well as proper, and several claimed that it was required by "lawyers' ethical obligation to zealously represent their client." That consensus prompted a cover story in the magazine *American Lawyer*, aptly titled "Sleazy in Seattle."[14]

In commenting on the *Fisons* case, another ethics expert, Monroe Freedman, asked the key question:

> What does this [consensus among experts] tell us? It tells us that lawyers throughout the bar (including those who later became judges) had known for decades that discovery rules were being systematically frustrated by disingenuous responses to discovery demands. It tells us that the Washington Supreme Court was itself being disingenuous in pronouncing itself shocked that such things were going on.

What the case also tells us is that whether or not the Washington justices were truly shocked, they should have been. As one Seattle law professor who supported sanctions noted, "There were kids out there dying because [Fisons's lawyers and managers] were hiding information so they could win a lawsuit."[15]

How often such ethically questionable conduct occurs is, of course, speculative. But the limited evidence available suggests that it is by no means atypical. In a recent ABA-sponsored study of litigation ethics, many lawyers and judges shared the view of one participant: "*Fisons* is not unusual at all. There is usually no consequence . . . to an attorney for hiding documents. What matters is keeping the client and winning the case." The most systematic recent research on discovery found that almost half of attorneys reported problems in obtaining relevant documents. In an earlier study, lawyers handling large cases reported that in about half the matters that were settled and in about 40 percent of those that were tried, they had significant information that was not discovered by other parties.[16]

Case histories of such adversarial abuses are also common, even in contexts presenting substantial risks to public health and safety. Hardball tactics in litigation involving asbestos, the Dalkon Shield, cigarettes, and vehicle design defects have placed the public at substantial risk and denied remedies for thousands of serious injuries. In many other less visible contexts, counsel for some of the nation's leading law firms and corporations have been involved in destroying or withholding material evidence. In another case somewhat similar to the one involving Fisons, Texaco lawyers failed to produce the minutes requested for personnel meetings at which racist discussions occurred. Instead, the company provided only edited versions of the minutes. Since plaintiffs were unaware that two versions existed, they had not specified their obvious desire for complete, unrevised minutes. And Texaco counsel took the position that it could give them "what they were asking for—nothing more, nothing less." After a disgruntled employee leaked original tapes of the meetings, Texaco settled the litigation to avoid punitive damages. The case was then worth a record $176 million, "nothing more and nothing less."[17]

Among lawyers, such partisan pathologies evoke two main responses. For practices that clearly violate procedural and ethical rules, attorneys want greater judicial control. Surveyed practitioners consistently favor a more active role for trial courts in overseeing the litigation process and in sanctioning abusive behavior. On other practices, lawyers are divided. Some see hardball strategies as largely inevitable by-products of an adversary system and confidentiality protections that, on the whole, well serve societal and professional interests. Other lawyers would like to see greater curbs on partisan abuses, but they are divided about what constitutes abuse. The compromise has been voluntary civility codes, which establish more ethically demanding norms than current procedural or ethical rules, but which are not intended to give rise to judicial sanctions, bar discipline, or malpractice liability.[18]

Each of these solutions has obvious limitations. The last two decades have witnessed greater efforts to curb abuse through managerial judging strategies. These include increased use of pretrial conferences, special masters to oversee discovery proceedings, and sanctions both for claims that are not "well grounded in fact" or based on "good faith arguments," and for actions that are intended to harass or to cause needless delay or expense. However, these judicial efforts have been constrained by the absence of adequate resources and incentives for oversight as well as by the difficulties of applying such standards. One study asked several hundred judges to consider ten hypothetical cases based on reported decisions. In six of those cases, the survey participants divided almost evenly on whether to impose sanctions. This indeterminacy in standards has made it easier for judges' own biases to affect decision making. One unwelcome effect of increased judicial control has been an excessive use of discovery sanctions to punish what some courts consider "frivolous" claims in controversial civil rights and public interest litigation. Yet reforms designed to reduce trial judges' discretion can create other problems. For example, during the late 1980s and early 1990s, federal courts tried requiring sanctions for all reported violations of discovery rules. The result was that lawyers had more incentives to contest alleged violations and to charge their opponents with abuse. Sanctions claims then turned into another weapon in litigators' arsenal and often compounded the expense and acrimony that they were meant to prevent. That experience prompted rule makers to make sanctions once again discretionary, not mandatory. The federal judiciary has recently adopted further changes that somewhat limit the scope of issues subject to discovery. But experts doubt that such tinkering will significantly affect abusive practices, given current incentive structures and enforcement difficulties.[19]

Judicial oversight has other limitations as a control on adversarial abuses. As one federal court put it, "Judges in general have neither the time, the resources, nor the will" to provide such oversight. Sorting out who is at fault and what constitutes evasion or bad faith often requires more knowledge about the merits of a case than overburdened courts can afford to acquire, particularly on matters that are likely to be settled before trial. One judge in the ABA litigation study put the point bluntly: "Discovery disputes are a nuisance. . . . Putting time into sanctions does not move a case to resolution." Substantially increasing judicial resources, reducing caseloads, and providing more special masters would obviously help. However, legislatures have been unwilling to make the necessary expenditures, and the public has been insufficiently informed or concerned to demand them.[20]

Moreover, even if courts had more resources to monitor misconduct, it is unclear how often they would do so effectively. Most judges dislike antagonizing lawyers by imposing sanctions; such penalties can escalate the dispute, compromise settlement efforts, risk reversal on appeal, and erode support in judicial elections or bar opinion polls. If attorneys cannot keep partisanship in check, a common judicial response has been to leave them to their own devices. Litigation then becomes a "contact sport with an absent referee." Even when courts do impose penalties, they are often insubstantial in relation to the stakes for the lawyer and client. *Fisons* is a classic illustration; the firm and client received a $325,000 fine in a case involving several million dollars in potential damages and legal fees. "Chump change" was how many lawyers viewed that penalty.[21]

In the absence of official oversight, bar leaders have sought ways of increasing voluntary self-restraint. Civility codes and professionalism courses have been the strategy of choice. The reason is obvious: They are a concrete response at little cost. Lawyers who oppose such efforts can largely ignore them. Yet without enforcement mechanisms, the effectiveness of civility standards is open to question. The bar's current enthusiasm for such standards rests on no evidence that they significantly influence behavior. A few jurisdictions require lawyers to certify that they have read the applicable civility code; none have attempted to assess compliance or even to measure awareness of its requirements. Nor have efforts been made to determine whether professionalism courses for practitioners affect behavior.

This reluctance to scrutinize effectiveness may in part reflect concerns about likely results. It seems implausible to expect that voluntary codes or occasional classes will attract disciples among those most in need of conversion. One such litigator expressed widespread views in a recent *National Law Journal* editorial. "It's a dangerous distraction for any lawyer to spend time thinking about what he owes to other lawyers. My objective has always been, and remains, to win for my client. Not by a little, but by a lot." Jerking around an adversary can have obvious payoffs, and as one practitioner put it, "My experience with jerks is that they like to be jerks." Others find the tactic profitable. One of the nation's most notoriously uncivil practitioners is also one of the highest earners. Texas personal injury lawyer Jo Jamail is legendary for foul language and sharp practices. By the mid-1990s he had a net worth estimated at $950 million.[22]

A related limitation of civility initiatives is that key provisions are vague and inconsistent. For example:

> [A lawyer should] learn and follow practices and civilities that encourage respect, diligence, candor, punctuality, and trust;
>
> [A lawyer should] be a vigorous and zealous advocate on behalf of [a] client while recognizing that, as an officer of a court, that excessive zeal may be detrimental to many clients' interests as well as to the proper functioning of our system of justice;
>
> [A lawyer should], within the framework of vigorous representation, advocacy, and duty to the client, be firm, yet tolerant and nonabusive of ineptness or the inexperience of opposing counsel;
>
> [A lawyer should] attempt to avoid bullying, intimidating, or sarcastic questioning of witness except as reasonably proper under circumstances reasonably related to trial tactics.[23]

Such standards command widespread support because they dodge the difficult issues. Who can disagree with rules that aren't really rules but only aspirations and that tell lawyers not to be bullies unless it becomes "necessary" or "proper"? The issue really worth discussion is how to determine when zeal is unnecessary or "excessive." When does "vigorous" representation demand taking advantage of opposing counsel's ineptness? On questions involving hard trade-offs between individual clients' interests and broader societal values, most civility codes are diplomatically vague. And those that favor broader concerns often are inconsistent with bar disciplinary rules.

These problems emerge clearly in a Missouri Supreme Court decision in which the justices divided almost evenly about duties of professionalism. The case involved a lawyer who obtained a default judgment for the plaintiff and then received a letter from the defendant's attorney requesting a schedule for discovery. That attorney was under the mistaken impression that an answer had been filed. The plaintiff's lawyer waited until after the time had passed for the defendant to set aside the judgment, and then notified opposing counsel of the adverse result. Four judges concluded that the lawyer had acted appropriately in protecting his client's interest, and upheld the default ruling. Three dissenters maintained that the lawyer should have notified opposing counsel of the mistake in time to set aside the judgment. The Chief Justice insisted that the failure to do so should "shock all right thinking lawyers."[24]

Such cases suggest the difficulties that arise when lawyers and judges want to have it both ways or remain ambiguous about which way they want it. Aspirational civility standards advise attorneys not to exploit their adversaries' inadvertent mistakes, but mandatory ethical rules demand deference to clients' legal objectives. On other issues, where civility and disciplinary provisions are similar, the rationale for redundant standards are by no means clear. If the problem is that lawyers too often violate the bar's current code, "the answer surely is not to devise another," particularly one without sanctions.[25]

Aspirational civility standards cannot adequately compensate for limitations in mandatory rules. If professionalism codes are to play a useful regulatory role, they should include fewer vague exhortations and more concrete obligations. Such codes should eliminate provisions that repeat or contradict mandatory rules, and provide more specific directives that courts or bar associations would be willing to adopt as enforceable standards. Several jurisdictions have moved in this direction. For example, the Los Angeles Superior Court has adopted local bar association guidelines on litigation conduct as part of its procedural rules. These guidelines include concrete examples of unacceptable behavior. Some federal judges also have relied in part on state civility codes when imposing sanctions. A few bar associations have established programs that refer claims of incivility to mediation or peer counseling.[26]

Other bar leaders have made promising efforts to reinforce civility standards. Associations such as the American Inns of Court have established trial advocacy and mentoring programs. In-house counsel of some prominent corporations have agreed to abide by civility codes and have made good on that commitment. For example, General Motors recently fired outside counsel for refusing to reschedule a deposition when the opposing attorney's mother had died and the timing was not crucial for GM's case. Client efforts to control costs through closer monitoring and non–hourly fee arrangements also have made some progress in curbing excessive litigation tactics.[27]

In the long run, however, major improvement in adversarial practices will require major changes in bar ethical codes, enforcement patterns, and incentive structures. Current codes are insufficiently demanding. Some ethical standards simply track existing civil procedure rules prohibiting actions that are frivolous or intended to harass, and these standards are almost never enforced in disciplinary proceedings. Other code provisions incorporate minimal prohibitions already applicable to all citizens concerning fraud, perjury, destruction of evidence, and related matters. Proposals for more ethically demanding requirements are not in short supply. Several were made and rejected during the ABA's debates over the Model Rules of Professional Conduct. For example, one proposal would have prohibited lawyers from "unfairly exploiting" an opponent's ignorance and obtaining an "unconscionable result." Another would have required lawyers to disclose adverse facts to a tribunal if they would "probably have a substantial effect on the determination of a material issue." Other commentators have proposed requirements that attorneys not misrepresent or conceal a relevant fact or legal principle and that counsel in civil cases follow the rules now applicable to prosecutors in criminal cases and turn over material evidence favorable to other parties.[28]

Opposition to such requirements rests on several concerns. One involves the issues of confidentiality discussed below. The others involve fairness, incentives, and enforcement. Attorneys steeped in the "sporting theory of justice" see no reason why opponents should freeload on their efforts. It seems unjust for their clients to subsidize both sides of a lawsuit, and it seems inefficient to undermine incentives for thorough preparation by opposing counsel. Yet the current system imposes equal if not greater inefficiencies by encouraging duplication of fact-finding efforts and by allowing attorneys to withhold material information that opponents have failed to discover through reasonable efforts. It is also by no means clear that some minimal disclosure requirements would significantly reduce opponents' efforts. Such requirements have not had that effect in criminal cases when clients have adequate resources for representation. Whatever other ethical problems arose with O.J. Simpson's lawyers, freeloading on prosecutorial efforts was not among them. And where clients cannot afford advocacy, any loss in incentives for their counsel may be offset by the value of information provided through mandatory disclosure provisions. In the federal courts that have chosen to require automatic disclosure of certain basic information, most surveyed lawyers and judges favor retaining those requirements, and few report negative effects. Other countries with adversarial processes also impose more demanding ethical requirements than the United States without demonstrable difficulties. As one British justice put it, litigation is a "serious business. It is not a form of indoor sport."[29]

If American lawyers viewed the adversary process more as a search for truth and less as a sporting event, then such requirements would not appear unjust. Why shouldn't clients be stuck with the facts? If the point of the justice system is promoting justice, why not prevent professional assistance in unreasonable outcomes? As Robert Gordon has suggested, the ultimate test for adversarial practices should be: "What would happen to the system if everyone did this? Would this practice. . . seriously interfere with efficient and accurate fact finding [and a just] resolution on the merits?" Subjecting lawyers to that test would require greater obligations of candor, cooperation, and civility. The result is likely to be less expense, acrimony, and injustice. Over the long run, clients in general, like the public in general, would benefit from a system in which fairness and truth were central objectives, not incidental by-products of lawyers' efforts.[30]

The main obstacle to such a system involves enforcement. If bar regulatory structures cannot prevent widespread noncompliance, then strengthening ethical rules has limited value. And the current oversight system is inadequate to that task. Judicial sanctions are too intermittent, inconsistent, and insignificant to deter abuse. Bar discipline for adversarial abuses is even less effective. Disciplinary officials almost never respond to such conduct without a formal complaint, and few judges or practitioners see much point in filing one. Disciplinary agencies generally decline to act while litigation is pending, and they rarely impose substantial sanctions or financial remedies that compensate victims of adversarial abuses. Why should lawyers or judges risk the hassle and antagonism of reporting when the response is unlikely to be adequate or to benefit them?

An apt illustration involves a demonstrably frivolous class action suit against Ford Motor Company. After the suit was dismissed because it had been filed in the wrong jurisdiction, Ford paid the lawyer $100,000 not to refile in the correct court. Reporters later asked Ford's lawyer why he had agreed to this undeserved payoff and had not filed a complaint with the bar. He explained that the company was better off avoiding the adverse publicity and expense of fighting the claim. "Won't this just encourage [the lawyer] to go after other big business targets?" asked one journalist. "Of course it will," defense counsel conceded, but "I represent Ford Motor Company, not the next guy. . . . I have a very narrow balance sheet to look at."[31]

There are, of course, limits to how much we can alter those incentives, but we have yet to exhaust some obvious possibilities. Courts and bar disciplinary agencies need greater resources and pressure to sanction misconduct. Judicial codes could require referral of ethical violations to disciplinary authorities, and, discovery sanctions or civil malpractice suits could also prompt investigation. More legislative and judicial remedies, such as attorney fee awards and punitive damages, should be available for frivolous claims and SLAPP suits. Some strategies developed for white-collar crime, corporate misconduct, and compliance with environmental standards could be equally appropriate in professional regulation. For example, in cases like *Fisons,* disciplinary agencies could require the law firm and in-house counsel to design regulatory plans to prevent future abuse. Such plans might include internal policies, educational programs, oversight committees, reporting channels, and ethical audit processes. Voluntary organizations like the Association of Business Trial Lawyers or the American Inns of Court could establish "best practice standards" that included such internal procedures and could certify firms that complied. Bar agencies also could make greater use of reputational sanctions, such as requiring lawyers to notify other clients of judicial sanctions or disciplinary action against them or their law firms. Trial judges could be evaluated on their responsiveness to adversarial abuses. Legal education should place more emphasis on professional ethics and collaborative problem solving skills. Research on the effectiveness of such strategies would permit a more sensible reform agenda.[32]

The prospects for that agenda will depend on securing greater commitment from those within the profession and greater pressure from those outside it. Judicial, legislative, and media leaders need to insist on fundamental changes in adversarial practices. And lawyers need to accept more responsibility for the performance of adversarial processes and bar oversight structures. As the ABA litigation study makes clear, a central problem in countering ethical abuses is the perception that the source of those problems lies everywhere and anywhere else. Judges blame attorneys for greed and incivility. In-house counsel put responsibility on plaintiffs' lawyers who bring frivolous claims and defense lawyers who turn procedural maneuvers into "cash cows." Plaintiffs' attorneys blame opposing counsel for stonewalling and judges for laxity. Defense counsel are equally critical of judges, and they also fault clients who want scorched earth tactics. In short, everyone agrees that it's "the other fella's fault."[33]

That perception needs to change. The problems are widely distributed, and accountability for solutions needs to be widely shared. Lawyers for Ford Motor Company do not represent just that client. They also hold a public trust as officers of the court and members of a largely self-regulating profession. Too many lawyers have failed to assume that responsibility, and too little effort has been made to hold them accountable.

RELATIONS WITH WITNESSES

If American lawyers truly considered the adversary system a search for truth, they would have quite different practices concerning witnesses. Under the current system, individuals who testify at trial must swear to tell the truth, the whole truth, and nothing but the truth. But attorneys who select, prepare, and cross-examine witnesses have no such goal. The advocate's role is to persuade, and where information is not helpful to that end, a lawyer has no reason and generally no obligation to disclose it. What emerges from the fact-finding process is not "the facts" but a skewed and often misleading selection of the facts.

Efforts to repackage reality are a standard part of preparing a witness to testify, and they present a wide range of ethical problems. At one extreme lie overt efforts to create false testimony, a practice which clearly violates bar ethical codes and criminal statutes. At the other end of the spectrum are unintended effects. Social science evidence makes clear that lawyers' discussions with witnesses can alter recollections and descriptions of events, even when everyone is seeking accuracy. The information that attorneys provide before asking a question, as well as the way they formulate and follow up that question, inevitably shapes the response. Between these extremes is a vast gray area in which lawyers guide clients down memory lane with certain destinations clearly in view.[34]

Some ethical difficulties arise from the common practice of explaining the law before discussing the facts. In effect, an attorney indicates what would constitute a successful claim or defense and only then asks the witness "what the facts happen perchance to be." A celebrated fictional account of the technique appears in the movie *Anatomy of a Murder*. After the lawyer describes how to prove temporary insanity, his client conveniently recalls information that fits the description.[35]

A less famous but more infamous real-world example involved a 1997 memorandum by the Dallas law firm Baron and Budd. Its litigation department drafted the memorandum to prepare clients for trial, and mistakenly included it in documents given to opposing counsel. The clients were plaintiffs seeking damages from exposure to asbestos products, which had occurred sometimes as much as twenty-five to thirty years earlier. The memo began with helpful explanations about what clients would need to say to make the defendant companies "want to offer . . . a settlement." When identifying particular asbestos products, "Remember to say you saw [defendant manufacturers'] NAMES on the product or on the containers. Try to remember how close you were. The more often you were around [them], the better for your case. It is important to maintain that you NEVER saw any labels on asbestos products that said WARNING or DANGER." For clients worried about being caught in a lie, the memo provided reassurance: "[Defendants] have NO RECORDS to tell them what products were used on a particular job." The memo also suggested examples of physical and economic damages resulting from asbestos-related diseases, and it reminded plaintiffs "never to mention" the existence of the memo itself. When the document nonetheless came to light, the firm suffered some embarrassment but no disciplinary or judicial sanctions.[36]

It is impossible to know how often lawyers provide such coaching and how often their assistance crosses the line between helping witnesses present what they know and helping them to know something else. Normally, all lawyers' oral and written instructions to a client remain confidential; they are shielded from disclosure by the attorney-client privilege. Written communications with other witnesses also may be protected as confidential work products. But most experts believe that unethical coaching is common and almost impossible to prove. Analogous problems arise with attorneys' frequent practice of drafting pretrial affidavits and declarations for witnesses to sign that include the facts necessary to prevail on a crucial motion. In theory, witnesses can edit their statements; in practice, the lawyer's version often prevails. And enough case histories have come to light to suggest that dubious drafting and suggestive coaching are by no means isolated examples.[37]

Another well-known instance involved a reporter for *American Lawyer* who posed as a client and interviewed thirteen randomly selected Manhattan lawyers. She explained that she had suffered injuries after a fall near a construction site. Her best recollection was that she had been day-dreaming at the time and had noticed no major debris or cracks that might have caused her accident. However, she implied that she might be willing to recall the event differently in order to make a good case. Five of the thirteen lawyers were equally willing. The most forthright stated, "Basically it's up to you—whether you're up to, well, quite frankly lying." When the reporter acknowledged a few reservations about perjury, he replied, "Everybody lies under oath. It comes down to your word against [the construction company's]." Other attorneys were somewhat more tactful. The most cautious suggested that she return to the site and "refresh [her] memory." When she indicated that she had done that already and found nothing, his advice was, in essence, "If at first you don't succeed . . ." As the attorney patiently explained, if the woman could recall some construction materials that had caused her fall, "then I can help you."[38]

However murky the line between helping witnesses recollect reality and helping them revise it, these examples fall clearly on the wrong side of the divide. But part of the reason that attorneys cross the line is that bar ethical codes and adversarial practices encourage skirting the edges. Many litigators agree with law professor Monroe Freedman's rationale for disclosing the law before discussing the facts. In his view, lawyers should not presume that a witness will make unlawful use of their advice. Before a client begins to remember essential facts, he "is entitled to know what his own interests are." To decide otherwise would "penalize the less well-educated defendant." A Baron and Budd litigator similarly explained that asbestos clients often are poorly educated and readily intimidated by opposing counsel. Yet as most legal ethics experts note, it is often asking too much of human nature to provide a strong motive for lying and then to expect the truth. While "well-educated" clients may be better able to deceive without assistance, a lawyer's role need not include giving everyone equal opportunities for deception.[39]

Similar problems often arise when attorneys suggest possible language or lines of testimony. Such preparation can, of course, have legitimate purposes. It can eliminate misleading descriptions, prevent unduly technical or rambling presentations, and help unsophisticated or nervous witnesses make more effective presentations. This assistance can significantly affect how decision makers view a case. For example, one study asked participants to watch a film of a collision and then to estimate the speed of the vehicles. If the question describing the collision used the term *smashed,* subjects' average estimate was 41 mph; the terms *hit* and *contacted* yielded 34 mph and 32 mph. The difficulty, however, is that when an attorney suggests language that might be helpful, a witness may be highly motivated to revise reality accordingly. And no violation of bar ethical rules occurs unless the lawyer "knows" that the testimony is false.[40]

Practicing attorneys have quite different views about what constitutes knowledge and how much coaching is appropriate. In one of the only surveys on point, litigators differed over whether it was acceptable to make any of the following statements in pretrial preparation of a witness:

> If there is any uncertainty in your mind, say you don't recall. It's almost impossible to prove that "I don't recall" is a false answer.
>
> I'm hearing you say that the green car was traveling very fast when it hit the truck. Why don't you say the green car smashed into the truck? Is that word OK by you?
>
> Before I ask you about your recollection, let me tell you what Mary Smith recalls.[41]

Of course, as experienced trial attorneys note, their own self-interest imposes some constraints on coaching behavior. Finding out from witnesses what really happened will prevent unpleasant surprises later. When lawyers imply that truthfulness is unimportant, parties may embellish in ways that ultimately prove counterproductive. But in too many cases, both lawyers' and clients' interest lie in carefully scripted court performances that bear limited resemblance to actual events. And judges, juries, and opponents often will be unable to separate fact from fiction. Although opposing counsel sometimes can ask nonclient witnesses about the preparation they received, the truthfulness of their responses is extremely difficult to gauge. The problem is compounded by witnesses who have learned the convenience of "I don't recall." President Clinton's deposition in the Paula Jones sexual harassment case was a textbook illustration. Although known for his mastery and recollection of technical details, Clinton's memory failed him on 267 occasions during that testimony.[42]

If adversarial proceedings are truly intended as a search for truth, they require a different approach to witness preparation. One possibility would be to modify ethical rules to permit greater inquiry by opposing counsel into coaching practices or to ban certain techniques, such as suggestions of particular language. Some experts believe that prosecutors could send an effective message by launching "sting operations" with undercover agents posing as clients willing to adjust their testimony. But given the difficulties of exposing unethical attorney practices, it makes sense to consider the approach of most European countries. They prohibit counsel from contacting witnesses prior to trial, and permit judges or investigating magistrates to conduct factual inquiries and to obtain unrehearsed testimony. Such prohibitions carry a price, but so does our current process. And as the concluding section of this chapter notes, a system that relied more on neutral judges and less on partisan advocates in the search for truth might have a better chance of finding it.[43]

Similar points are applicable to the cross-examination of witnesses. A century ago, Anthony Trollope suggested:

> One would naturally imagine . . . [that] clear evidence would be best obtained from a man whose position was made easy and whose mind was not harassed; but this is not the fact; to turn a witness to good account, he must be badgered this way and that . . . he must be confounded till he forget his right hand from his left, till his mind be turned into chaos. . . . What will fall from his lips when in this wretched collapse must be of special value, for the best talents of practiced forensic heroes are daily used to bring it about.

Bar ethical rules impose relatively few constraints on this process. They prohibit lawyers from asking questions that are irrelevant or that have no substantial purpose other than to "degrade, "embarrass," or "burden" a witness. But attorneys often have another substantial purpose: they seek to confuse and discredit truthful witnesses or to discourage them from testifying in the first instance. The bar has rejected proposed standards prohibiting attorneys from undermining testimony that they believe is truthful. Indeed, leading trial practice manuals offer techniques designed to do exactly that. For example, a Practicing Law Institute publication promises a "fun-filled way to learn how to scorch witnesses and score points." Irving Younger's *Ten Commandments of Cross-Examination* advises lawyers, "Never permit the witness to explain his or her answers." Save damaging interpretations of the witness's answers for closing arguments "when the witness is in no position to refute them."[44]

Other strategies, seldom endorsed in theory but commonly followed in practice, involve the introduction of prejudicial information. Facts that have little relevance to the issues in dispute often influence judges or juries, and cross-examination on those points during pretrial proceedings or interviews may deter parties from pursuing legal claims. Rape and sexual harassment cases are among the most notorious examples. A standard defense in these cases is to show that the complainant is somehow responsible—that she fantasized, provoked, welcomed, or acquiesced in the abuses that she claims. This "nuts and sluts" defense can be highly effective. Jurors' perception of the conduct and character of victims is the most important factor in predicting the outcome of sexual assault cases. That perception is often based on factors that bear no relation to a defendant's guilt. What women were wearing or drinking and whether they appeared to be neglectful mothers or promiscuous partygoers may be technically irrelevant but highly effective points for the defense.[45]

In an effort to curb the victimization of victims, state and federal statutes now prohibit the introduction of a complainant's prior sexual history except in certain limited circumstances. However, some jurisdictions permit exceptions that can swallow the rule; lawyers can introduce evidence of previous sexual conduct that establishes a pattern of conduct or that judges find more probative than prejudicial. So, for example, in a Glen Ridge, New Jersey, case involving a gang rape of a retarded girl with a baseball bat, defense counsel presented testimony about prior behavior that painted the victim as promiscuous. Even when courts exclude evidence about complainants' sexual background from trial proceedings, inventive lawyers can leak such information through press reports, pretrial records, and indirect questioning. In the rape prosecution of William Kennedy Smith, defense counsel placed the complainant on trial and ensured widespread coverage of her Victoria's Secret underwear, out-of-wedlock child, bar-hopping history, and reputed "wild streak." Similar tactics gained national prominence in a New York City police brutality case. Defense counsel's opening argument suggested that the injuries to a Haitian immigrant could have occurred through a same-sex consensual encounter rather than a police assault. Although there was no convincing evidence of such an encounter, as became clear when the defendant confessed midtrial, the lawyer insisted that his allegations were consistent with an advocate's obligation to "do anything in his power to defend the client."[46]

Defense counsel in sexual harassment proceedings often take a similar view and are willing to discredit or deter a plaintiff with harassing tactics of their own. Women who allege physical or psychological damage from harassment routinely face humiliating questions about possible alternative causes for their distress—everything from closeted lesbian relationships to abortion experiences or intimate marital difficulties.

Plaintiffs' attorneys sometimes can respond in kind, as Paula Jones's lawsuit against President Clinton made abundantly clear. Jones's allegations were dismissed without a trial for lack of credible evidence of injury, but not before destructive foraging expeditions concerning Clinton's consensual extramarital relationships.[47]

The lessons of those well publicized cases are not lost on other potential litigants. Part of the reason that over 90 percent of sexual assault and harassment victims never file complaints is that they have no desire to compound their injuries in order to prove them. They realize, as one district attorney acknowledged, that in most cases "'Trash the victim' is the only real form of defense . . . no matter what the law says." Even when courts attempt to minimize harm to witnesses through limits on courtroom questions or press statements, the sanctions for violations are too often inadequate to ensure compliance. Almost never do abusive questions or prejudicial leaks result in bar disciplinary action. The typical response, a judicial reprimand or modest fine, pales in relation to the potential payoffs. The same is true of judges' other common response to objectionable cross-examination: striking inappropriate material from the record and instructing jurors to disregard it. But it is impossible to "unring the bell." Social science research finds that such instructions can even be counterproductive. They may draw special attention to the evidence and increase its perceived value.[48]

Proposals to impose more effective constraints on misleading or degrading tactics have met with little enthusiasm from the organized bar. Prevailing ideologies and incentive structures push in the opposite direction. To be sure, few lawyers would support an ethical rule that expressly authorized advocates to "do everything the law allows to disconcert, distress, divert, disturb, deflect, deceive, disorder, delude, dupe, and distract" their opponents. But in practice, many attorneys have supported adversarial norms that permit exactly that. In a survey of lawyers handling rape cases, one public defender summarized widespread views: "The bottom line is getting my client off. [I am] more concerned with this one guy and his freedom than the ethical issue of sexism." Another litigator, when questioned about his humiliating cross-examination of a sex harassment victim, offered a similar rationale: "It's certainly something I'd prefer not to do—but I don't allow myself the luxury of regret." Yet there is nothing noble about such self-denials and nothing inherent in the lawyer's role that requires them. The general public is by no means clamoring for gladiatorial tactics. In one of the rare comparative surveys of attitudes within and outside of the bar, almost three-quarters of lawyers thought that it was appropriate for litigators to discredit a witness whom they believed was giving accurate and truthful testimony. A majority of nonlawyers disagreed.[49]

A regulatory structure more responsive to ethical principles and less hostage to client interests would strike a different balance concerning relations with witnesses. Bar ethical codes should prohibit attorneys from discrediting or degrading a witness whom they believe is testifying truthfully. Of course, lawyers sometimes will be unsure which witnesses fall in that category. And as discussion in chapter 3 suggested, a system requiring proof beyond a reasonable doubt for criminal cases authorizes defense attorneys to raise legitimate doubts even for a client they believe is guilty. But not all doubts are legitimate. And neither should lawyers in criminal or civil proceedings exploit the vulnerabilities of truthful witnesses whatever the price. Some circumstances may call for special restraint, such as where the individual testifying is very young, lacks education or English language skills, or is discussing intimate sexual matters. Lawyers should consider the harmful consequences for those witnesses, for others who might be deterred from becoming witnesses, and for the accuracy of fact-finding processes. Similar considerations should also guide courts in more actively policing litigation tactics. For example, attorneys should have to demonstrate a clear and convincing need for questions likely to prove especially intrusive or humiliating. "Getting the client off" should not be the only value, and it ranks too high among believers in the sporting theory of justice.

Similar considerations are applicable to the selection of witnesses. Federal Judge Richard Posner comes directly to the point: "There is hardly anything not palpably absurd on its face that cannot now be proved by some so-called experts." What experts are prepared to sell, lawyers are prepared to buy. And we all pay the price for the distortions that result.[50]

Attorneys' reliance on expert testimony has increased dramatically in recent years, partly in response to the growing technical complexity of many cases. Specialists provide testimony on a wide range of issues, such as the nature and cause of injuries, the reliability of evidence, and the mental capacity or dangerousness of defendants. Standards for admitting expert testimony are quite permissive, and they allow almost any specialized evidence that will assist the trier of fact. Such testimony need not meet with "general acceptance" among other specialists; the evidence need only rest on a "reliable foundation." That standard leaves lawyers ample opportunities to shop for biased testimony. They can select experts on the basis of how helpful they will be to a client's case, not on the basis of their qualifications or the merits of their positions. To identify helpful witnesses, attorneys can rely on consulting organizations or advertisements highlighting favorable results from the expert's testimony. As one such organization promises, if the "first doctor we refer doesn't agree with your legal theory, we will provide you with the name of a second." Lawyers also can reduce their search costs by hiring only experts who come clearly labeled, such as a well-known Texas "Doctor of Doom." In over seventy capital punishment cases, he concluded, sometimes without even personally examining the defendant, that the man was a remorseless "sociopath" who would kill again. Juries were persuaded to impose the death penalty in all but one of those trials.[51]

Bar leaders often condemn "junk science" that creates 'junk law." But they generally insist that the adversary system is capable of exposing it. As Chief Justice Rehnquist put it in *Daubert v. Merrell Dow Pharmaceutical:* "Vigorous cross-examination, presentation of contrary evidence and careful [jury] instruction . . . are the traditional and appropriate means of attacking shaky but admissible evidence." Yet those traditional measures are often inadequate. The ethics of experts vary, and the representativeness of their positions or extent of their biases may be difficult to demonstrate. The *Fisons* case is an apt example. There, the defendant law firm was able to line up nationally recognized scholars and bar leaders willing to put the best possible spin on hardball tactics. The plaintiffs had no ready means of showing that these views were atypical. In many cases, each side produces its own team players: experts carefully preselected and prepared to supply the party line. Particularly where the issues are esoteric or highly technical, such battles of the experts are not a self-evidently effective way to expose truth; they may, as David Luban notes, simply "pile up the confusion."[52]

Moreover, even if parties are successful in challenging an expert's testimony *at* trial, the mere fact that such a witness is available may get the case *to* trial. The consequence may be to impose substantial costs, or to extort a substantial settlement, on the basis of implausible but adequately pedigreed claims. For example, in Paula Jones's suit against President Clinton, a critical issue was whether her claim of damages was sufficiently credible to justify a trial. The support for her claim came from an "expert" with a degree in education and counseling who briefly interviewed her some six years after the alleged harassment. He asserted that she was suffering from "sexual aversion." Although the trial judge refused to credit that assertion and dismissed the case, many other judges reportedly would have permitted the suit to go to trial. If a proposed witness has any colorable claim of expertise, courts generally allow the case to proceed and let the jury determine how much weight to give the contested testimony.[53]

A final problem with relying on "traditional" adversarial methods to expose flaws in expert evidence is that not all parties can afford effective challenges. Resource disparities are particularly pronounced in criminal and personal injury proceedings. Prosecutors' offices and corporate defendants usually can afford substantially more expert assistance than their opponents. In a rare case like O. J. Simpson's, defense lawyers were able to demonstrate substantial weaknesses in the expert testimony offered by the prosecutor. But they spent several million dollars in the process. The vast majority of criminal defendants have no access to such assistance.[54]

Resource inequalities are compounded by bar ethical codes and judicial rulings that prohibit experts from charging fees that are contingent on successful outcomes. In principle, these prohibitions make perfect sense; they attempt to prevent witnesses from shading their testimony in an effort to encourage large verdicts. But in practice, the rule against contingent fees does not remove the incentives for experts to be helpful, and it carries a substantial cost. Many of these individuals have ongoing relations with lawyers who have retained them and have a tacit understanding that they will seek reimbursement only in cases that are successful. Cross-examination will not expose such arrangements, because in pretrial or trial proceedings the witness can testify truthfully that their fee agreements call for payment whatever the outcome. Attorneys who are unwilling or unable to arrange such subterfuges, or who are litigating matters that will not yield monetary awards, often cannot adequately finance a battle of the experts. And valid claims may be among the casualties.[55]

Various proposals for reform are worth considering. One possibility is to build on the approach of civil law countries like Germany. There, courts decide whether an expert is necessary and, if so, whom to select. Judges typically choose from a list approved by an official licensing body or by another public agency. Parties may object to a particular individual on grounds of bias and request appointment of a different expert or hire their own. Other possibilities would be to have courts appoint a panel of experts from a list chosen by the litigants or to have opposing parties each select one expert and have courts choose a third. More modest reform proposals include allowing explicit contingency agreements for experts' fees, subject to full disclosure and court approval; encouraging more judicial appointments of neutral experts under existing rules; and permitting only expert testimony that reflects accepted views within the field. Any of these reforms would push us in the right direction. Not all facts are created equal, and the public deserves a process more responsive to the differences.[56]

CONFIDENTIALITY

"If I had to choose between betraying my country and betraying my friend, I hope I should have the guts to betray my country." This was E. M. Forster's view, and for many lawyers, the principle extends more often to clients than to friends. The stakes may seldom involve a nation's betrayal, but they often present serious threats to innocent third parties, as the following cases reflect.

- A defendant convicted of rape is released on bond pending completion of a sentence recommendation. As a result of a clerical oversight, no date for sentencing is ever set. He refuses to contact the court, and his lawyer is aware of that fact.

- Lawyers representing a computer leasing firm learn that their assistance has helped a client complete fraudulent loan agreements totaling almost $60 million. The lawyers resigned but declined to explain their reasons to the client's new counsel. That firm unknowingly assisted the completion of another $15 million in faulty loans before the fraud was exposed. After the clients were convicted of criminal fraud, the first lawyers were sued for nondisclosure by defrauded lenders.

- A lawyer for the defendants in a personal injury action requests that the plaintiff have his injuries assessed by a medical expert. That doctor submits a confidential report to the lawyer indicating that the plaintiff has a life-threatening condition that his own physician has failed to detect. The lawyer has an opportunity to settle the case for a modest sum if he does not disclose the condition.

- After a lawyer promises complete confidentiality, his client reveals that he committed a murder for which another man has been sentenced to death. That man was convicted of murdering a young female employee in a trial marred by anti-Semitic prejudice. The client refuses to disclose his guilt or to allow the lawyer to do so.

- A lawyer working for a kidney dialysis company learns that its German subsidiary has just sent a shipment of machines that fail to meet U.S. Food and Drug Administration standards. The machines could put some patients at risk by leaving excessive levels of potassium and phosphate in their systems. The company president indicates that he will accept the shipment for resale to a customer whom he believes cares more about price than quality. After the lawyer threatens to disclose the defects, he is fired, and the machines are resold.[57]

None of these are hypothetical cases. They all involved real people and real lives. And in none of them would the bar ethical rules prevailing in most jurisdictions require disclosure. In general, these rules permit disclosure only where necessary to prevent future criminal acts, or criminal conduct that would result in imminent death or substantial bodily harm. Since it is not a crime for clients to refuse to incriminate themselves, or to violate FDA regulations, or to withhold information that another party has failed to request, lawyers generally would not be authorized to reveal their clients' confidences.

In all but one of the cases, the attorneys did not do so. The exception involved the lawyer for the kidney dialysis company. He practiced in Illinois, which is one of the few states that requires disclosures necessary to prevent any client conduct that would result in death or serious bodily harm. The lawyer reported the defective machines to the FDA and then sued the company for wrongfully terminating his employment. The Illinois Supreme Court rejected his claim. A majority of state supreme court justices agreed that the lawyer had "no choice" but to reveal the client's misconduct. However, because he had no alternative, the court concluded that he also needed no protection against the employer's retaliatory discharge. Lawyers should expect that they may sometimes "have to forego economic gains in order to protect the integrity of the profession." In the court's view, it was more critical to protect companies from unfair litigation than to protect employees from unfair discharges. If corporations had to fear lawsuits from disgruntled former lawyers, and the disclosure of confidences as part of the proceedings, "employers might be less willing to be forthright and candid with their in-house counsel." This risk appeared more important to a majority of justices than supporting attorneys who forfeited their jobs to save lives.[58]

The Minnesota Supreme Court made a similar assessment in the case involving the life-threatening injury. There, the plaintiff eventually learned of his condition during an army medical examination and sued to vacate the settlement of his personal injury action. The trial judge granted that request on the ground that he had been a minor at the time of settlement and that informed consent by the court had been required for the terms of the agreement. However, in affirming that decision, the Minnesota Supreme Court made clear that lawyers generally would have no ethical obligation to disclose such information to an opponent; their disclosure responsibilities ran only to the court. If the plaintiff had been an adult, his sole remedy would have been malpractice actions against his own physician for not discovering the condition and his attorney for not seeking discovery of the medical expert's report. Never did the court even acknowledge the possibility that the plaintiff might have died before learning about his condition and appropriate treatment, let alone about his potential malpractice actions. In a later interview explaining his decision, the judge indicated that he had a personal relationship with a senior partner at the defendant's law firm and didn't want to expose the firm to criticism.[59]

None of the other cases reached a court. Lawyers in the commercial leasing transactions paid $10 million to settle the claims by defrauded lenders. The sentencing oversight was not discovered until ten years after the defendant had been free on bail. The lawyer justified his refusal to disclose the oversight on the ground that his client may not in fact have been guilty and did not seem like "the kind of guy [who] would [rape] on a regular basis."[60]

The dilemma involving the erroneous criminal conviction later came to light in the lawyer's autobiography. In 1915, Arthur Powell, a prominent Atlanta practitioner, heard his client confess to a murder for which Leo Frank had been convicted. Powell contacted the governor and asserted Frank's innocence, but would not reveal details or the source of his information. Although the governor commuted Frank's death sentence, there were insufficient facts to demand a new trial. A lynch mob hanged Frank and formed a group that subsequently became part of the Ku Klux Klan. Seventy years later, Frank was pardoned posthumously. Powell defended his action on the ground that the constitution guaranteed the right to counsel, including the right to confidential assistance, and that lawyers were bound by their oath of office to obey constitutional mandates. However, Powell also added, "I would be strongly tempted to break my oath before I would let an innocent man hang, but would know that I was violating the law and my oath if I did so."[61]

These cases are not isolated incidents. In one recent variation on the *Frank* case, a man wrongly convicted of murder sat on death row for twelve years while the attorney for the guilty man remained silent. Not only did the lawyer fail to disclose that his client had committed perjury at the trial, but the lawyer also advised the client against later confessing to his crime.[62]

Attorneys' silence concerning client misconduct has contributed to some of America's worst public health and financial disasters. For considerable periods, lawyers knew much more about the dangers of asbestos, the Dalkon Shield, and tobacco than either regulatory agencies or the users of these products. Tobacco companies deliberately channeled compromising scientific research through their law firms in order to claim that it was privileged and exempt from disclosure. By making unfounded claims of privilege, lawyers prevented the timely release of thousands of documents revealing fraudulent activity. Attorneys' active assistance or passive acquiescence in misconduct by savings and loan associations contributed to catastrophic losses that are projected to cost taxpayers $200 billion. Federal trial judge Stanley Sporkin asked the appropriate question in response to such abuses by Lincoln Savings and Loan: "Where were [the lawyers] when these clearly improper transactions were being consummated? Why didn't any of them speak up or disassociate themselves from the transactions?"[63]

Two explanations seem particularly plausible. One involves money. More than eighty firms collected an estimated $70 million for representing the parent company of Lincoln Savings in its five years of tussles with the Federal Bank Board. According to one insider, "For a half a million dollars you could buy any legal opinion you wanted from any law firm in New York." Another explanation involves professional ideology and regulatory structures. The prevailing view of lawyers' responsibilities, reinforced by bar ethical codes, gives high priority to client confidences at the expense of other values.[64]

The American Bar Association's Model Rules of Professional Conduct and their predecessor, the Model Code of Professional Responsibility, prohibit lawyers from revealing confidential information except in limited circumstances. The Model Rules do not *require* disclosure of confidential information except where necessary to prevent fraud on a tribunal. Nor do the Rules even *permit* such disclosure to prevent noncriminal but life-threatening acts or to avert massive economic injuries. Lawyers may, of course, advise clients to rectify their conduct. And in cases involving organizational clients, lawyers may refer matters involving serious legal violations to the organization's highest authority. But if clients refuse to take appropriate corrective action, attorneys' only recourse is generally to withdraw from representation and to disavow any of their own prior statements to third parties that might assist criminal or fraudulent conduct.[65]

These ethical rules shield far more compromising information than the laws of evidence concerning the attorney-client privilege. The privilege only exempts lawyers from testifying in court concerning communications that come directly from clients and that do not involve future crimes or frauds. The ABA's Model Rules demand confidentiality in all contexts regarding information from all sources if it relates to client representation and does not involve physically dangerous criminal activity. Although state ethical codes generally incorporate more exceptions to confidentiality requirements than the Model Rules, these exceptions still are strikingly limited. A majority of codes permit disclosure of information necessary to prevent any criminal acts by a client and some permit disclosure of future frauds or rectification of past frauds committed during the course of representation. About a dozen states require disclosure in certain cases, typically criminal conduct likely to result in death or bodily injury. However, for the most part, lawyers have discretion to keep information confidential except in the relatively rare circumstances in which they know of a client's criminal intent or fraud on a court. Lawyers also have discretion under the Model Rules and all state codes to reveal confidential information when necessary to defend themselves from accusations of wrongful conduct or to collect unpaid fees.[66]

From the profession's perspective, these rules make eminent sense. They give lawyers maximum scope to protect their own interests and those of paying clients. From the public's perspective, however, it is not self-evident why attorneys have the right to reveal anything to collect a bill but not the responsibility to make limited disclosures that could prevent far more significant injuries. And none of the bar's traditional responses provide adequate justifications for prevailing ethical rules. These rationales for confidentiality run parallel to conventional rationales for the advocate's role. One justification involves the importance of confidentiality in protecting individual rights. A second involves the value of confidentiality in promoting just resolution of legal disputes and compliance with legal obligations. Neither are fully convincing.

Rights-based arguments for confidentiality build on several assumptions about social values and client conduct. The first is that legal representation provides essential protection for individual rights, and that effective representation depends on clients' willingness to disclose relevant information. A related assumption is that clients generally will be unwilling to make such disclosures without assurances that the information will remain confidential. According to bar leaders, the trust and candor necessary for professional relationships cannot survive if lawyers assume significant whistleblowing obligations. Although these arguments are not without force, they fail to justify the scope of current confidentiality protections. Concerns about individual rights cannot explain why confidentiality principles should shield organizational misconduct. Nor do such concerns explain why the rights of clients should always take precedence over the rights of everyone else, particularly where health and safety are at stake. In practice, traditional confidentiality principles yield perverse results; they categorically favor clients who withhold inculpating information out of guilty motives at the expense of innocent third parties whose physical or financial well-being depends on disclosure. The exceptions to bar confidentiality obligations are similarly hard to justify. If a less self-interested group were responsible for adopting confidentiality rules, it seems highly unlikely that we would end up with the current versions. Would anyone other than judges require disclosure to prevent a fraud on a court but not to save a life? Would anyone outside the bar permit disclosures to help lawyers collect a modest fee but not to prevent a massive health or financial disaster?[67]

Attorneys generally claim that clients insist on confidentiality and that without its protection, they would withhold relevant information. But current rules are riddled with exceptions and indeterminacies that few clients comprehend. The most systematic research available suggests that adding further limitations would not alter most clients' behavior. For example, a New York study by law professor Fred Zacharias found that attorneys almost never informed their clients about rules governing confidentiality. Many clients substantially misunderstood these rules, and only about a third reported giving information to their lawyers that they would not have given without a guarantee of confidentiality.[68]

Other research also suggests that even clients who might like to withhold compromising information may be unable to do so, whatever the bar's ethical responsibilities. In many cases, individuals will not know what material would be legally damaging, their lawyer will have other sources for such information, or their need for informed legal assistance will outweigh the risks of disclosure. Historical, cross-cultural, and cross-professional data make clear that practitioners have long provided assistance on confidential matters without the sweeping freedom from disclosure obligations that the American bar has now obtained. Businesses routinely channeled compromising information to attorneys before courts recognized a corporate privilege, and most European countries manage without one now. Many Americans also are reasonably candid with accountants, financial advisers, private investigators, and similar practitioners who cannot promise protection from disclosure obligations. When evaluating the appropriate scope of a privilege for other professionals such as psychiatrists, legal decision makers generally have concluded that the benefits of absolute confidentiality are too speculative to outweigh concrete risks to third parties.[69]

Moreover, when lawyers' own needs to reveal information are at issue, defenders of sweeping confidentiality protections rarely pursue the logic of their position. If disclosures to protect innocent third parties will erode client trust, why won't disclosures to protect lawyers' financial interests be equally damaging? As Geoffrey Hazard and Susan Koniak note, "Such a preference for lawyers as compared with third party victims seems very difficult to justify, to put it mildly. As compared with other victims, the lawyer is likely to be in a superior position to prevent the wrong . . . [and] probably runs a lesser risk of suffering actual injury if the fraud is consummated." Attorneys have no lack of strategies short of disclosure for dealing with deadbeat clients. Lawyers can charge large retainers in advance, refuse to perform services or to release client files, or institute collection proceedings. Nonlawyers typically have fewer options.[70]

In short, the rationale for current confidentiality rules has more to do with professional than public interests. As the history of bar debates over these rules makes clear, attorneys' overriding objective has been to minimize their own risk of civil or disciplinary liability. The prevailing combination of broad confidentiality requirements with limited discretionary exceptions serves this purpose. Discretionary provisions give attorneys the option to disassociate themselves from criminal or fraudulent conduct, while reducing risks of accountability if they choose not to do so. To avoid any ambiguity on this point, the commentary in the Model Rules and in many state codes provides that "the lawyer's exercise of discretion not to disclose information . . . should not be subject to reexamination." Yet from a public policy standpoint, lawyers' decisions on confidentiality *should* be reexamined. If the rationale for broad confidentiality obligations is that society as a whole benefits, then society should decide whether the gains outweigh the losses. As philosopher Sissela Bok notes, the professions are too insular and self-interested to make appropriate assessments.[71]

The difference between lawyers' and nonlawyers' views on confidentiality emerges clearly in the limited research on point. For example, Zacharias's survey asked participants to consider a hypothetical case in which a lawyer learns of a confidential study concerning an airplane that his client manufactures. That study suggests that one of the plane's parts might weaken and cause explosions at high altitudes. However, the part meets federal standards, and the client's board of directors concludes that the safety risks are too inconclusive to require disclosure. Under these circumstances, over three-quarters of surveyed lawyers indicated that they would not reveal the information, a decision consistent with the New York Bar ethical code. By contrast, 85 percent of clients believed that attorneys *should* disclose, half believed (incorrectly) that attorneys already had discretion to do so, and only 15 percent indicated that disclosure would affect their willingness to rely on attorneys. Similarly, in studies of negotiation ethics, about a third more nonlawyers than lawyers believed that it was inappropriate for attorneys to misrepresent their authority to settle a case or to withhold information necessary to correct a vulnerable opponent's misunderstanding of a material fact.[72]

As these survey findings suggest, decision makers concerned less with their professional liability and more with the public interest undoubtedly would end up with different rules and a different, more accountable process for formulating them. To gauge the likely results, it is useful to consider a variation on philosopher John Rawls's classic thought experiment. If decision makers stood behind Rawls's "veil of ignorance" and had no idea what position they would hold in society, what rules on confidentiality would they adopt? What factors would be most relevant to their decisions? While reasonable people might vary somewhat in their priorities, consensus seems likely on certain critical points. Confidentiality rules should take account of the likelihood and significance of harms from nondisclosure, the potential for minimizing those harms through strategies other than disclosure, and the likely effects of disclosure on lawyer-client relationships.[73]

Legal ethics experts and drafting committees that have attempted to balance such concerns from a disinterested perspective have recommended various reforms. Proposed early drafts of the Model Rules would have required lawyers to reveal conduct likely to present imminent physical danger to third persons, crimes or frauds in which the lawyers' services had been used, violations of the law by organizational clients, or information likely to affect the determination of a material fact. Other proposals, modeled on securities regulation, would obligate lawyers to disclose material evidence and to refrain from making materially misleading statements. Any of these reforms would be steps in the right direction, as would limiting lawyers' rights to disclose confidential information in their own disputes with clients. If attorneys had to make some threshold showing of compelling circumstances that justified such disclosure, it could reduce the risks of clients being pressured to pay unjustified fees or to drop legitimate malpractice claims in exchange for continued confidentiality.[74]

The effectiveness of such reforms is difficult to predict. Critics often argue that whistle-blower requirements would be widely violated and that such noncompliance would threaten the credibility of other ethical rules. There is clearly some basis for those concerns. In states with the most demanding disclosure requirements, they are seldom invoked or enforced.

But it does not appear that the absence of formal sanctions has compromised the legitimacy of other ethical obligations. Nor does it follow that the legal profession would be better off without codified requirements of candor and fairness even if enforcement is limited. Such requirements at least can raise ethical expectations, remove excuses, support claims by third parties, and encourage lawyers who wish to resist client or collegial pressures.[75]

But to achieve major improvements, bar rules also need to be reinforced through other legal and organizational strategies. To that end, the profession needs more legislative, judicial, and administrative agency initiatives that require or protect whistle-blowing. For example, the Securities and Exchange Commission and the federal Office of Thrift Supervision have attempted to impose modest reporting responsibilities on lawyers to ensure that they do not lend assistance to fraudulent client conduct. Such obligations could be expanded and extended to other contexts, particularly those involving health and safety. Useful models are available from requirements applicable to other occupations such as medicine and engineering, and to legal advisers in other nations. A related strategy is to provide whistle-blowers with greater safeguards against reprisal. Building on legislation that now protects government employees, legislatures could prohibit discharge of any individuals, including lawyers, who report activity reasonably believed to be illegal or against public policy.[76]

Courts also should provide greater support for whistle-blowers by allowing wrongful discharge claims where attorneys are fired for reporting, or for refusing to participate in, illegal activity. Although some courts have permitted such claims, others have denied relief or allowed remedies only for wrongful terminations that can be proved without disclosure of confidential information. For example, according to the Illinois Supreme Court, lawyers can be counted on to "do the right thing" and to report illegal conduct despite the absence of legal safeguards against retaliation. The historical record offers little support for that assumption. Whistle-blowers routinely experience harassment, dismissals, transfers, or blacklisting. Many individuals are unwilling to pay that price, particularly in organizational contexts where responsibility is fragmented and close collegial relationships would be jeopardized. To counter these pressures, greater job protections are essential, as are greater civil penalties for those who remain silent. Other professionals are increasingly held accountable for knowing facilitation of fraud or conscious avoidance of facts suggesting fraud. Lawyers should be subject to similar standards.[77]

Increased organizational support for attorneys' disclosure of misconduct is equally critical. Most research finds that internal institutional incentives are more likely to promote ethical behavior than occasional sanctions by external regulatory agencies. Law firms and other organizations that employ lawyers should encourage reports of client or collegial abuses by establishing specific ethical guidelines, education programs, and reporting channels. Lawyers who cut ethical corners should be penalized in performance evaluations and compensation decisions.[78]

Reform on all these fronts—in professional codes, legal standards, and organizational structures—is no modest undertaking. It means fundamental rethinking of our sporting theory of justice and fundamental restructuring of the incentives that sustain it. Yet at least partial progress is a realistic goal. Many individuals, both within and outside the profession, are frustrated by adversarial pathologies. The challenge is to tap their disaffection in pursuit of concrete strategies for change.

Adversarial practices have their value, but they have too often been viewed as ends in themselves and their defects too often excused. The structures that now lead to adversarial abuses are not necessary to preserve the virtues that most Americans find in current processes: protection of individual rights, incentives for effective preparation, and checks on judicial bias and governmental power. Other legal systems have preserved such values without the level of obfuscation and incivility that American lawyers have accepted. In a prominent *New York Times* account of "Why Lawyers Lie," New York lawyer Floyd Abrams put the relevant question: "It is time to ask whether it really leads to justice to have a system in which lawyers spend far more time avoiding truth than finding it. And it is never too late to ask whether we can continue to justify every sort of legal game in which the players lose sight of why they started playing in the first place and the spectators forget that what they are watching was not supposed to be a sport at all."[79]

CHAPTER 5

TOO MUCH LAW/TOO LITTLE JUSTICE: TOO MUCH RHETORIC/TOO LITTLE REFORM

I n 1770, a New Hampshire census report noted that Grafton County included "6,489 souls, most of whom are engaged in agriculture. . . . There is not one lawyer, for which fact we take no personal credit, but thank an Almighty and Merciful God." To many contemporary observers, such a prospect would doubtless seem appealing. A majority of Americans believe that the United States has too many lawyers and that lawyers file too many lawsuits. Bar leaders also rank litigiousness at the top of the list of problems facing the profession. The conventional wisdom is that the nation has too much law and too little justice and that the legal profession contributes more to the problem than to the solution.[1]

Yet underlying this apparent consensus are contested assumptions and competing values. Problems in the distribution of legal services remain unsolved partly because there is no agreement, except at the rhetorical level, about what the problems are. Efforts to pin down the difficulties raise more questions than they resolve. On what basis do we conclude that America has too many lawyers or lawsuits? Too many in comparison to what? Other countries? Other eras? Why should our concern center on the number of lawyers? Why shouldn't we instead focus on the price and quality of what lawyers do? If, as the following discussion suggests, this nation's litigation rates are not exceptional, then our difficulties look different than popular discussion implies. For most Americans, the most significant problem involves not too much but too little: too little access to justice and too few choices about legal services and dispute resolution processes. And for most policy makers, the problem involves too much: too much posturing that is uninformed about legal needs and unreflective about the competing interests at issue.

The reasons have much to do with how readily folklore passes for fact in discussions about our perennial litigation "crisis." In media portraits and political debates, systematic research typically plays at best a walk-on role; skewed statistical sound bites and unrepresentative anecdotes are the main attraction. Distorted profiles of the problem lead to distorted perceptions of the solution. Our concern should focus less on the amount of law and more on its distribution. Too many consumers cannot meet their legal needs at a price they can afford. Too few consumers have a voice in policy processes that might promote more effective alternatives. Our greatest difficulty is not that we have too many lawyers but that we have given them too much control over legal policy. Once again, the result has been a system that too often serves the profession at the expense of the public.

TOO MANY LAWYERS

The number of American lawyers has almost tripled over the last three decades and now approaches nine hundred thousand. However, complaints about the number—whatever its magnitude—have remained unchanged for centuries. Even the metaphors remain the same; attorneys appear, and reappear, as "cursed caterpillars" and "plagues of locusts" "sapping the vitality out of American enterprise," burying the nation under an "avalanche of suits, and creating 'bloodbaths' for businesses." Media accounts repeatedly and uncritically rely on assertions like Dan Quayle's claim that America has 70 percent of the world's attorneys. Informed estimates, however, put the figure somewhere between a quarter and a third, which is roughly the United States' share of the world's combined gross national products. Cross-cultural comparisons are also misleading because they fail to reveal the number of individuals in other countries who are not licensed members of the bar but who receive legal training and perform tasks that the United States reserves for lawyers.[2]

Critics' endlessly favorable references to Japan are particularly in need of qualification. This hypothesized haven of cooperation has fewer than twenty thousand licensed lawyers while America produces thirty-five thousand new lawyers every year. Yet such comparisons overlook key facts. Many

Japanese business and government employees receive university legal training and provide legal services but never obtain licenses to practice in court because bar exam pass rates are set at around 2 percent. Indeed, some Japanese commentators complain that their country overproduces legal advisers and at a higher rate than America. Japan has approximately twice as many graduates of law programs per capita as the United States.[3]

Of course, even adjusting for differences in population and in occupations delivering legal services, the United States has relatively more providers of such services than other industrial nations. Many individuals assume that this concentration of lawyers is largely responsible for America's heavy reliance on law. Popular humor collections replay endless variations on this theme. A common (and not necessarily apocryphal) example portrays a solo practitioner starved for business in a small town. A second lawyer then arrives, and they both prosper.

However, this conventional account may have the central causal connections backwards. While attorneys certainly encourage and capitalize on America's legalistic culture, it is naive to hold them responsible for its origins. According to most researchers, the United States' disproportionate share of lawyers is more the effect than the cause of its dependence on complex, decentralized legal processes. As later discussion indicates, other countries pursue similar regulatory and compensatory goals through centralized bureaucratic structures which require fewer expensive legal professionals.[4]

To many Americans, our heavy reliance on lawyers seems wasteful and inefficient. Prominent critics like former Harvard University president Derek Bok conclude that the legal profession simply absorbs too much "human talent." Unlike other professionals, such as engineers, lawyers reportedly cannot "make the pie grow larger; [they] only decide how to carve it up."[5]

Yet such descriptions, however effective rhetorically, are unconvincing factually. As a characterization of attorneys' role in corporate planning, regulatory compliance, civil liberties litigation, or criminal defense, the pie metaphor is highly misleading—"pie in the sky," as one critic puts it. Lawyers supply as well as divide social goods: They provide essential safeguards of personal rights and governmental accountability. Attorneys who sue to protect an inventor's patent claims are not just "dividing the pie." They also are enforcing a system of incentives that rewards innovation and increases the pie.[6]

Moreover, many laments about litigiousness overlook concerns about access. As Rutgers Law School dean Roger Abrams notes, the problem for most Americans is not that there are too many lawyers but rather that "there are too many lawyers trying to serve the same clients." Corporations and individuals with deep pockets or large potential claims may encounter a glut of would-be advocates. Ordinary Americans with ordinary needs do not. And for the poor, access to a lawyer is impossible for all but the most acute problems. Although four-fifths of Americans believe that indigents have a right to free counsel for civil cases, courts and policy makers have decided otherwise. The best estimates suggest that the nation supplies about one legal aid attorney for every nine thousand poor persons, compared with one lawyer for every three hundred residents.[7]

Whether America is overloaded with lawyers is a question that cannot be answered in the abstract. Nor is it the crucial question. The critical issue is not "how many?" but "how well?" How effectively is the legal profession meeting the nation's legal needs? What are the alternatives? Could some legal problems be addressed adequately by nonlawyer specialists at lower cost? Would greater competition from such practitioners offer a better array of consumer choices? These are not, however, the questions that dominate public debate. And until that changes, we will be left with too much rhetoric and too little reform.

TOO MUCH LITIGATION

Judging from mainstream media accounts, America suffers from a perpetual crisis of "legal hypochondria." Among its symptoms is an unseemly outbreak of mixed metaphors. The nation endures "avalanches," "bloodbaths," and "epidemics" of litigation rising to "bubonic plague proportions." The basis for this diagnosis is largely anecdotal. It draws heavily on what commentators label "news as vaudeville"—on the aberrant, amusing "fuzz and wuzz" of court proceedings. A twenty-five-year-old victim of "improper parenting" seeks damages from his mother and father. A suitor, who is fed up when stood up, sues his date. A customer having a "bad hair day" wants the beautician to pay. A woman tries to dry her poodle in a microwave following a shampoo and demands compensation from the manufacturer for the unhappy outcome.[8]

Such cases receive disproportionate attention—and for obvious reasons. In an increasingly competitive media market, the line between news and entertainment increasingly blurs. Serious coverage of the legal system struggles to survive among livelier rivals: talk radio, tabloid trash, and docudramas. As a result, factual content often is dumbed down and spruced up in ways that preempt informed debate. The public gets anecdotal glimpses of atypical cases without a sense of their overall significance. The problem is exacerbated by political polemics that take considerable poetic license. According to former California governor Pete Wilson, the "lawyer's briefcase has become a weapon of terror." Texas governor George W. Bush denounces "junk lawsuits that clog our courts" and damage awards that "terrorize small business owners." Dan Quayle replays a seemingly inexhaustible supply of homespun homilies. In his portrait of our "crazily litigious country," a base-ball crashes through a window and "the 'victim' . . . sues the neighbor. Or the baseball's manufacturer. Or the glassmaker. Or usually all three." As the line between fact and fiction grows increasingly fuzzy, the world begins to resem-ble the one that politicians like Kentucky senator Mitch McConnell inces-santly describe, where "everyone is suing everyone."[9]

Yet these embellished accounts fail to establish that America has an exceptional number of legal frolics or that they occupy a substantial amount of judicial time. Courts in many cultures provide outlets for petty griev-ances and develop strategies for sanctioning or summarily dismissing mer-itless claims. The United States' current collection of loony litigants might look less alarming if the public had a fuller historical and cross-cultural pic-ture. The nine thousand slander suits that once confronted Belgrade courts surely dwarf any American counterparts.[10]

Moreover, what qualifies as a frivolous claim depends on the eye of the beholder. While a few commonly cited examples meet almost anyone's def-inition, the line between vindictiveness and vindication is often difficult to draw. Sexual harassment claims were once routinely dismissed as matters beneath judicial notice. In some quarters, the situation has not significant-ly improved. Press commentators have a field day with harassment "witch trials" and "corporate McCarthyism," which assertedly allow radical femi-nists to "sue anybody about anything." To some (usually male) judges, it is a mistake to allow antidiscrimination law to redress the "petty slights of the hypersensitive." Yet only through these ostensibly petty claims have Americans finally begun to recognize the real costs of harassment. Women pay the highest price in terms of direct economic and psychological injuries, but all of us pay more indirectly. Harassment costs the average *Fortune* 500 company an estimated $6 million annually in turnover, worker absences, and lost productivity.[11]

Many of the media's favorite examples of trivial claims and outrageous verdicts rely on highly selective factual excerpts. A textbook illustration involves a recent multimillion dollar punitive damages award against

McDonald's for serving coffee at scalding temperatures. To most journalists, this case served as an all-purpose indictment of the legal profession and legal process; an avaricious lawyer paraded a petty incident before an out-of-control jury and extracted an absurd recovery. Newspaper editorials, radio talk shows, and magazine commentaries replayed endless variations on the theme summarized by the national Chamber of Commerce: "Is it fair to get a couple of million dollars from a restaurant just because you spilled hot coffee on yourself?"[12]

On closer examination, the question no longer looks rhetorical. The plaintiff, a seventy-nine-year-old woman, suffered acutely painful third degree burns from 180 degree coffee. She spent eight days in the hospital and returned again for skin grafts. Only after McDonald's refused to reimburse her medical expenses did she bring suit. At trial, jurors learned of seven hundred other burn cases involving McDonald's coffee during the preceding decade. Although medical experts had warned that such high temperatures were causing serious injuries, the corporation's safety consultant had viewed the number of complaints as "trivial." The jury's verdict of $2.3 million was not an arbitrary choice. Its punitive damages award represented two days of coffee sales revenues, and the judge reduced the judgment to $640,000. To avoid an appeal, the plaintiff then settled the case for a smaller undisclosed amount. McDonald's put up warning signs, and other fast-food chains adopted similar measures. While evaluations of this final result may vary, it was not the patently "ridiculous" travesty that media critics described.[13]

Nor is the McDonald's litigation an isolated case. In pursuit of fetching illustrations, commentators often let facts fall by the wayside. And stories "deficient in drama" sometimes "have drama grafted on." A well-documented example involves a *60 Minutes* profile of an ostensibly outrageous verdict. After a ladder slipped when placed in horse manure, the injured plaintiff recovered $300,000, reportedly because the manufacturer had failed to warn about such perils. This slip and fall had comic potential too good to be true. Or so the producers might have discovered if anyone had bothered to look at the trial record. In fact, the ladder was defective and the victim's fracture and cracked vertebrae had caused permanent injury. When questioned about the failure to check the facts, news anchor Harry Reasoner denied the need to do so. After all, he noted, "We were only trying to present [this defendant's] perspective."[14]

Yet such simplifications of the story miss what the real story should be. All too often, anecdotes substitute for analysis and masquerade as reflective of broader trends. Since stories are easier to sell than statistics, coverage of the litigation "epidemic" tends to be long on folklore and short on facts. The problem is compounded by cognitive biases. Because vivid incidents are especially easy to recall, our tendency is to overestimate how frequently they occur. When stories displace data on statistical trends, the public ends up with highly distorted impressions. This is not to imply that objectively "correct" data are always available. But some accounts of legal processes are more closely connected to evidence than others. And the legalization debate has been a sinkhole for sloppy statistics.[15]

A case in point involves the perennially popular assertion that the United States is "the world's most litigious nation." Scholars have been debunking this assertion so often that it is startling how much bunk survives. Much of what passes for "evidence" relies on a statistical sleight of hand. Commentators point to dramatic growth in certain kinds of cases, such as bankruptcy and product liability suits in federal courts. But federal filings account for only 2 percent of American litigation. And in state courts, product liability suits have been declining. While business leaders raise the most complaints about legal hypochondria, disputes between businesses are the largest and fastest growing category of civil litigation. Experts also agree that current litigation rates in the United States are not exceptionally high, either in comparison with prior eras or with many other Western industrial nations not known for contentiousness. Higher per capita caseloads occurred in previous centuries in some American communities. United States court filings now are in the same range, when adjusted for population, as those in Canada, Australia, New Zealand, England, and Denmark.[16]

In any event, litigation rates are a highly imperfect measure of cultural combativeness or legal hypochondria. Uncontested divorces account for much of the recent growth in civil caseloads. Yet this increase appears less a reflection of greater litigiousness than of increased expectations for marital satisfaction, decreased tolerance of domestic violence, and simplification of legal procedures. Nor do such cases constitute a major drain on judicial resources: In one representative survey, the average uncontested divorce hearing took four minutes.[17]

By focusing excessive attention on excessive litigation, critics bypass an equal if not greater problem: Most Americans lack the information or resources to assert legitimate claims. The exact extent of the problem is, of course, difficult to quantify. Whether individuals believe that a matter requires legal assistance is highly subjective. Yet while different methodologies yield somewhat different results, virtually all recent studies reveal a large universe of unmet needs. State and national surveys generally suggest that over four-fifths of the legal problems of low-income households are not addressed. Among moderate income families, a recent ABA study found that about 60 percent of civil legal needs were never taken to the justice system; in about 40 percent of those cases, parties were unsatisfied with alternative efforts at resolution.[18]

Other surveys of specific legal problems reveal similarly high levels of unmet needs. For example, the most systematic research finds that only about 10 percent of accident victims make any claims for compensation and only 2 or 3 percent file lawsuits. So too, a review of some thirty thousand New York hospital records disclosed that only about 12 percent of patients who sustained injuries from negligent medical care brought malpractice actions and only half of those received compensation. The tort liability system reimburses only about 4 percent of victims' direct costs of accidental injuries. Moreover, if the public were to hear as much about frivolous corporate defenses as it hears about frivolous plaintiffs' claims, its perception of the problem might be quite different.[19]

American legal institutions offer least to those who need help most. Barriers to the justice system impose enormous hardships on vulnerable groups: domestic violence victims in need of protective orders; impoverished families improperly denied medical benefits; elderly claimants with unresolved social security or pension problems. Yet these garden-variety needs remain unacknowledged in public debate and unaddressed in public policy. Our folklore fixates on the loony litigant with a rapacious lawyer. The far more common plight—inadequate access to any lawyer, rapacious or otherwise—remains out of sight and out of mind.

TOO MUCH LAW

According to conventional wisdom, America not only has too many lawsuits. It also has too much law. Recent statistical trends encourage that perception. Since the 1960s, legal services have more than doubled their share of the gross national product. Each year, state courts issue almost 100 million legal decisions, state legislatures pass over twenty-two thousand laws, and administrative agencies generate thousands of volumes of regulations and reports. Not only do we have more law but the law we have is more pervasive. It is not always a welcome guest. When a six-year-old "sex harasser" can be suspended for a smooch, legal rights have overstayed their visit.[20]

Recent increases in the reach and volume of law reflect broader cultural trends. Most are by no means unique to America. As patterns of life become more complex and interdependent, the need for law becomes correspondingly greater. In Western industrialized countries, improvements in the standard of living have also led to increased expectations about the role of legal institutions in maintaining that standard. Throughout the last century, many societies have come to expect what Stanford law professor Lawrence Friedman labels "total justice." Industrial accidents, discriminatory conduct, environmental damage and inadequacies in social services that were once accepted as a matter of course now prompt demands for legal remedies.[21]

Moreover, as commentators since Alexis de Tocqueville have noted, the United States has relied more heavily on law and lawyers to solve social problems than most other societies. Americans traditionally have distrusted centralized power and have checked its exercise through a system of privately initiated litigation. This nation turns to courts for needs that other countries meet through administrative measures and governmental services. For example, accident victims in many Western industrialized societies can rely on guaranteed health insurance and no-fault wage replacement systems rather than personal injury lawsuits. Yet those who lament litigiousness rarely focus on the forces underlying it or on the trade-offs that alternative governmental structures would require.[22]

TOO MUCH EXPENSE

The assumption underlying popular debates is that the United States would be better off if it relied less on law, lawsuits, and lawyers. For centuries, Americans have heard about the legal system's "staggering expense and delay," and such concerns are now widely shared. Over four-fifths of Americans believe that litigation is too slow and too costly, and about three-quarters believe that it is damaging the country's economy. Half of surveyed corporate leaders think that product liability suits have a major impact on their companies' international competitiveness. California's top executives repeatedly single out liability law as the factor most likely to hurt the state's business climate.[23]

In assessing such concerns, it is important to separate two related but distinct questions. First, are the total costs of legal liability excessive in comparison with their benefits, and are they a threat to American economic health? Second, are the transaction costs of resolving particular types of legal claims excessive, given the value they provide and the alternatives that could be devised? Most public debate has been ill informed on both those questions and has leaped from misinformed factual premises to misguided policy proposals.

Although we lack reliable assessments of the total costs of civil liability, some reasonable estimates are available for the tort system. These figures are far lower than most popular debate assumes and do not reveal a substantial effect on economic productivity. For example, Brookings Institution studies estimate that tort liability could represent no more than 2 percent of the total costs of U.S. goods and services, an amount "highly unlikely" to have a substantial effect on American competitiveness. Other research suggests that businesses' total liability for all legal claims, including torts, is only about 25 cents for every $100 in revenue. Corporate risk managers report relatively little adverse effect from these legal costs on larger economic indicators such as gross revenues or market share. In most managers' experience, the major impact of tort claims has been to improve product safety and warning efforts.[24]

Yet such systematic findings have little effect on popular perceptions. Part of the reason is that they seldom reach mainstream audiences. Reputable statistical research is readily displaced by more colorful profiles of runaway verdicts. Recent surveys find that media accounts significantly overrepresent successful claims and large damage awards. The verdicts for reported cases are between four and twenty times larger than the average for all cases that go to trial. Such skewed coverage reflects both audience preferences and journalistic convenience. As earlier discussion noted, the news, after all, needs to be new. So exceptional awards attract disproportionate coverage. They are also easier for reporters to identify, since plaintiffs' lawyers have an obvious interest in publicizing large victories rather than humiliating losses or modest settlements. And as noted earlier, when events are especially vivid, people tend to overestimate their frequency. The combined effect of selective reporting and selective recall leads to misperceptions of the likelihood of large recoveries, particularly in tort contexts. Even relatively well informed individuals, including lawyers, legislators, and insurance adjusters, overestimate the amount of litigation as well as the size and likelihood of plaintiffs' verdicts.[25]

Although business leaders constantly bemoan excessive punitive damage awards, they fail to acknowledge the low frequency of such awards. In fact, plaintiffs recover punitive damages in less than 1 percent of all cases and only 2 to 3 percent of the product liability and medical malpractice suits that attract most criticism. Such damages are more common in disputes between businesses, a point on which corporate leaders are diplomatically silent. Moreover, damage awards are by no means as excessive or arbitrary as popular portrayals suggest. Typical awards are modest: In mid-1990s personal injury cases, the median judgment was under $50,000. Contrary to widespread assumptions, jury decisions are not systematically biased against corporations with deep pockets. Nor are these verdicts out of line with the judgments of experts, such as judges and physicians, who evaluate the same facts. Although large tort damages are the target of most public outrage and reform proposals, seriously injured victims are in fact more likely to be undercompensated than overcompensated. For example, one study of Florida medical malpractice cases found that plaintiffs on the average recovered just over half their costs, and those with the most severe injuries received only a third. Similar patterns of undercompensation hold for victims of unsafe products and of automobile and airline accidents.[26]

Not only does popular debate exaggerate the frequency of excessive verdicts. It also exaggerates their consequences. Again, much of the "evidence" that reaches the public is anecdotal, and the morals of these stories are highly misleading. John Stossell's ABC News special entitled "The Trouble with Lawyers" is a case study in the use and abuse of case studies. The program more than fulfilled its opening promise that "If you think there are too many lawyers making too much money off too many lawsuits, this program is for you."[27]

Throughout the broadcast, Stossel condemned litigiousness but finessed the sticky questions about whether litigation is actually increasing, whether it is excessive in comparison with other countries, or how much it affects the national economy. "Whatever the numbers are," he noted, "and they are hard to pin down, fear is up." Since data are irrelevant and only perceptions matter, the viewer gets lots of poignant illustrations of litigation phobia. First comes the Arizona couple who "cooked thousands of free Thanksgiving dinners for the poor, until . . . someone got a stomach ache and threatened to sue." Then follows the parents who "are afraid to coach Little League because they could get sued over a pop fly." Discussion concludes with seemingly unnecessary investments in product safety and unwarranted withdrawals of medically valuable products. Stossel, like other critics, is appalled that "[e]very football helmet costs $100 more because of lawsuits." The result, he explains in a companion *Wall Street Journal* editorial, "is that some financially strapped schools don't have football programs. The kids play in the streets. Is that safer?" What he fails to mention are the students who now play other sports that *are* demonstrably safer or the significant number of students who were killed annually in football accidents before helmets were redesigned.[28]

Such skewed presentations are not atypical. The American Tort Reform Association spends millions of dollars to popularize poignant illustrations of the costs of liability insurance. One campaign features forlorn children at a closed swimming pool; the title for the picture reads, "The Day They Canceled the Fourth of July." A representative op-ed piece in the *Wall Street Journal* comes directly to a similar point in its running head: "Lawyers May Kill My Daughter." The editorial lambastes the potential withdrawal of silicone products following breast implant litigation without acknowledging the contested safety issues surrounding such decisions. Almost no one, except lawyers themselves, discuss lawsuits that save daughters through product removal or modification. Even well-known cases quickly drop from view. Editorialists are not, for example, counting the tragedies prevented from toxic shock syndrome, flammable pajamas, and the Dalkon Shield.[29]

Nor does most mainstream commentary on this issue challenge questionable assertions from biased sources. Press accounts often report as uncontested facts some widely disputed claims by medical associations and insurance companies. For example, in an effort to block patient rights legislation, the American Association of Health Plans ran commercials claiming that a "feeding frenzy" of trial lawyers were "pressuring Congress for new ways to sue your health plan. Think that won't hurt you? Better think again. If trial lawyers get their way, health care for millions of Americans could simply disappear." In fact, the Congressional Budget Office has estimated that right to sue provisions would increase premiums by less than 2 percent, an amount unlikely to have significant effects on coverage decisions. Doctors claim that excessive malpractice litigation and insurance costs have discouraged many physicians from delivering babies and have routinely encouraged expensive and unnecessary medical tests. Yet a systematic review of the evidence by the federal government's Office of Technology Assessment found no such relation between insurance premium increases and withdrawals from obstetrics practice. It also concluded that "a relatively small proportion of all diagnostic procedures, certainly less than 8 percent overall—is performed primarily due to conscious concern about malpractice liability risk." Determining whether such precautions are worth the expense involves complex clinical and value questions that current debates seldom raise, let alone resolve.[30]

Exaggerated portraits of liability expenses also compound the problem that critics describe. Systematic overestimation of liability costs can encourage unnecessary tests or product removals. And disproportionate focus on excessive jury awards can fuel disproportionate concerns about excessive litigation. Policy makers assume that people sue too often and win too much, that frivolous claims are clogging the courts, and that verdicts are out of control. Such assumptions underpin tort reform legislation that limits damages and proposals that would require losing litigants to pay their opponents' legal costs. Yet as earlier discussion made clear, the most pervasive problem with the American tort system is undercompensation, not overcompensation of victims. Recent reform initiatives compound that injustice. Limiting damages often provides inadequate deterrence for misconduct and it strikes hardest at those with the most severe injuries, who generally fail to recover most of their losses. Requiring unsuccessful litigants to pay their adversaries' legal fees might reduce frivolous claims, but at the cost of discouraging meritorious ones as well. Those most likely to suffer would not be corporations that can absorb the risks of paying opponents' costs as a tax-deductible business expense. The real losers would be people of moderate means, some of whom had strong claims but could not risk subsidizing both sides of an unsuccessful suit.[31]

Supporters of fee-shifting initiatives often fail to discuss this problem. Instead, they emphasize that "loser pay" systems are the norm in other nations. But what proponents almost never acknowledge is that those countries typically have more comprehensive legal assistance, social welfare, and medical insurance programs. Such programs cushion the deterrent effects of fee shifting by reducing reliance on privately financed litigation to subsidize the costs of injuries. Nor does mainstream debate on fee-shifting policies consider Florida's unsuccessful experience. After five years, the state abolished its loser-pays system in medical malpractice cases. Although the threat of additional legal fees did somewhat reduce the number of malpractice cases filed, it also increased the number that went to trial. Plaintiffs fought harder because the stakes were higher. And since a significant number of losing plaintiffs had insufficient assets to pay opponents' costs, defendants' overall expenses were also higher. Whether comparable results would occur in other litigation contexts or whether they would be avoidable under more carefully designed systems are questions subject to debate. But that debate is too often missing, and it is essential for rational policy choices.[32]

TOO MUCH RHETORIC

In short, most contemporary debates about litigiousness are focusing "on the tip of the iceberg, and the wrong iceberg, at that." The relentless focus on "too much"—too much law, litigation, lawyering—deflects attention from issues of too little—too little access to legal assistance and too little informed debate about the performance of the justice system. The public's concerns about expense and delay are well taken, but popular debate misconceives the underlying causes and misdiagnoses the appropriate responses.[33]

Significant costs are inherent in a legal system that values interests apart from efficiency and speed, such as opportunities for participation, public trials, and development of precedents to guide future cases. For example, no-fault processes can provide quicker and cheaper ways of compensating victims, but the price may be reducing deterrence and responsibility for wrongful conduct. Alternative dispute resolution methods may cut costs but offer insufficient procedural protections. Few Americans are adequately informed about these trade-offs. As Yale law professor Peter Shuck notes, the legal profession "has failed to educate the public about the complexity of the systems in which we live. . . . [W]e can't realize all our ideals at the same time or to the same extent." We can, however, be clearer about our priorities and more knowledgeable about how the legal system and legal profession might better advance them.[34]

That is not to understate the difficulties in getting a more accurate picture to the public. As H. L. Mencken once noted, "What ails the truth is that it is mainly uncomfortable and often dull." It is also less accessible for journalists under deadlines than the simplified sound bites put out by politicians and business lobbying groups. But there are strategies for minimizing the distortions that now preempt thoughtful policy debates. One possibility is to make the press a more sophisticated consumer of claims about the legal system and the legal profession. We could support more legal education for reporters by both law and journalism schools. The profession also could establish organizations, modeled after Fairness and Accuracy in Reporting, that would attempt to counteract distorted coverage on legal profession issues. A related strategy would be to help legal experts become more adept at presenting material to the general public and to create nonpartisan institutes that could make responsible research more accessible.

How much these strategies would influence public opinion and policy choices is open to question. On many issues affecting access to justice, Americans are not only poorly informed but deeply divided. Yet it seems plausible to hope that a more informed debate might yield a reasonable degree of consensus around certain key points. Three general principles seem likely to command broad support. First, individuals should have reasonable opportunities for access to legal services and dispute resolution processes for significant legal needs. Second, those processes ought to satisfy basic criteria of substantive and procedural fairness. And third, those services ought to meet reasonable expectations of competence and cost-effectiveness.

Underlying these basic principles are, of course, a host of complexities. "Reasonable" is one of the law's classic "weasel words," and what it requires in particular cases will be open to dispute. "Equal access to justice" is a particularly unhelpful slogan. As political theorist Richard Tawney once observed about issues of equality more generally, it is unclear what would terrify supporters most, "the denial of the principle or the attempt to apply it." Given the broad range of problems that could be considered legal and the wide disparity of skills among lawyers, any serious attempt to equalize access would require massive public subsidies. More modest demands to expand, if not fully equalize, access usually skirt the sticky points. How much are we prepared to pay for process? How do legal services compare with other demands on our collective resources?[35]

These are not questions that can be resolved in the abstract. But they should be more explicitly confronted in the context of specific policy debates. Those debates need both a broader set of questions and a more informed basis for addressing them. The issue is not simply whether America has "too much" or "too little" law but who gets to decide. All too often, the profession has controlled decisions affecting access to the legal system and has made trade-offs that serve its own interest at the expense of the public's. Americans have had too few choices about how best to meet their legal needs and too little information about the choices that are, or should be, available. Despite a recent expansion of options, particularly for sophisticated clients, too many individuals are still locked out of the market for cost-effective services as well as the policy process that could promote them.

TOO FEW CHOICES: ALTERNATIVE DISPUTE RESOLUTION PROCEDURES

Four-fifths of Americans believe that going to court costs too much, and their perceptions clearly have some basis in fact. Law is a pricey pastime, partly because law is a pricey profession. Sobering reminders come from a series of RAND studies of tort litigation. Over half of insurance companies' payouts in surveyed cases covered transaction expenses; less than half compensated victims. In asbestos litigation, delivering $1 to injured plaintiffs has cost more than $2.50. Such steep transaction expenses have multiple causes, but part of the problem involves inadequacies in legal services and dispute resolution procedures.[36]

Debates about the structure of legal processes often suffer from the same limitations as debates about litigiousness: too much sweeping rhetoric and too little careful factual analysis. Critics of the current legal system frequently present alternative dispute resolution (ADR) as an all-purpose prescription. It becomes *the* preferred solution for excessive expense, delay, and combativeness. Critics of ADR offer similarly sweeping assessments. In their analysis, alternative dispute resolution offers "apartheid justice"—a second-class strategy for bypassing rather than addressing inadequacies in the current structure.[37]

To make sense of this debate, the public needs fewer categorical pronouncements and more contextual evaluation. The last two decades have witnessed a dramatic growth in the range and sophistication of ADR methods, such as arbitration, mediation, adjudication by privately retained judges, and summary jury trials of key issues. These methods vary considerably in structure and offer different strengths and limitations. Not all respond effectively to the concerns fueling the litigiousness debate.

Discussions of ADR too often invoke overly simplified or idealized models. For many ADR advocates, the relevant comparison is between a courtroom trial, with all its costs, and a more informal, participatory process with all its virtues. From this perspective, adversarial proceedings look far less attractive than alternatives that can assist parties to identify underlying interests, promote cooperative relationships, explore possibilities for mutual gains, and discover strategies that may prevent or resolve future disputes. Informal processes that reflect parties' own priorities may also foster greater legitimacy and compliance. Yet as ADR critics note, 90 percent of cases settle without the full expense of trial, and many ADR processes are no less costly or contentious than traditional adjudication. For example, proceedings before privately selected arbiters, judges, or jury panels rely on conventional adversarial frameworks. Opportunities for delay and obfuscation can be comparable to those plaguing current litigation processes. Moreover, imbalances of wealth, power, and information may skew outcomes under any dispute resolution system, including ones that rely on nonadversarial approaches. Research comparing mediation and adjudication does not disclose consistent differences in costs, speed, or participant satisfaction.[38]

Rather, such research underscores the importance of context both in structuring and evaluating dispute resolution processes. What makes a given procedure effective depends on the participants' needs, the societal values, and the quality of programs at issue. A recent RAND Institute survey found no significant advantages for mediation over adjudication in federal pilot programs, but these programs were not well designed to accomplish the objectives that most ADR proponents seek. For example, the systems under review often provided insufficient training for mediators and inadequate opportunities for participation by parties.[39]

Other research underscores problems in arbitration and mediation procedures that are mandatory rather than voluntary or that fail to address major disparities in power and resources. For example, processes geared toward conciliation are not well suited for families with a history of abuse. And compulsory labor arbitration systems that involve employers who are repeat players may systematically disadvantage employees who are not. In one study involving such cases, the odds of an employer winning were about 5 to 1. Only repeat players had incentives to investigate the past decisions and predispositions of ostensibly "neutral" decision makers. And arbitrators who want repeat business have obvious incentives to favor participants who can supply it.[40]

Even where parties are more evenly matched, ADR is not always a desirable substitute for adjudication. Processes designed to satisfy private parties lack public accountability and may undervalue public interests. ADR methods do not require appointed or elected officials to enforce norms that are subject to democratic or judicial oversight. Informal procedures aimed at private settlements may provide insufficient development of legal precedents, inadequate deterrence of unlawful conduct, or ineffective safeguards for third-party interests. Much would be lost if socially important cases like *Brown v. Board of Education* routinely resulted in privately mediated settlements, however acceptable those outcomes might be to the individual parties.[41]

Yet as earlier discussion emphasized, the issue in evaluating legal processes should always be: compared to what? Critics who denounce ADR as second-class justice need to consider how often first-class justice is available and on what terms. The deficiencies common in alternative dispute resolution are chronic in conventional adjudication as well. Private settlements are the norm, not the exception, and procedural protections that are available in theory are often missing in practice. Imbalances of wealth, power, and information skew outcomes even in cases receiving the closest judicial oversight. As the title of Professor Marc Galanter's now classic article put it, the "Haves Come Out Ahead" in most legal settings.[42]

If any single lesson emerges from the burgeoning research on dispute resolution, it is that no single method is uniformly superior. Yet the current legal process is heavily weighted in favor of a single adversarial structure, which does not always serve either the parties' or the public's interest.

Alternatives to that system are too often imposed rather than chosen, such as mandatory mediation for child custody cases or arbitration of disputes involving less than a threshold amount of damages. Parties with needs that poorly fit the prescribed process can obtain an alternative only by paying its full costs, an option that not all individuals can afford. Such an opt-out structure also deflects energy from reform efforts. If the most powerful consumers of legal processes can buy themselves an alternative, there is less impetus for improving the current system.[43]

What the public needs instead is a broader range of procedural choices and the information necessary to make them. Participants' preferences should be respected, but they should be balanced against other social values. Proposals along these lines are not in short supply. Many ADR experts have developed promising blueprints for "multidoor courthouses" that would "fit the forum to the fuss." These courthouses would allocate different types of cases to appropriate dispute resolution processes based on several key criteria: the nature of the controversy, the relationship between the parties, the priorities that the participants attach to various features of the dispute resolution process, and the societal interests at issue. For example, crucial features of the controversy include the remedies being sought and the novelty or complexity of relevant law. Cases involving relatively small monetary damages and the application of settled legal precedents may not justify the expense of full-scale adjudication. In other contexts, the relationship between the parties may argue for procedures that are best able to address power disparities or to foster long-term working relationships.[44]

Participants' own preferences should also weigh heavily in the choice of process. Much may depend on the relative values that parties assign to maintaining privacy, expediting a decision, minimizing costs, maximizing recovery, obtaining a favorable precedent, or participating in remedial choices. An equally important, sometimes competing, consideration involves the public interests that may conflict with private choices. Whatever the parties' own preferences, adjudication may be desirable for cases raising significant questions of legal interpretation, social policy, or recurrent violations. More judicial oversight may also be appropriate for private dispute resolution that fails to meet reasonable due process standards. For example, courts could decline to enforce contract provisions requiring arbitration of disputes before a decision maker selected by a trade association representing one of the parties.[45]

Of course, consensus is often easier to reach on general considerations that should guide procedural choices than on what those choices should be in specific contexts where competing values are at stake. An especially sticky question involves the relationship between public interests and private preferences. Under what circumstances should courts or legislatures require certain dispute resolution processes for specific categories of cases or subsidize only those processes? Before we can satisfactorily resolve those issues, we need better information about how ADR principles work in practice. Some lessons may be available from jurisdictions that are moving toward multi-door courthouses. For example, the District of Columbia gives parties a formal opportunity to register their procedural priorities. After considering those individual preferences, along with other relevant characteristics of participants and their disputes, an administrator makes a process recommendation to the judge. Options include adjudication, mediation, arbitration, mini-trials, or early evaluation by a neutral expert. The judge then consults with the parties in order to select an appropriate process for resolution.[46]

We need more experimentation with such ADR programs and more systematic information about their effectiveness. How well do they respond to public concerns about expense, efficiency, fairness, and access? How much protection do they provide for societal interests that compete with party preferences? Although we lack adequate answers to those questions, more general research on dispute resolution suggests that expanding ADR choices would move us in the right direction. Most studies indicate that individuals' satisfaction with the legal process is heavily dependent on their assessments of its procedural fairness, and that some participation in the selection of procedures increases perceptions of fairness. Incorporating more alternative methods within the legal system is also likely to increase its accountability. If individuals have choices, they also have leverage in making their concerns heard and in improving the processes available.[47]

TOO FEW ALTERNATIVES TO LAWYERS

Similar observations can be made about expanding consumer choices among providers of legal services. Indeed, such observations have been made by almost all the scholars and bar commissions that have systematically studied access to nonlawyer assistance. Virtually no experts believe that current prohibitions on such assistance make sense. What consumers need, rather, is a framework that expands choices, reduces obstacles to self-help, permits qualified nonlawyer services, and provides effective regulation.[48]

Current bans on unauthorized practice of law by lay competitors are sweeping in scope and unsupportable in practice. Nonlawyers who engage in law-related activities are subject to criminal prohibitions that are inconsistently interpreted and unevenly enforced. The definition of illegal activities varies by jurisdiction, and attorneys in some states have a monopoly over routine services like completion of real estate closing forms that nonattorneys perform effectively in other states or even in other parts of the same state. The dominant approach is to prohibit individuals who are not members of the state bar from providing personalized legal assistance. For example, independent paralegals may type documents but not answer even the simplest legal questions. Courthouse facilitators are instructed to provide legal "information" but not advice and to refrain from answering "should" questions, such as "Which form should I file?" The American Bar Association recently voted to increase enforcement of unauthorized practice laws, a decision inconsistent with the prior recommendations of its own expert Commission. According to its Model Rules of Professional Conduct, "whatever the definition, limiting the practice of law to members of the bar protects the public against rendition of legal services by unqualified persons." "How well" and "at what cost" are questions too often overlooked.[49]

As experts have long noted, many nonlawyer specialists are equally or more qualified than lawyers to provide assistance on routine matters. These specialists are a diverse group. Some, like accountants or real estate brokers, already are subject to licensing requirements. Their work often involves assistance on legal issues, and competent performance necessarily involves technical violations of unauthorized practice prohibitions. Other nonlawyer providers are independent paralegals or former legal secretaries with considerable expertise in areas like uncontested divorces and administrative agency representation. Comparative research finds that these lay specialists can perform as effectively as attorneys. In the one reported survey of consumer satisfaction, nonlawyers rated higher than lawyers. As one judge noted, paralegals with training in specialized areas are a "refreshing change" from attorneys who lack such background. One recent law graduate made a similar point about the difference between his work and that of paralegals: He "billed the client nearly twice as much per hour and [only] they knew what they were doing."[50]

Such assessments should come as no surprise. Three years in law school and passage of a bar exam are neither necessary nor sufficient to ensure competence in areas where the need for routine services is greatest. Schools generally do not teach, and bar exams do not test, ability to complete routine forms for divorces, landlord-tenant disputes, bankruptcy, immigration, and welfare claims. For many of these needs, retaining a lawyer is like "hiring a surgeon to pierce an ear." Other countries typically permit nonlawyers to give legal advice and to provide assistance on routine matters, and no evidence suggests that these lay specialists are inadequate. Training and experience apart from law schools can offer adequate preparation for practitioners in many areas where unmet needs are greatest. A case in point involves Great Britain's Citizen's Advice Bureaus, which provide effective low cost assistance with nonlawyer staff.[51]

This is not to discount the problems that result from unqualified or unethical lay assistance. Some unlicensed practitioners, including disbarred attorneys, misrepresent their status and exploit vulnerable consumers. Immigrants are particularly common targets, both because they are often unfamiliar with American legal practices and because they are unlikely to report abuses. However, the appropriate response to these problems is regulation, not prohibition. Consumers need frameworks that offer a reasonable degree of protection without foreclosing choice.[52]

Current unauthorized practice restrictions are ill-suited to that task because they focus only on whether nonlawyers are providing legal assistance, not whether they are doing so effectively. Strong consumer demand for low-cost services make such restrictions difficult to enforce. As a result, most lay practice goes unregulated, and when abuses occur, the public has inadequate remedies. Similar problems can arise with ADR practitioners who are not subject to licensing or ethical rules. Most states impose greater requirements to become a hairstylist than a mediator.[53]

A sensible regulatory framework would provide both less and more protection—less for attorneys and more for consumers. Nonlawyers like accountants or real estate brokers who are already licensed by the state should be allowed to provide legal assistance related to their specialties. And lawyers who are licensed by other states should be permitted to provide services that comply with local ethics rules. Many of these individuals already are providing such services. Problems in their performance should be addressed by strengthening the requirements governing their activities, not by curtailing cost-effective assistance through overbroad unauthorized practice prohibitions.

For currently unlicensed service providers, states should develop regulatory frameworks responsive to public needs, which may vary across different practice areas. Where the risk of injury is substantial, in contexts such as immigration, consumers may benefit from licensing systems that impose minimum qualifications and offer proactive enforcement. In other fields, it could be sufficient to register practitioners and permit voluntary certification of those who meet specified standards. States also could require all lay practitioners to carry malpractice insurance, contribute to compensation funds for defrauded clients, and observe basic ethical obligations governing confidentiality, competence, and conflicts of interest.[54]

Such a regulatory framework would offer a number of advantages over current structures. Experience here and abroad suggests that increased competition between lawyers and nonlawyers is likely to result in lower prices, greater efficiency, and increased consumer satisfaction. Regulating the activities of lay practitioners should help curb abuses that currently go unremedied, while encouraging innovative partnerships between lawyer and nonlawyer specialists. Such partnerships could increase access to cost-effective assistance by enabling organizations to provide multidisciplinary legal services. Such opportunities for "one-stop shopping" would be of particular benefit to businesses seeking consolidated financial assistance and to other groups such as elderly, juvenile, or immigrant clients who need assistance cutting across occupational boundaries.[55]

Previous collaborative efforts have bumped up against the bar's prohibitions on fee splitting and partnerships between lawyers and nonlawyers. In effect, the Model Rules of Professional Conduct allow attorneys to work for organizations controlled by nonattorneys only as long as these in-house counsel represent the organization, not its outside clients. Efforts to liberalize these rules have met with no success. The American Bar Association's House of Delegates has rejected proposals that would enable companies like Sears to employ lawyers to provide simple low-cost services. And it has tabled reforms that would permit lawyers to form partnerships with nonlawyers such as accountants in order to offer consolidated financial assistance. Opponents' stated concern is that such arrangements might compromise the independent judgment of lawyers and undermine compliance with bar ethical rules governing confidentiality and conflicts of interest. These are legitimate concerns, but they can be addressed by regulation that does not curtail competition or prevent consumer choice.[56]

The issue of multidisciplinary collaboration has attracted increasing attention largely due to increasing competition from accounting firms. Other Western industrialized nations generally permit nonlawyers to provide some law-related services and to employ or form partnerships with lawyers. As a consequence, the Big Five accounting firms dominate the global legal market with over sixty thousand employees in over 130 countries. These accounting firms are also making increased inroads in the American market. Federal law provides that tax advice and representation in tax court does not constitute the practice of law. This exception to traditional unauthorized practice prohibitions enables lawyers to provide services for clients of accounting firms as long as the work can be defined as tax, not as legal assistance. Over the past decade, the Big Five have taken increasing liberties with this definition and have expanded their in-house legal staff to provide many of the same services as law firms on matters involving finance, estate planning, intellectual property, ADR, and litigation support. The American legal profession faces growing difficulties competing with these accounting organizations, which often offer a wider range of financial services, greater economies of scale, and more effective marketing and managerial capacities. The result is that the world's largest providers of legal services are no longer law firms. Or as law professor Geoffrey Hazard indelicately puts it, accountants are "eating our lunch."[57]

That realization has triggered what is variously perceived as a turf battle or a holy war. Opponents of multidisciplinary practice paint the struggle in apocalyptic terms. At stake are the independence and core values of the profession, now threatened by an invasion of profit-maximizing infidels. Critics worry that lawyers will become accountable to supervisors from a different tradition with less rigorous standards governing confidentiality, conflicts of interest, and pro bono service. Law will truly become just another business, and clients will pay the price when professional judgments are driven by the bottom line. Supporters of multidisciplinary practice see the struggle in less lofty terms. From their perspective, the stakes are status and money. Professionalism is window dressing for protectionism; lawyers unable or unwilling to compete are attempting to miscast personal interests as public values.

A more productive debate must start from different premises. Opponents' concerns are real, but they are not limited to the multidisciplinary context, and they can be addressed by regulation rather than prohibition. American lawyers already face many pressures and constraints that compromise professional independence. In-house counsel need to please nonlawyer management. Outside counsel need to please important clients, third parties who refer clients or pay their fees, and supervisors preoccupied with billable hours. Court-appointed counsel for the poor need to balance competing cases and resource demands. No evidence suggests that the threats to independent judgment in multidisciplinary practice are qualitatively different from those in other settings.[58]

As a recent ABA commission also acknowledged, strategies short of prohibition are available for addressing the pressures likely to arise in multidisciplinary practice. The commission recommended holding MDP lawyers to the same ethical standards governing conflicts and confidentiality as those applicable to the bar generally, and imposing special audit provisions to prevent nonlawyers from interfering with lawyers' professional judgments. The attorney-client privilege could be extended to cover these settings, or clients could be warned about its unavailability. An alternative approach, more workable for accounting firms, would be to follow their less stringent conflict-of-interest procedures. These procedures create screens between professionals representing competing concerns and seek informed client consent to the dual representation. Such structures have not proven inadequate here or abroad, and sophisticated clients have not pressed for reforms or alternatives. Unless and until problems with multidisciplinary partnerships arise, the bar has no convincing justification for restricting their availability. In effect, the profession should learn from competitors, not shield itself from competition.[59]

Related reforms should focus on creating a more coordinated and comprehensive system of access to justice. Efforts should center on increasing information about legal rights, services, and processes, making those processes more accessible, and expanding opportunities for low-cost assistance. One set of strategies should enable Americans to meet more of their own needs through their own efforts. Again, we do not lack for promising models. For centuries, critics have denounced the unnecessary formalities, archaic jargon, and cumbersome rituals that discourage individuals from resolving legal problems themselves. Some of these excessive complexities seem linked to the early British bar's practice of charging by the word, and to the American bar's desire to preserve its own business. Simplified forms and streamlined procedures could expand individuals' opportunities to handle routine matters such as governmental benefits, probate, uncontested divorces, landlord-tenant disputes, and consumer claims. Expanded hours, childcare assistance, and multilingual services would also make courthouses more accessible.[60]

More assistance for self-representation would serve similar objectives. A few courts and legal aid providers are now pioneering interactive computer kiosks and on-line self-help systems. Users obtain basic information and assistance in completion of routine forms. Such initiatives are steps in the right direction, but further efforts are necessary to make them effective for those whose unmet needs are greatest. These efforts should include free or low-cost workshops, hotlines, courthouse advisers, and walk-in centers that provide personalized multilingual assistance at accessible times and locations. Support could come from a mix of public and private sources: judicial administration funds, foundation grants, bar pro bono contributions, law school clinics, and legal services outreach projects.[61]

Although the organized bar has endorsed procedural simplification and self-help services in principle, it generally has failed to do so in practice. Countless commissions, committees, and task forces have recommended such initiatives with striking regularity and few results. The resistance comes largely from lawyers who doubt that these reforms would be good for business, and from judges who depend on lawyers' cooperation or campaign support. Such reforms would, however, be good for the public—and for the profession's public image. Since surveyed lawyers identify poor image as a paramount concern, the profession as a whole may have much to gain from access-to-justice initiatives. Business lawyers face little economic risk from self-help activities. Other attorneys might benefit from providing discrete "unbundled" services to groups that now are priced out of the market. Lawyers can provide limited low-cost assistance that does not involve full representation: advice about legal options; evaluation of proposed settlements; development of negotiating strategies; and referrals to other service providers such as accountants, mediators, and health professionals.[62]

If the bar is unwilling or unable to provide such services efficiently, then critics may well be right: we do have too many lawyers. We clearly have too little justice, at least for middle- and low-income Americans, and the bar's traditional solutions have fallen far short. Its preferred responses, like government-subsidized legal aid and voluntary pro bono contributions, deserve greater support, but realistically they cannot come close to meeting current needs. Fundamental restructuring is necessary for legal services and legal processes.

Policy debates both within and outside the profession too seldom confront this reality and the choices that it demands. Simplistic sound bites have displaced systematic analysis. Equal justice is the kind of principle that we find easier to proclaim than to define, let alone finance. If we are seriously concerned about America's balance of law and justice, then we need to translate more of our rhetorical commitments into policy priorities.

CHAPTER 6

REGULATION OF THE PROFESSION

I n an influential history of the legal profession sponsored by the American Bar Association, former Harvard Law School dean Roscoe Pound assured ABA leaders that their organization was not the "same sort of thing as a retail grocers' association." If he was right, it was for the wrong reason. Lawyers, no less than grocers, are motivated by their own occupational interests. What distinguishes the American bar is its ability to present self-regulation as a societal value. Lawyers retain far more control over their own oversight than any other occupation. Such freedom from external accountability too often serves the profession at the expense of the public.[1]

The following discussion explores limitations in the regulatory processes governing admission, discipline, malpractice, fees, advertising, and related matters. For the most part, these processes have been developed and administered by the profession. That insularity compromises their effectiveness. The problem is not that bar policies are baldly self-serving. Lawyers and judges who control regulatory decisions generally want to advance the public's interests as well as the profession's. Rather, the difficulty is one of tunnel vision, compounded by inadequate accountability. No matter how well intentioned, lawyers and former lawyers who regulate other lawyers cannot escape the economic, psychological, and political constraints of their position. Without external checks, these decision makers too often lose perspective about the points at which occupational and societal interests conflict. This chapter explores those conflicts.

THE RATIONALE FOR REGULATION

The conventional rationale for regulation rests on what economists describe as imperfections in the market for legal services. One cluster of problems involves the difficulties for many consumers in judging the value of legal services. Most individual (as opposed to business) clients are one-shot purchasers. They seldom consult an attorney, and their lack of experience, coupled with the difficulties and expense of comparative shopping, makes it hard to assess the quality of assistance. Even some sophisticated corporate consumers report problems in determining the necessity or efficiency of services. In the absence of external regulation, too many clients may receive incompetent, overpriced, or unethical representation. A related problem is that when purchasers cannot accurately compare the services available, performance standards are likely to decline. Lawyers will lack adequate incentives to invest time, education, and resources in providing quality representation unless regulators step in to set minimum standards. Competition will encourage attorneys to cut corners, and a "market for lemons" will result.[2]

An additional difficulty involves "free riders"—attorneys who benefit from public trust without adhering to the standards that maintain it. If no regulatory body effectively enforces those standards, individual attorneys lack economic incentives to comply. They can enjoy the bar's general reputation while shirking the obligations it implies. The result may be a "race to the bottom" among lawyers, with consumers as the ultimate losers.

A final category of problems concerns "externalities"—the external costs to society and third parties from conduct that may be advantageous to particular clients and their lawyers. For example, the public has an interest in seeing prompt and just resolutions of disputes even in circumstances where individual clients would willingly pay attorneys to delay or obstruct truth-finding processes.[3]

Although there is widespread agreement that these problems call for some regulation, there is no comparable consensus on what forms that regulation should take and who should decide. The market for legal services is both specialized and stratified. Not all protections appropriate for unsophisticated consumers are necessary for business clients. Nor are the trade-offs between maximizing quality and minimizing expense the same for all purchasers. Designing a regulatory system that will effectively accommodate these diverse interests involves complex and contested choices. And it poses equally controversial questions about who should make them.

Historically, the profession itself has controlled the regulatory process. For centuries, courts have asserted "inherent power" to regulate the practice of law. One rationale for this authority is that judges need to control the conduct and qualifications of lawyers in order to ensure the proper administration of justice. A second justification is that self-regulation preserves the separation of powers and protects the independence of the legal profession from government domination. As a practical matter, American courts have delegated much of their regulatory authority to the organized bar, which defends its autonomy on similar grounds. According to the preamble of the ABA's Model Rules of Professional Conduct, "An independent legal profession is an important force in preserving government under law, for abuse of legal authority is more readily challenged by a profession whose members are not dependent on government for the right to practice."[4]

These arguments have considerable force, but they cannot justify the current regulatory structure. Protecting the bar from state control clearly serves important values, and nations that lack an independent legal profession have had difficulty safeguarding individual rights and checking official misconduct. But professional autonomy and government domination are not the only alternatives. Many countries with an independent bar impose far more checks on its self-regulatory powers. They have built a public voice into the development and enforcement of professional standards. Governmental efforts to increase lawyers' accountability do not necessarily pose significant risks of retaliation or threats to the proper administration of justice. Indeed, American courts often recognize as much and increasingly permit some regulation of attorneys by legislatures and administrative agencies.[5]

Yet on the whole, lawyers retain considerable control over their own regulation. Bar codes of conduct claim to protect the public, but the public has had almost no voice in their formulation or enforcement. Only one nonlawyer served on the commissions that drafted the American Bar Association's Model Code of Professional Responsibility and the Model Rules of Professional Conduct. Only one was included on the thirteen-member Ethics 2000 Commission that recommended revisions. The ABA House of Delegates, which has power to accept or amend model ethical codes, is composed exclusively of lawyers. And state supreme courts, which ultimately adopt, reject, or modify ABA standards, rely heavily on recommendations from their local bars, typically without public involvement. Although nonlawyers often have token representation on other regulatory bodies such as discipline committees, these lay members are almost always selected by the profession. Almost never do they have the information, resources, leverage, or accountability to consumer groups that would be necessary to check bar control. Indeed as a report for state supreme court chief justices candidly acknowledges, "Over time these lay representatives become goodwill ambassadors for the bar."[6]

The limitations of such a structure are obvious. Experts here and abroad have long documented the self-regarding tendencies of self-regulating occupations. As former Stanford Law School dean Bayless Manning has noted, American lawyers normally are "splendidly scrupulous" about creating safeguards against conflicts of interests. But that sensitivity vanishes when the profession's own governance structure is at issue. The vast majority of surveyed lawyers favor bar control over regulatory processes despite the obvious potential for bias.[7]

In justifying this control, lawyers often claim that ultimate governance authority rests with state judges, who do not face the same conflicts of interests as practitioners. Yet the history of self-regulation suggests the limitations of such oversight. Most judges are by training and temperament sympathetic to bar interests. Moreover, their reputation, effectiveness, and reelection may depend heavily on support from lawyers. Seldom has the judiciary attempted to impose regulation that might seriously compromise lawyers' status, income, or power.

As a result, bar standards of conduct have been insufficiently demanding and inadequately enforced. These limitations in professional oversight have, in turn, encouraged other, more ad hoc forms of regulation. Legislators, agency officials, and insurance companies have made some attempt to strengthen rules of conduct and to modify self-protective bar policies. However, some of these groups, like other regulatory bodies, are subject to capture by those they seek to regulate. And their efforts have led to a patchwork of sometimes conflicting ethical mandates. Attorneys in different states and different specialties may be subject to different requirements. This lack of uniformity presents obvious problems as more and more legal representation involves multiple states and multiple sources of regulation.[8]

There are no simple solutions to any of these problems. The public generally lacks sufficient information or incentives to press for fundamental changes in bar regulation. The profession, however, is highly motivated and well positioned to resist such changes. But recent reform efforts suggest that some progress is possible and that further efforts are essential to increase public accountability in regulatory processes.

ADVERTISING AND SOLICITATION

Although many attorneys view advertising and personal solicitation of clients as a recent and regrettable development, it is, in fact, restrictions on such practices that are recent. Lawyers in ancient Greece and Rome were not shy about promoting their services. Neither were distinguished eighteenth- and nineteenth-century American attorneys, including Abraham Lincoln, who used leaflets and newspaper listings. However, after the turn of this century, bar leaders increasingly became concerned with the profession's public image, and early codes banned almost all forms of advertising and personal solicitation. Until the 1970s, courts and ethics committees condemned a wide range of practices, including not only "ambulance chasing" but also ostentatious office signs, Christmas cards that mentioned the lawyer's profession, and boldface type in telephone books. These sweeping prohibitions helped preserve the dignity of established lawyers, but at the cost of restricting competition and foreclosing information about legal assistance among unsophisticated consumers.[9]

These restrictions have come under increasing challenge. Over the past quarter century, state and federal courts have forced significant liberalization of bar ethical rules. In essence, the Supreme Court has held that truthful advertising is entitled to First Amendment protections. However, states may restrict potentially misleading information, largely prohibit personal solicitation, and impose other regulations that are narrowly drawn to further a "substantial state interest." But what constitutes a substantial interest remains open to dispute, and it is by no means clear that the current rules well serve public concerns.[10]

State bars have imposed various restrictions, including bans on dramatizations, visualizations, endorsements, and "self-laudatory" presentations. Almost all jurisdictions prohibit in-person or telephone solicitation of a prospective client "with whom the lawyer has no family or professional relationship when a significant motive is pecuniary gain." Some states impose further bans on targeted mail to accident victims and their relatives for thirty days after the accident. These rules are significantly more restrictive than those governing other forms of commercial speech. For example, the Court has upheld bans on personal solicitation by lawyers, but not accountants, on the theory that lawyers are more skilled manipulators and that their clients are less sophisticated. The Court also has upheld bans on targeted mailings concerning legal services but not other products, on the ground that the state has a substantial interest in protecting "flagging reputations" of lawyers and preventing the "erosion of confidence in the profession that such repeated invasions [of privacy] have engendered." The flagging reputations of other professionals have not enjoyed similar protections. Nor have sweeping prohibitions on dramatizations, endorsements, or self-laudatory portrayals been upheld in other occupational contexts.[11]

Such selective restrictions are difficult to justify as consumer protection. Empirical research generally finds that advertising for professional services increases competition and reduces prices without diluting quality. Lower prices tend to heighten demand, expand volume, and encourage economies of scale. Although the bar defends bans on targeted mailings as necessary to protect recipients' privacy, that objective could presumably be served by narrower means. Some states, for example, require lawyers to disclose on the outside of envelopes if they contain a commercial solicitation. The problem with rules that now prohibit such mailings, as well as personal contacts by plaintiffs' lawyers, is that these prohibitions do not apply to insurance agents and defense lawyers. The result is that accident victims and their families often are pressured into accepting inadequate settlements before they have obtained legal advice. Unsurprisingly, victims represented by a lawyer receive much higher recoveries than those who negotiate directly with insurance companies.[12]

In short, many restrictions on lawyers' commercial speech seem designed less to protect the public than to protect the profession's public image. Most attorneys oppose mass media advertising, and a significant number of practitioners and judges appear to agree with former Chief Justice Burger that selling law like laxatives is one of the most "unethical things a lawyer can do." However, as constitutional law scholar Kathleen Sullivan has noted, the evidence for bar concerns is "severely wanting." Most research, including the ABA's own national study, finds that advertising is not a major factor in shaping public impressions of the bar and that dignified advertisements reflect favorably on the profession. In surveyed states, over 90 percent of all complaints to the bar about advertising come from other lawyers, and only 1 or 2 percent of consumers' complaints about attorneys involve advertising. The study that the bar has invoked to justify its ban on targeted mailings found that only about a quarter of consumers reported lower regard for the profession as a result of the solicitation.[13]

That is not to suggest that all of lawyers' concerns about public image and public protection are misplaced. Offensive personal solicitation of victims and their families immediately following an accident is far too frequent. Mass disasters have attracted swarms of lawyers, patrolling hospital corridors or lurking behind potted palms in hotels where victims' relatives are staying. The bar has legitimate interests in policing such abuses as well as in preventing misleading advertisements. But some of the resources now spent on regulating merely tasteless marketing could be better used in sanctioning serious misconduct. As discussion below indicates, bar disciplinary authorities lack the capacity to handle most client complaints about malpractice, negligence, and overcharging: they can ill afford to worry whether lawyers should drive a hearse promising "No Frill Wills" or use jingles modeled on the Monopoly game's "Get Out of Jail Free" card.[14]

A more sensible regulatory structure would vest authority over commercial speech in a more disinterested institution than the organized bar. Consumer commissions should determine what constitutes misleading advertising or abusive solicitation. Rather than banning all forms of personal contact by plaintiffs' lawyers and none by defendants' agents, regulatory authorities should make both groups subject to reasonable time, place, and manner restrictions. For example, a sensible proposal by the Federal Trade Commission would prohibit any personal solicitation that involves harassment, coercion, undue influence, or communication with persons who are "unable to exercise reasonable considered judgment" or who have expressed a desire not to be contacted.[15]

The organized bar also should expand the mass disaster programs now available in only some jurisdictions. These programs provide written advice about legal rights, including information about how to report unlawful solicitation, as well as free consultation with volunteer pro bono attorneys who do not accept paid cases arising from their services. Such an approach would better serve both public and professional interests. As bar surveys repeatedly demonstrate, the best way for lawyers to improve their image is to improve their conduct, not restrict their speech. More pro bono services and more effective responses to consumers' concerns would do more for lawyers' flagging reputations than banning commercial practices that most Americans find unobjectionable.

ADMISSION

For most of this nation's history, bar admission standards were notably permissive. Until the twentieth century, law school was not required, apprenticeships were often undemanding, and entrance exams were seldom rigorous. One bar candidate's report gives a flavor of the process in the mid-nineteenth century. His examiner, Abraham Lincoln, was taking a bath during the exam. After a few "meager inquiries" concerning simple issues, such as the definition of a contract, Lincoln certified the applicant as "smarter than he looks to be" and therefore fit for admission.[16]

By contrast, most states now require graduation from an accredited law school, passage of a demanding bar exam, and proof of good moral character. In theory, these requirements serve to protect the public from incompetent or unethical attorneys. In practice, they are highly imperfect means of accomplishing either. As chapters 5 and 7 suggest, three years in law school are neither necessary nor sufficient to ensure competence for many routine specialized tasks. The same is true for bar exams. And in many respects, they are an even more arbitrary screening device.[17]

Current exams test only some of the skills necessary for competent lawyering. In most states, passage requires only minimal writing capacity, knowledge of basic legal principles, and an ability to function under extreme time pressure. Few exams make any effort to measure other key abilities involving research, drafting, or negotiation. Rather, the process places a premium on rote memorization and superficial analysis. As a recent report to the Conference of State Supreme Court Justices noted, current exams "fail to provide an effective measure of the basic competence of new lawyers." Bar review cram courses appropriately warn candidates that too much knowledge is a dangerous thing. According to one veteran instructor, "The key to getting the question right is to avoid thinking for yourself." Legal ethics professors give similar advice about passage of the multiple choice professional responsibility exam. The conventional wisdom is "If in doubt, pick the second most ethical course of conduct."[18]

This screening method is both over- and underinclusive. It excludes individuals with sufficient experience and practice skills to offer routine assistance for routine needs, while providing no assurance that those who pass are, or will remain, competent in their chosen fields. Most of the problems that clients have with attorneys do not arise from deficiencies that exams assess. Rarely do these problems involve a lawyer's inadequate knowledge of the law or of the relevant ethical rules. Rather, as the discussion below indicates, the deficiencies typically reflect poor office management, neglect, overcharging, unrealistic caseloads, or related problems, which are often rooted in personal difficulties such as financial pressures and substance abuse.[19]

Although bar exams do measure some relevant skills, the current grading system does not capture relevant distinctions. No effort has been made to correlate performance on admission exams with performance in practice. The most that bar officials can establish is a correlation between examination scores and law school grades. That relationship is scarcely surprising, since both measure similar skills. How well either predicts success as a lawyer is something else again and has yet to be demonstrated. Charles Evans Hughes failed the New York bar exam six times. He later became chief justice of the United States Supreme Court. And the list of less celebrated failures is extensive.[20]

The inadequate link between exam and job performance is of special concern because minority applicants have disproportionately low passage rates. Part of the problem is that these applicants are least able to afford the time and expense of bar review courses and multiple attempts at passing. Although courts have rejected claims that the exam process is racially discriminatory and insufficiently predictive of competence in practice, their reasoning has relied on evidence that has been found deficient in other occupational contexts: unsupported testimony by administrators who believe that their questions are unbiased and relevant. But even assuming that exam performance demonstrates some necessary lawyering skills, the current grading process is arbitrary at best. One California study found that a third of bar examiners disagreed about whether a particular set of answers failed or passed, and that a quarter of examiners, when presented with the same paper a second time, reversed their earlier decision.[21]

The selection of passing scores raises further difficulties. States that use the same multiple choice tests vary considerably in the scores they find acceptable and in their ratios of successful to unsuccessful applicants. The number of candidates who pass ranges from under 35 percent to over 90 percent. Unsurprisingly, success rates tend to be lowest in the states with the highest concentrations of lawyers, where new competitors are particularly unwelcome. By contrast, other jurisdictions pass such a large proportion of candidates that they become known as the "Tijuana[s] of the law admission world." No evidence suggests that these states experience exceptional problems with lawyer performance. If states swapped cutoff scores, the majority of applicants passing the bar in permissive jurisdictions would fail, and the majority of those failing in stringent jurisdictions would pass. So too, as statisticians point out, higher grading standards do not guarantee higher competence in a system where about 95 percent of candidates who keep taking the exam eventually pass. In states with low success rates, students simply "study harder" and more applicants have to take the test multiple times.[22]

The bar's current ways of assessing moral character raise similar concerns. In principle, such requirements make perfect sense; the public has an obvious interest in protection from unethical lawyers. In practice, however, bar screening processes are incapable of accurately identifying such individuals and often are highly idiosyncratic and unnecessarily intrusive. An inherent problem involves timing; the current process comes both too early and too late. Screening takes place before most applicants have faced circumstances comparable to those arising in practice but after candidates have invested so much time and money in legal training that examiners are reluctant to deny admission. The most systematic research available suggests that about 99 percent of bar applicants eventually gain entrance. However, the process also imposes substantial burdens on candidates, and a significant number are deterred, delayed, or demeaned. Some evidence also suggests that Ivy League graduates receive more cursory investigation than other applicants and that candidates of color receive more stringent review than white counterparts.[23]

States generally have lengthy questionnaires concerning any incidences of dishonesty, disrespect for law, mental health difficulties, or "dishonorable," "immoral," or "improper" conduct. Bar inquiry frequently extends to juvenile offenses, parking violations, child support payments, and civil disobedience. Violation of a fishing license statute ten years before application was sufficient to cause one local Michigan committee to decline certification. But in the same state at about the same time, other examiners admitted individuals convicted of child molesting and conspiracy to bomb a public building. Some applicants have been denied admission for belonging to communist or racial supremacy organizations and for refusing to answer questions about their membership. Decisions have been particularly inconsistent concerning drug and alcohol offenses, sexual conduct, bankruptcy, political affiliations, and mental health treatment. Sexual orientation has been an issue in states that criminalize sodomy; other states expressly avoid inquiry.[24]

These decisions raise problems not only of inconsistency and intrusiveness but also of inaccuracy. Psychological research makes clear that moral behavior is highly situational. While individuals differ in their responses to temptation, contextual pressures have a substantial impact on moral conduct. Attorneys' compliance with ethical rules depends heavily on factors that cannot be anticipated at the time of admission, such as exposure to temptation, client demands, and financial or peer pressure. Prior behavior is relevant but often misleading because it is necessary to know a great deal about how and why individuals responded to earlier situations in order to gauge how they will react in somewhat different future circumstances. Examiners seldom if ever have that kind of knowledge.[25]

The same is true for predictions based on mental health and related difficulties. Many jurisdictions include broad, intrusive questions about almost any mental health treatment and require applicants to release all medical records. Some applications ask about any incidents of intoxication in the last seven years; others want information about any conditions significantly affecting applicants' ability to cope with the "ordinary demands of life." In states where litigants have challenged these inquiries under the Americans with Disabilities Act, bar examiners have been unable to show that past mental health assistance predicts future problems in practice. About half of those who seek such assistance do not have a diagnosable illness. Those who do may pose fewer risks than candidates with undisclosed and untreated problems. Except in extreme cases, even mental health experts cannot reliably predict future difficulties based on past treatment. Untrained bar examiners are scarcely likely to do better. And the presence of overly broad questions discourages some applicants from seeking professional counseling that might jeopardize their admission.[26]

A comparison of bar admission and disciplinary processes raises further doubts about current character requirements. Bar disciplinary officials do not require practicing lawyers to report their parking violations, overdue child support payments, political affiliations, or psychiatric treatment. Yet if such conduct is relevant for applicants, why is it not even more relevant for licensed attorneys? Even more to the point, why doesn't the bar devote more of its resources to sanctioning misconduct involving clients? Behavior occurring after individuals become officers of the court surely is a more reliable indication of fitness to practice than behavior occurring before admission. Yet the reverse double standard now prevails: applicants must satisfy higher standards than practicing attorneys. Such selective screening seems geared less to public protection than to public image.[27]

A final problem in bar admission structures involves their effect on interstate practice. Except in limited circumstances requiring court approval, attorneys may provide representation only in jurisdictions where they are admitted to the bar. According to some judicial rulings, attorneys may not even offer advice by phone or computer concerning matters in a state where they are not licensed. Such prohibitions cannot serve client needs that routinely cross state boundaries. Nor are these prohibitions possible to enforce in a technological age that makes such boundaries increasingly irrelevant. Attorneys who attempt to avoid unauthorized practice by obtaining admission in multiple jurisdictions bump up against substantial obstacles. Many states require passage of their own bar exam. Some require residency, including a local office. And many will waive exam requirements only for lawyers from jurisdictions that also provide waivers. Such reciprocity rules are difficult to justify from any consumer protection perspective. If experienced out-of-state attorneys are competent to practice, it shouldn't matter how their local bars treat competitors. The situation is tolerable only because bar agencies seldom have sufficient information or resources to enforce prohibitions on out-of-state practice. However, the threat of sanctions deters many attorneys from providing cost-effective representation on multistate matters. And many clients have to subsidize their lawyers' affiliation with local counsel who provide no significant function other than compliance with protectionist bar admission requirements.[28]

In short, the current licensing system cannot be justified on rational policy grounds. It persists largely due to professional interests and public inertia. Once admitted to the bar, lawyers have little incentive to eliminate arbitrary or overbroad restrictions if the effect would be to increase the number of potential competitors. For example, 80 to 90 percent of surveyed attorneys want to retain a bar exam, even though two-thirds agree that it does not adequately measure competence. Many lawyers think that there already are too many new lawyers, and they are wary of easing restrictions on entry. The public generally shares that view and has too little understanding or incentive to challenge bar admission policies.[29]

Yet at least some reform may be possible, largely because many attorneys are dissatisfied with the inconsistencies and barriers resulting from exclusively state-controlled admissions systems. A majority of surveyed lawyers would prefer a national bar exam. If the profession moved toward a national system, then other aspects of the admission structure could come under review. Any rational reform strategy would attempt to make competence and character evaluations more closely relate to performance in practice. One possibility would be to eliminate bar exams and require only graduation from an accredited law school. Such a system would, of course, involve certain risks. The absence of concern about bar passage rates might push tuition-hungry schools toward overly permissive entrance and graduation requirements. That has not, however, been the experience in states like Wisconsin, which have long exempted law graduates of state universities from bar entrance exams. Further experimentation with such systems seems warranted. In any event, if bar exams are to remain part of the admission process, their structure requires rethinking. A wider range of skills should be assessed. And as chapter 5 argued, states should also devise licensing systems that would permit specialists with less than three-year law school degrees to perform routine legal services.

Similar considerations are applicable to character requirements. Although neither the public nor the profession is likely to favor eliminating such inquiries altogether, they should be limited to recent histories of serious misconduct or current mental health impairments. Bar officials should eliminate overly intrusive inquiries, particularly on matters involving psychological counseling, sexual orientation, and political beliefs. Applicants are entitled to greater consistency and notice concerning conduct that could justify denial or deferral. Resources now spent on ineffective efforts to predict misconduct should be redirected to disciplinary programs that could deter or remedy it. If, for example, an avowed racist engages in discriminatory conduct as an attorney, he can be sanctioned for those actions; he should not be excluded for expressing racist beliefs. Only a more constrained and consistent administration of moral character requirements can avoid trivializing the values at issue.

Finally, states should move either to a national system of admission or to a more effective means of accommodating interstate practice. Under a national structure with uniform examination and character requirements, states still could discipline attorneys for misconduct and impose additional requirements necessary to test knowledge of local rules. Alternatively, states could retain licensing authority but admit out-of-state lawyers who meet threshold requirements or permit those lawyers to engage in limited professional activities with clients' informed consent. For example, the American Law Institute's *Restatement of the Law Governing Lawyers* suggests that out-of-state lawyers should be able to engage in local practice that involves matters reasonably related to their home-state practice. The bar should prosecute only nonadmitted lawyers who engage in substantial continuing representation that jeopardizes legitimate public interests. Local practitioners' desire to minimize competition does not satisfy that standard.[30]

CONTINUING LEGAL EDUCATION

Question: How can lawyers achieve tax deductions and employer reimbursement for
> a week at Club Med in Mexico,
> a thirteen-day European cruise,
> a Giants baseball game,
> courses in sports nutrition, cardiovascular health, overeating, and Tibetan relaxation methods?
Answer: Call it Continuing Legal Education.[31]

Continuing legal education (CLE) for practicing lawyers began in the mid-1970s in the aftermath of Watergate, largely in response to concerns about lawyers' ethics and competence. About forty states now require attorneys to complete instruction, generally ranging from ten to twelve hours per year. In most jurisdictions, some of the coursework must focus on ethics. A minority demand coverage of other topics such as bias in the profession, substance abuse, and emotional distress.[32]

Such requirements have been relatively uncontroversial. Who could object to having lawyers make modest efforts to stay current in their fields and address significant ethical issues? The answer is not, however, self-evident, given the courses listed above. In order to gain acceptance from the bar, CLE requirements are minimal, and user-friendly approaches are endless. Courses on substance abuse and emotional distress can focus on stress reduction, diet tips, and finding "joy and satisfaction in the legal life." Sports law can be absorbed at sporting events, along with complementary hot dogs and peanuts. "Opportunities to exchange views on legal developments with . . . Superior Court Judges" can briefly interrupt snorkeling and windsurfing at luxury resorts.[33]

The problem is not simply that some courses stretch the concept of "legal education." The more fundamental difficulty is that the system itself cannot ensure that educational goals are being met. As a District of Columbia task force noted, "There have been no reliable, scientific demonstrations of the efficacy of continuing legal education." Research in other professions such as medicine and engineering has found no relationship between performance and participation in continuing education. Neither is it self-evident that passive attendance at ungraded courses will significantly increase competence in practice.[34]

Nor have bar officials made adequate attempts to monitor compliance with minimal requirements. Many states make generous provision for "self-study." Attorneys may certify that they have watched videos, listened to audiotapes, completed interactive computer programs, or written publishable articles. Since no passage of exams is required, bar officials cannot verify whether any significant "study" actually occurred. Nor is the problem solved by requiring physical attendance at courses, since no one checks to see if participants are sober, engaged, or even awake. According to one seasoned veteran, "Almost any lawyer will tell you [that] CLE credits are much easier to swallow when washed down with Bloody Marys." Another added that "requiring a knave to listen to five hours of lectures on ethics per year will give you a bored knave, not an honest attorney."[35]

This is not to suggest that all CLE is unproductive. As both a perpetrator and participant in many programs, I have sometimes seen their value. One memorable example occurred after I had given a lecture on ethics and a man in his mid-fifties approached the podium. He had graduated from law school before professional responsibility instruction was required and had subsequently become the CEO of a large company. My lecture suggested that perhaps some issues were escaping his attention. "I gather from your talk that the bar has a code of ethical conduct. Where can I get a copy?" For some participants, CLE may be a useful wake-up call, and a purely voluntary system is unlikely to reach those who need it most. A little knowledge may be a dangerous thing, but total ignorance is scarcely better.

However, states should retain the current mandatory system only if they can establish that it is a cost-effective means of promoting competence in practice. Lawyers are now spending millions of hours and dollars on programs of questionable value. They persist largely because CLE is a good public relations gesture and a cash cow for the bar organizations that administer them. But in representative surveys, most practitioners find the current approach unsatisfactory. And if the goal is truly public protection, not just public image, the system requires reassessment. One possibility might be to require both less and more. States could demand fewer hours but impose greater quality controls. Bar officials should require passage of an exam and deny credit for courses that bear little demonstrated relationship to performance in practice. More programs should target the deficiencies that cause the greatest disciplinary problems, such as client neglect and financial improprieties. Providers could themselves be held to educational requirements that ensured some basic level of effectiveness. Under such a system, greater incentives should be available for law schools and legal employers to develop CLE programs, since these institutions have independent interests in maximizing quality.[36]

Alternatively, states could combine required and voluntary approaches. CLE could be mandatory for new lawyers and for other practitioners who have violated ethical rules. Attorneys who are subject to disciplinary, judicial, or malpractice sanctions could be required to take appropriate courses. Other attorneys who voluntarily complete CLE classes and pass a basic test could receive certification of their coursework. That credential could become part of a broader certification structure. For example, lawyers who complied with such "best practices" requirements could use their compliance to attract clients and to reduce their malpractice insurance premiums. An increasing number of lawyers are now willing to complete demanding educational requirements in order to become certified as specialists in particular fields of practice. States could encourage this trend by expanding specialization programs, publicizing their value to consumers, and improving their educational quality.[37]

As a concept, continuing legal education is hard to oppose. Its potential value is self-evident for a profession confronting rapidly changing laws, evolving practice technologies, and widespread ethical problems. But as currently administered, the system leaves much to be desired. Too many practitioners end up in circumstances evoking W. H. Auden's description of those who "had the experience but missed the meaning." Legal education should truly be a continuing commitment, not the token gesture that many practitioners now experience.

COMPETENCE AND DISCIPLINE

"Too slow, too secret, too soft, and too self-regulated": That is how the public views the discipline system, according to the American Bar Association's own research. Less than a third of Americans think the legal profession does a good job disciplining lawyers. And as a prominent ABA Commission acknowledged, much popular criticism is "justified and accurate." Similar acknowledgments have surfaced in virtually every study that the bar has undertaken. Yet all of those studies have also concluded that the profession should retain control over the regulatory process. For example, only 20 percent of surveyed California lawyers believed that the disciplinary system was doing an effective job, but some 90 percent believed that the bar should continue to conduct disciplinary activities.[38]

In justifying this continued authority, bar leaders have emphasized the importance of ensuring that "those individuals . . . who pass judgment on attorney conduct be knowledgeable regarding the practice of law." But in fact, disciplinary complaint processes proceed on precisely the opposite basis. They rely almost exclusively on clients as a source of information about ethical violations. Those with the most knowledge concerning many violations—lawyers and judges—rarely report misconduct. And bar rules requiring reports are almost never enforced.[39]

This failure to disclose ethical violations reflects a combination of social, psychological, and economic factors. Part of the problem is that many professional standards are formulated in highly general terms. What constitutes an "incompetent" performance or "unreasonable" fee is difficult to assess except at the extremes, and lawyers usually have no incentive to gather the relevant information. Disciplinary structures reflect classic free rider/common action problems. Reporting misconduct by another lawyer serves society and the profession as a whole, but it seldom benefits complainants or their clients. Although implicit threats to file a grievance sometimes can provide useful bargaining leverage, more often they impose time-consuming burdens or start feuds that yield no personal advantage. For many practitioners, a reluctance to appear "holier than thou" or to expose the profession's "dirty linen" to public scrutiny also discourages disciplinary reports.[40]

As a consequence, bar agencies depend almost entirely on complaints from clients, along with felony convictions, as a basis for disciplinary investigations. These sources are highly inadequate. Clients frequently lack sufficient information or incentives to file grievances. Many individuals have little understanding of their rights and remedies in disputes with lawyers, and only two states provide a centralized source of consumer advice. Some forms of attorney misconduct, such as discovery abuse, benefit a client; others will not yield effective remedies. Bar disciplinary agencies generally dismiss about 90 percent of complaints without investigation or because they lack probable cause or fall outside agency jurisdiction. Grievances involving neglect, "mere" negligence, or fee disputes generally are excluded on the grounds that disciplinary agencies lack adequate resources, and other remedies are available through malpractice suits or alternative bar-sponsored dispute resolution processes. However, as subsequent discussion suggests, malpractice litigation is too expensive for most of these matters, and only a minority of states have alternative dispute resolution procedures for client grievances. The procedures that are available usually are voluntary. Clients most in need of assistance seldom find their attorneys willing to cooperate. Many disciplinary agencies also are reluctant to pursue powerful bar leaders or public officials. One survey of some 380 cases of serious prosecutorial misconduct found that none resulted in disciplinary actions.[41]

A further problem involves the inadequacy of sanctions. Less than 2 percent of complaints result in public sanctions such as reprimands, suspensions, or disbarment. Seldom does the disciplinary system provide remedies like reimbursement that benefit the client. Although some grievances clearly are without basis and reflect dissatisfaction with outcomes rather than deficiencies in attorney performance, the infrequency of significant sanctions also reflects fundamental problems in the regulatory process. The vast majority of disciplinary agencies are underfunded and understaffed. To varying degrees, these agencies depend on good relations with the profession, which controls their budget and monitors their performance. Many of the judges and bar leaders who regulate the regulators have a "there but for the grace of God go I" attitude toward all but the most serious misconduct. Rarely do disciplinary committees or courts that review committee findings want to withdraw attorneys' means of livelihood or to antagonize the local bar. Reported cases include too many examples like the San Francisco lawyer who was recently disbarred, but only after being privately disciplined for abandoning client matters, sanctioned four times by federal appellate courts, and found guilty of fraudulently overcharging clients some $280,000.[42]

Bar disciplinary processes also reflect the same problems of idiosyncratic judgments that plague moral character admission procedures. Ordinary client grievances often are taken less seriously than conduct occurring in nonprofessional contexts for which other civil or criminal sanctions are available. For example, South Carolina suspended a lawyer who pocketed $1,800 from her daughter's Girl Scout cookie account, while other jurisdictions imposed only probation or ethics courses for practitioners who took similar liberties with client funds. Similar priorities are apparent in two cases decided within days of each other by the Indiana Supreme Court. One decision concerned a lawyer who "deceived clients, failed to promptly deliver unearned fees and other funds rightfully belonging to a client, neglected his clients' cases, and abused his clients' trust." The other decision involved a lawyer who "knew [that] marijuana was growing on his premises and failed to destroy the plants." In the first case, the attorney received a forty-five-day suspension; in the second, the attorney was disbarred.[43]

Related problems in disciplinary processes involve delay and secrecy. Most jurisdictions have no time limits for resolving cases and decline to proceed if any other legal proceedings involving the misconduct are pending. The resulting delays can prevent successful prosecution and expose more clients to misconduct. Except in three states, bar disciplinary agencies will not disclose the existence of a complaint unless they find a disciplinary violation or probable cause to believe that a violation has occurred. Lawyers with as many as twenty complaints under investigation have received a clean bill of health when a consumer has asked for information about their records. Nor do potential clients have a ready way of discovering even public sanctions after the process is completed. Not all states publish disciplinary actions, and none do so in publications designed to reach the general public. There is no centralized national information bank that consumers can consult about a lawyer's full record of disciplinary or malpractice complaints.[44]

The processes for allowing disciplined attorneys to return to practice are equally problematic. An attorney recently disbarred in New Jersey for stealing $38,000 from his law firm was admitted in Pennsylvania twelve months later. In all but a few states, disbarred lawyers can also reapply for reinstatement in the same jurisdiction within a few years. Half of those who do so are readmitted, even though about 40 percent of these readmitted attorneys have a history of stealing client funds. Lawyers typically are not required to disclose their disciplinary history to clients, and few do so voluntarily. "I don't tell them I have hemorrhoids [either]," was one attorney's explanation.[45]

The profession's long-standing failure to address problems in the disciplinary process argues for an alternative system that provides more public accountability. The design of that system does, however, pose special challenges. As bar leaders note, the history of legislative regulation of the professions does not suggest that more direct political control necessarily yields better public protection. Legislatively created oversight agencies often suffer from the same problems of underfunding, delays, and capture by regulated groups as bar authorities.[46]

California's experience illustrates other problems with unduly politicizing the disciplinary process. There, a combination of poor management, high dues, and unpopular lobbying activities made the organized bar vulnerable to challenge from both within and outside the profession. Unlike other states, the California legislature has power to determine bar dues. When Governor Pete Wilson vetoed the 1997 dues bill, the bar was forced to rely on voluntary contributions from its members. Only a quarter paid, and most bar activities including discipline were suspended for a substantial period. To knowledgeable commentators, the governor's action seemed primarily designed to punish the bar for opposing part of his own political agenda. Wilson's unhappy personal experience with bar exams (he failed at least twice) reportedly contributed to his animosity. And the partisan maneuvers that followed his veto do not build confidence in a politicized regulatory process.[47]

Yet it by no means follows that all efforts to increase the public accountability of professional regulation are inherently flawed. Other nations provide useful models. New South Wales, Australia, has an independent office that handles complaints, and Great Britain has provided oversight through an ombudsman and an advisory commission on the legal profession with half its members drawn from outside the bar. A common American proposal is a commission with broad-based membership ultimately subject to state supreme court control but independent of the organized bar. For example, a bill unsuccessfully proposed by a California task force of regulatory experts would have created a Commission on Attorney Discipline and Competency. Its members would have included lawyers and nonlawyers with experience in consumer protection, appointed by different constituencies such as the bar, the California Judicial Council, the governor, and the Speaker of the California Assembly. Such checks and balances in the appointment process would produce a regulatory structure more responsive to the public interest than the prevailing system.[48]

Even without such structural reform, substantial improvements are possible, but they are likely to require significant pressure from outside the bar. The ABA has recommended some useful incremental strategies, but few states have adopted its most significant proposals: comprehensive alternative dispute resolution systems for complaints now excluded from disciplinary processes, and a consumer's bill of rights, including opportunities to appear before disciplinary agencies and to appeal dismissal of grievances. These reforms would be steps in the right direction, but they fall well short of the changes that are necessary. Further efforts are essential on three fronts: disciplinary agencies and legal employers need more information about misconduct, consumers need more information about disciplinary processes, and the bar needs more enforcement resources and authority.[49]

One obvious strategy for expanding agencies' and employers' knowledge base is to enforce rules requiring lawyers to report ethical violations. The only state that has attempted to do so has seen dramatic improvements. In *In re Himmel*, the Illinois Supreme Court suspended an attorney for failing to disclose that his client's previous lawyer had unlawfully withheld settlement funds belonging to the client. Reports of misconduct dramatically increased following that decision and substantially exceed those in other jurisdictions. Other states should follow Illinois's lead. They should also require all legal employers to develop adequate internal ethics policies and reporting channels, as do some organizations here and abroad.[50]

Disciplinary agencies also should make greater efforts to encourage clients to report and discover misconduct. Promising strategies include publicizing complaint processes, helping consumers file grievances, and requiring attorneys to provide clients with information about their rights and their remedial options. A related set of strategies should focus on increasing the public's knowledge about the ethical records of attorneys. Consumers now have access to a national information bank for information about disciplinary and malpractice records of doctors. The bar should provide or assist a similar on-line clearinghouse and toll-free hotline. Such a data bank could disclose lawyers' disciplinary and malpractice records, as well as provide advice about consumer remedies. Regulatory agencies also should take more proactive steps to discover misconduct. For example, enforcement officials should initiate investigations based on malpractice judgments, random audits of client trust fund accounts, and court-imposed sanctions for litigation-related abuse.[51]

These disciplinary processes should be open to public scrutiny from the time that complaints are filed. The bar has long resisted such scrutiny on the ground that disclosure of unfounded complaints would unjustly prejudice lawyers' reputations. However, Oregon's extended experience with public proceedings does not disclose such problems. Nor are such claims accepted in other contexts. The American justice system generally proceeds on the assumption that charges of misconduct should be matters of public record, whether or not they prevail on the merits. Society tolerates some risk to privacy and reputation in order to ensure public accountability. Lawyer disciplinary systems should stand on similar footing. Surveyed consumers express deep suspicion about closed door proceedings—and with good reason. A system that dismisses over 90 percent of complaints and withholds information about their content does not inspire confidence. Such concerns prompted the ABA's own expert commission to recommend public disclosure of all disciplinary complaints. The bar's rejection of that proposal is impossible to explain on grounds other than members' self-interest.[52]

Any system in which lawyers regulate lawyers also requires significant external oversight, and consumer organizations should become more active in that process. For example, a public-interest group could publish a book on lawyers modeled on the "Questionable Doctors" directory by the Public

Citizen Health Research Group. It lists some thirteen thousand physicians who have been disciplined by state or federal agencies for substandard care but who are still practicing. Another effective oversight strategy could be a discipline monitor who would be independent of the bar but have access to its records. The California legislature appointed a consumer protection expert to serve in that role during the late 1980s and early 1990s, and his annual reports prompted significant reforms. One illustration involved his initial finding that the state bar did not publicize a telephone number for disciplinary complaints or even list one in the Yellow Pages. Once a number had been listed, the monitor reported that callers encountered prolonged busy signals or were placed on hold for lengthy periods. In the end, the public got a complaint line that worked. More substantial improvements have occurred in other countries that rely on ombudsmen to oversee bar grievance processes and that require legal employers to develop internal compliance structures.[53]

A final set of reforms should focus on expanding the discipline system's enforcement capabilities. Most states need significantly more professional staff, investigatory resources, and remedial options. Greater emphasis should center on preventive strategies such as substance abuse assistance and law office management programs. Lawyers accused of minor misconduct, such as neglect and overbilling, should be required to participate in low-cost mediation or arbitration programs at a client's request. The performance of these programs, including measures of consumer satisfaction, should be subject to independent evaluation.

Sanctioning options for more serious misconduct also should be expanded. Only a few jurisdictions allow permanent disbarment or discipline against law firms as well as individual lawyers. No jurisdiction authorizes fines. All of these sanctions should be available to regulatory bodies. Organizational liability is appropriate where responsibility for misconduct is broadly shared and reflects failures to provide adequate supervision, ethical reporting channels, or safeguards against financial mismanagement. In such cases, disciplinary bodies should have authority to order institutional correctives or to impose economic sanctions that will prompt similar results. Although the bar traditionally has opposed fines on the ground that they appear more like punishment than public protection, that distinction is unconvincing. Few lawyers are likely to experience financial penalties as more punitive than existing sanctions such as suspension or disbarment. The rationale for adding fines is that they can help deter misconduct without removing lawyers' means of livelihood, and they can be used to subsidize the disciplinary process or to reimburse clients. However, for offenders with serious repeated misconduct, permanent disbarment is appropriate. At the very least, clients should have notice before they retain a lawyer who was once disbarred. Redemption may always be possible in theory, but consumers should not have to depend on it in practice.[54]

This reform agenda will require more pressure from both within and outside the bar. Legislatures, administrative agencies, and consumer organizations all need to become more involved in lawyer regulation. If, as bar leaders repeatedly insist, their overriding concern is protecting the public, then the public deserves a greater role in the regulatory process.

MALPRACTICE

The failure of bar disciplinary processes to provide effective consumer remedies has led to increasing reliance on malpractice litigation. The growth in claims over the last two decades also reflects the same factors that have fueled tort actions against other professionals: consumer activism, a search for "deep pockets" to sue following financial scandals, and an escalating number of lawyers specializing in malpractice work. Some commentators also believe that competition within the profession has increased incompetent practice by encouraging lawyers to cut corners and to handle matters beyond their expertise. The result is that 10 to 20 percent of attorneys face malpractice exposure in any given year, and insurance payouts are estimated at $6 billion.[55]

Despite the growth of malpractice claims, the obstacles to recovery remain substantial. The best available evidence indicates that over half of claims result in no remedy and another quarter bring payments of under $10,000. Since few lawyers find it worthwhile to sue uninsured attorneys and over a third of practitioners have no insurance, a large number of potentially valid claims are never filed. Many victims of incompetent or unethical practice also cannot satisfy the profession's highly demanding standards of proof. Most successful claims involve obvious errors such as missing deadlines, neglecting to file documents, or mismanaging funds. In less egregious cases, plaintiffs frequently must show that their lawyer's performance fell below prevailing practices in the community. This burden is difficult to meet, since no reliable evidence is available on how lawyers generally handle many legal tasks. Nor do most defendants lack for fellow practitioners willing to testify that the disputed conduct was within normal bounds. Courts do not allow recovery for mere "errors of judgment." And in many jurisdictions, not even violations of bar ethical rules are sufficient to establish malpractice. The rules themselves state that they are not intended to define standards for civil liability, and some courts have even excluded evidence of noncompliance.[56]

Plaintiffs who can show that their lawyers' performance was deficient face another obstacle. They must prove that this deficiency caused quantifiable damage. That burden typically requires a trial within a trial; claimants need to establish that but for the lawyer's malpractice, they would have been successful in the matter on which they sought legal assistance. For criminal matters, barriers to recovery are even higher and usually insurmountable: clients generally must prove that they were actually innocent of the crime charged and that their attorney's inadequate performance was responsible for their conviction.[57]

A further limitation of malpractice remedies involves restrictions on who can recover for violations of professional standards. The bar has long resisted liability to nonclients, and courts have often agreed. The traditional view has been that making attorneys accountable to third parties would erode loyalty to clients and introduce "undesirable self-protective interests" into professional relationships. Recent decisions have carved out exceptions to this rule, but most nonclients still lack remedies for malpractice. In general, courts permit recovery only where the lawyer undertakes responsibilities that foreseeably affect third parties and where enforcement of those responsibilities appears consistent with client interests. So, for example, damages have been available to individuals who failed to benefit from a deceased client's will because of a lawyer's incompetence. However, opposing parties usually cannot recover for dishonest or abusive conduct on the theory that lawyers' concern about such accountability might interfere with their zealous advocacy for clients. Similar reasoning has sometimes served to deny remedies to buyers or investors who reasonably rely on attorneys' negligent misrepresentations. Such decisions hold lawyers to lesser standards than used car dealers.[58]

All of these remedial limitations require rethinking. Given the weaknesses in bar disciplinary processes, malpractice proceedings play a crucial regulatory role. That role should be strengthened by providing remedies for violations of bar ethical rules and for performance that does not conform to a reasonable person's expectations of competence. Victims of malpractice should not have to establish that it was the sole cause of their losses. A fairer alternative would be the test applicable in England and France, as well as in American medical malpractice cases: plaintiffs who demonstrate that the defendant's substandard performance deprived them of a substantial possibility of recovery would be entitled to damages adjusted to reflect the likelihood of success. Third parties should also be able to recover for malpractice unless the lawyer can show that such a remedy would run counter to specific and legitimate client interests. The possibility of financial liability could help deter misconduct that now appears profitable, such as discovery abuse or misrepresentation to third parties. The result is likely to be an increase not just in attorneys' "self-protection" but in public protection as well.[59]

A system truly concerned with public safeguards also would require malpractice insurance for all practicing attorneys. Only Oregon now imposes such a requirement, and an estimated 30 to 40 percent of the nation's other lawyers are unwilling or unable to obtain coverage. Since most uninsured attorneys either lack substantial personal assets or manage to shelter them from liability, they are rarely sued for malpractice. This invulnerability encourages them to forego coverage and leaves many innocent victims without remedies. A case in point involves Walter Palmer, a Massachusetts lawyer who stole an estimated $3 million from the estates of a dozen elderly and working-class clients before finally being disbarred. He managed to shield his own property, including an expensive summer home, from malpractice claims by registering it under a state statute designed to protect the elderly from exploitation of the sort he practiced himself.[60]

The problem of inadequate remedies is compounded by other factors as well. One is the bar's recent trend toward limited liability partnerships. These structures absolve nonsupervising lawyers of any personal financial responsibility for their colleagues' malpractice, which deprives victims of remedies if those responsible lack adequate insurance coverage. Moreover, even individuals with valid claims against fully insured attorneys recover only a portion of their losses because the process involves such high legal costs and fees. Overall, claimants end up with less than half of what insurance companies pay out. The damages that victims ultimately collect are less than the combined fees of plaintiffs' and defense lawyers involved in malpractice litigation.[61]

Yet despite the problems in the current structure, the bar has opposed proposals to streamline the claims process or to expand insurance coverage and lower costs by requiring all lawyers to have malpractice policies. Rather, the ABA has recommended only "further study" of such proposals, and they have been rejected by state bars. The reasons have less to do with public than professional interests. Many lawyers worry that broadening the availability of remedies and requiring insurance would raise their expenses and increase the frequency of malpractice claims. However, no such increase has occurred in Oregon, which is the only state with mandatory insurance.

Claim rates there are average, and insurance premiums are below those of comparable jurisdictions. Part of the reason for Oregon's success is that it operates a nonprofit Professional Liability Fund that insures all the state's attorneys and incorporates effective prevention initiatives. Because participation is required, the system can eliminate expensive marketing and brokers' commissions. The combination of modest premiums and efficient services has yielded high satisfaction: over four-fifths of the state's attorneys support the state's program. Other jurisdictions should follow the lead of Oregon and the European communitys' code of conduct, and impose similar malpractice insurance requirements.[62]

Both the profession and the public also stand to gain from more preventive efforts and remedial options. Additional voluntary and mandatory assistance should be available to help attorneys avoid problems leading to malpractice claims: conflicts of interest, financial mismanagement, noncompliance with deadlines, inadequate communication with clients, and personal difficulties such as substance abuse. More low-cost dispute resolution procedures are necessary for small claims that fall through the cracks of the current structure. Bar compensation funds should be expanded to reimburse victims who cannot recover from their attorneys. Although most states now provide some limited reimbursement, they generally require proof of fraud or dishonesty and place a cap on payments. As a result, coverage is available for only a small fraction of client losses. In Illinois, for example, only about a third of claims receive reimbursement, and the average amount is only about $3,300. Requiring lawyers to subsidize more adequate compensation funds would not only assist innocent victims. It would also encourage efforts to reduce the need for such funds through reforms in disciplinary, malpractice, and insurance systems. Making lawyers bear more of the costs of professional misconduct may supply a necessary incentive for effective changes.[63]

FEES

Fewer than 5 percent of Americans believe that they get good value for the price of legal services, and the reasons for that perception are readily apparent. Billing excesses fall across a spectrum, reflecting everything from flagrant fraud and "creative timekeeping" to sloppy accounting and inefficient staffing. Audits of "legal expenses" have revealed massages during litigation, dry cleaning for a toupee, running shoes labeled "ground transportation," Victoria's Secret lingerie, and men's suits for an out-of-state trial that took longer than expected. Days in which lawyers bill more than twenty-four hours are no longer rare. The record goes to a class action attorney who logged over a thousand hours by charging some five thousand asbestos clients for the same twenty-minute task. When heiress Doris Duke died, leaving over a billion dollars to charity, two dozen law firms embarked on what one attorney candidly described as "a feeding frenzy." Some of the nation's leading practitioners, staying at leading hotels, charging at premium rates, managed to duplicate each other's work and keep each other employed, which diverted an estimated $20 million from charitable causes.[64]

The frequency of billing abuses is difficult to gauge, since they can often constitute the "perfect crime." It is impossible to verify whether some tasks are necessary and whether they require, or actually consume, the time that lawyers charge for completing them. However, auditors find demonstrable fraud in 5 to 10 percent of the bills they review and questionable practices in another 25 to 35 percent. Such practices include inflating hours, overstaffing cases, performing unnecessary work, and double billing two clients for the same task or time. In recent surveys, 40 percent of lawyers acknowledge that some of their work is influenced by a desire to bill additional hours, and about half of in-house corporate counsel and chief executives believe that their law firms are overbilling.[65]

Of course, complaints about attorneys' fees have an extended history. For some two thousand years, efforts have been made to restrict lawyers' charges or to ban them entirely. In this country, such restrictions have tended to be short-lived or readily evaded. By the mid-nineteenth century, most state legislatures had abandoned the effort, and statutory fee limitations now apply only to a narrow category of cases, such as indigent criminal defense, veterans' benefits, and contingency fees in medical malpractice. Although bar associations have long been involved with fee regulation, their initial concern was more with underbilling than overcharging, and their solution was to set minimum, not maximum, charges for specified tasks. According to the ABA's 1961 Committee on Professional Ethics, "The evils of fee cutting ought to be apparent to all members of the Bar," and habitually charging rates lower than those established by bar fee schedules could be "evidence of unethical conduct." The ABA Practice Manual recommended that lawyers present their clients with these lists of minimum charges in attractive folders suggesting a "degree of dignity and substance." Black leather with gold lettering was preferred.[66]

However packaged, these fee schedules were designed to discourage comparison shopping and competitive pricing. The Supreme Court eventually recognized as much, and in 1975 declared that promulgation of minimum fees constituted illegal price fixing under federal antitrust laws. However, by that time, most attorneys had shifted to time-based rather than task-based forms of billing. Beginning in the 1940s, management experts discovered that lawyers who used time records to set charges earned more than lawyers who relied on more traditional but less precise measures, such as the difficulty or perceived value of the work. At least initially, hourly billing also appealed to many clients. It seemed to offer an objective basis for establishing fees and comparing attorneys' rates. A detailed statement itemizing hours appeared to be a clear advance over a bar-established minimum charge or the common practice of indicating only the amount due "for services rendered."[67]

Although hourly based billing remains the dominant method of setting fees, its deficiencies have grown increasingly apparent, and bar enforcement structures have offered inadequate responses. Most state ethical codes require fees to be "reasonable," and they provide a long list of factors to consider in assessing reasonableness, such as the time, labor, and skill involved, the results obtained, and the customary charges for similar services. The indeterminacy of this standard, coupled with the high costs of enforcement, have made courts and disciplinary agencies reluctant to monitor fees. As noted earlier, bar agencies generally do not even consider fee complaints unless they present evidence of serious fraud or overreaching. Nor do most offer alternative dispute resolution processes. Although many corporate clients have sufficient experience and bargaining leverage to protect themselves, unsophisticated consumers are far more vulnerable. Monitoring fees can be expensive, and the difficulties of proof, coupled with the unavailability of low-cost remedies, has compounded risks of overbilling.[68]

The basic problem arises from the difference in lawyers' and clients' interests. An attorney's goal is to maximize profits; a client's goal is to maximize value and minimize costs. If lawyers are charging by the hour and lack other equally profitable uses for their time, they have an incentive to string out projects for as long as possible. And if their billings affect power, promotion, and compensation within firms, those incentives intensify. When hours determine fees and fees determine so much else, efficiency is not a virtue.

The problem is compounded by the amount of work that firms increasingly demand. When time-based billing began, the expectation was that lawyers would charge between twelve and fifteen hundred hours per year. Current rates generally range between eighteen hundred and two thousand, and the averages are considerably higher in large firms. Moreover, most estimates indicate that about a third of lawyers' office time cannot be billed honestly to clients; administrative matters, firm meetings, personal needs, and keeping current with legal developments all occupy a substantial chunk of time. To generate two thousand billable hours, attorneys typically need to work ten hours a day, six days a week. As Chief Justice Rehnquist has noted, if lawyers are expected to bill at current levels, "there are bound to be temptations to exaggerate the hours put in." Or, one audit expert adds, you either "have no personal life or you're going to synthesize those bills."[69]

In the face of such pressures, rationalizations for padding come readily to hand. Some lawyers insist that their work really is "worth more" than the time that it requires. Others use upward "adjustments" to compensate for hours and expenses that they assume they forgot to claim. Another possibility is to blame the client: attorneys often rationalize inflated charges as a response to those who unreasonably limit or haggle over fees. When all else fails, lawyers can always blame each other. As Webster Hubbell explained when his wife questioned whether he really had marked up his time, "Yes, I did. So does every lawyer in the country."[70]

Even lawyers who resist such rationalizations find some exaggeration hard to escape. Most attorneys bill in six- or fifteen-minute intervals, but few do so contemporaneously. When they later get around to completing time sheets, it is difficult as well as economically inconvenient to remember all the nonbillable matters that interrupted client work. Doubts are likely to be resolved on the side of overreporting, and the definition of "work" may expand accordingly. Almost 90 percent of surveyed partners report that they bill for "social conversations" with clients, although over 90 percent of corporate executives say they don't expect to be billed for such time. As one practitioner observes, among lawyers with high billable hour quotas, "filling out time sheets is [their] most creative professional activity."[71]

Moreover, at many firms, these quotas reach levels that are unlikely to yield cost-effective services. Geoffrey Hazard points out that no profession can get "serious mental effort out of its members at the rate of 2,000 hours per year." Not all hours are created equal, and part of the time that burned-out practitioners log is far more profitable for the firm than for the client. Of course, managing partners recognize as much. And lawyers will often reduce hourly charges that appear plainly excessive in light of the results obtained, at least for valuable clients offering repeat business. But not all clients are in a position to bargain for such reductions, particularly since not all inflated charges are clearly apparent. Even sophisticated consumers may have difficulty knowing whether some work was inessential or inefficiently performed.[72]

Related problems arise from the incentives that billable hours create for overstaffing. From a law firm's perspective, many hands make large bills. From a client's perspective, more is not necessarily merrier. Rather, the effect is similar to the New Yorker cartoon in which a beleaguered executive faces a room of well-heeled attorneys and clients and asks, "Has anyone lost their lawyer? I seem to have ended up with two." A well-known recent example is the bankruptcy proceeding where a federal judge denied over half a million dollars in fees to one of Los Angeles's leading firms, Gibson, Dunn, and Crutcher. Typical of the firm's work was one groundless motion in which twenty attorneys engaged in "duplicative and seemingly endless reviews and revisions of [an] ill-conceived objection."[73]

Reported cases also reveal frequent problems involving lawyers who are overqualified or underqualified for the tasks at hand. Some attorneys charging several hundred dollars per hour have busied themselves photocopying, tagging exhibits, unpacking boxes, or checking the coffee and pencil supplies in conference rooms. Having senior attorneys complete routine documents can grossly inflate expenses. For example, when asked to estimate their fees for preparing a standard guardianship application, some large firms sought up to $2,300 for work that others anticipated completing for several hundred. As that example suggests, overbilling also can occur when lawyers are underqualified to perform specialized tasks. Ignorance of the law never stops some attorneys from taking a case and educating themselves at clients' expense. Although courts occasionally reduce fees that are well above what qualified practitioners charge, it generally takes an egregious abuse to prompt relief. A recent case in point involved a Massachusetts lawyer with no criminal defense experience who nonetheless agreed to represent a business client's son on drunk driving charges. The lawyer was successful, but his self-education took two hundred hours and his fee was $50,000. For the first time ever, the Massachusetts Supreme Court publicly censured a lawyer for excessive charges.[74]

Remedies are equally infrequent for other fee abuses. One involves unit billing, in which tasks are charged in minimum time segments, sometimes as long as twenty minutes. Under such systems, a ninety-second phone message from a partner billing $500 an hour can cost a client $100. Some law firms extract maximum benefits from billing minimums with policies like "if you even think about a [case] whether in your car, in the shower, or on the golf course, it gets [this basic] . . . . charge."[75]

Another strategy involves billing multiple clients for the same time or tasks. For example, some lawyers taking a cross-country flight have charged one client for the travel time and another for the work done on the plane. Similarly, attorneys who have researched a single issue, such as the meaning of a particular term in an insurance policy, have billed more than a hundred clients for that task. Although the American Bar Association Ethics Committee has condemned such practices, its opinions are not binding, and many practitioners disregard its ruling. In their view, if they are travel-ing on behalf of one client and choose to work for another instead of watch-ing a movie, why shouldn't both pay? But if the rationale for billing for trav-el is that it represents time that otherwise could have been devoted to addi-tional work, and then attorneys in fact use the time for such work, why should they be paid twice? Billing for recycled tasks can be even more prob-lematic if it falsely represents that lawyers have spent time on a project such as drafting a document when in fact they simply copied material that was charged to another client. Even assuming that attorneys have a justifiable claim to double bill under some circumstances, it is difficult to defend their frequent practice of not disclosing that practice to the client. More than two-thirds of surveyed corporate counsel believe that double billing is always unethical, and 90 percent think that it is unethical when the client is not informed. If the practice is as defensible as some practitioners main-tain, they should be willing to justify the practice to those paying for it. And if clients cannot be persuaded, lawyers should not bill covertly for a charge that they could not collect openly.[76]

The same is true for another common practice: including undisclosed markups on expenses such as photo duplicating, faxes, and secretarial over-time. Lawyers increasingly have transformed such services into additional profit centers, and the result often have been charges that substantially exceed market prices. A textbook illustration appeared in the *American Lawyer* magazine's account of "Skaddenomics"—the surcharges prevailing at the Skadden Arps firm. One especially vivid example involved "much ado about danish": Clients paid for coffee and pastries at a 200 percent markup over standard retail prices. In a similar case, a million dollar bill for photo-copying reflected rates of a dollar a page, and consumed almost one-sixth of the total recovery. When sophisticated clients have limited the markup rate that they are willing to pay, some lawyers have compensated by billing for services normally considered part of overhead, such as pencils or "file stor-age." To escape auditors, these charges may appear under unilluminating labels. One unusually vigilant client discovered that the "HVAC" appearing on his bill referred to heating, ventilating, and air conditioning on week-ends. Although the ABA Ethics Committee has condemned such surcharges, they remain common for clients who don't know enough to object. And where ignorance is bliss, it is folly for firms to economize. If lawyers can profit from each page they duplicate, why shouldn't everyone get copies of everything, as often as possible?[77]

Other fee-related problems involve nonrefundable retainers and referral payments. Some lawyers demand such retainers when they accept a case, in order to compensate for the use of their reputation and their agreement to reserve future time for the client. If the matter is resolved before they perform significant work, none of the unearned retainer is refundable except in the few jurisdictions that ban such fee arrangements. Many lawyers also demand a substantial referral payment when they forward a case to another attorney outside their firm. Bar ethics rules generally permit this practice as long as the total fee is reasonable and the payments are "in proportion to the services performed" or both lawyers "assume responsibility for the representation." In fact, many lawyers assume only nominal responsibility, provide no services, and pocket one-third of the total fee. Since ethical rules do not require attorneys to inform clients of the actual division of labor or the size of the kickback, such excessive fees may go unchallenged. Yet as Geoffrey Hazard has noted, such referral payments, like nonrefundable retainers, enable lawyers to "get paid for no work."[78]

A related problem can arise with contingent fees. Under these arrangements, a lawyer receives a percentage of the client's recovery, typically around one-third. No payment is due if the claim is unsuccessful. Although such fee agreements are often beneficial to a client, they also pose obvious risks of abuse. A lawyer's return may bear no necessary relationship to the amount of work performed or to the risk actually assumed. In many cases where liability is clear and damages are substantial, a standard one-third recovery will provide a windfall for the attorney. If defendants make an early settlement offer, plaintiffs' lawyers can end up with huge fees for minimal routine services. In some widely publicized cases, the amount of work actually done was so insignificant that it would amount to an hourly rate between $20,000 and $40,000.[79]

Among plaintiffs' lawyers, such windfalls provoke occasional embarrassment but many rationalizations. A typical response is caricatured in one often retold anecdote about a man injured in a fall through an open sewer hole. He retains a famous attorney who wins the case and pockets two-thirds of the judgment in fees and expenses. The client is appalled: "But I was the one who was injured." The lawyer responds: "But *I* was the one who convinced a jury. Anyone can fall down a manhole." Of course, contingency fees also have some clear advantages over hourly billing and serve a crucial social function. Most important, they provide access to the courts for clients who could not afford time-based charges. Such arrangements also give lawyers an opportunity to spread risks of nonrecovery and an incentive to pursue cases vigorously. This incentive is particularly critical in contexts such as representation of plaintiffs in personal injury and discrimination cases, where contingency fees are most common. These clients typically are one-shot purchasers of legal services who lack the leverage and experience to provide effective oversight of their attorneys' performance. By giving lawyers a stake in maximizing efficient outcomes, contingency agreements offer some important protections against meter running or inadequate representation.

Such protections are, however, by no means complete. Contingency fees often create conflicts of interest between lawyers and clients. Attorneys' interests lie in gaining the highest possible return on their work; clients' interests lie in gaining the highest possible recovery. Most research suggests that for claims of low or modest value, lawyers generally want a quick settlement; it doesn't pay to prepare a case thoroughly and hold out for the best terms available for the client. Conversely, in high stakes cases, once lawyers have invested substantial time, they may have more to gain from gambling for a large recovery than clients with limited incomes and substantial needs. Even well-intentioned attorneys may have difficulty preventing their own interests from affecting their advice. And many unsophisticated clients necessarily rely on that advice in evaluating settlement offers.[80]

Such conflicts of interest pose particular difficulties in class action cases. As chapter 5 noted, these cases can serve crucial public interests by deterring and remedying misconduct where individual victims would otherwise lack sufficient information or incentives to sue. But such cases also pose significant risks of abuse because most members of large plaintiff classes also lack sufficient information or incentives to monitor lawyers' charges. The same is true of trial judges, despite their formal responsibility to ensure the reasonableness of fee agreements in class action settlements and to award fees under statutes authorizing such remedies. Effective oversight of compensation often requires more time-consuming review than overburdened judges can readily supply. Many courts face staggering caseloads, and the prospect of prolonging a case by overturning a fee agreement is seldom appealing.[81]

Adequate judicial review is particularly difficult when defense counsel acquiesce in excessive charges. Although defendants often have an interest in challenging such fees in order to discourage nonmeritorious claims, the path of least resistance is sometimes a cheap settlement for injured parties with a generous payout for their lawyers. That prospect is particularly inviting if the remedy can be structured so that most plaintiffs will not take advantage of damages to which they are theoretically entitled. The structure of choice has been the coupon settlement, in which prevailing parties receive a discount against future purchases of the defendants' products. In some cases, the amounts are too trivial to justify efforts to collect them. In other cases, such as one involving General Motors trucks with dangerous gas tanks, most plaintiffs would not be buying another GM truck within the relevant redemption period. Because attorneys fees for prevailing parties are generally based on the damages officially awarded, not those actually claimed, lawyers may be well compensated by coupon settlements that are little more than sales promotions for defendants' own products.[82]

Such strategies received the treatment that they deserved in Dave Barry's account of the "Adhesive Denture Menace." This national peril arose after a manufacturer recalled certain adhesives containing traces of benzene, a potential carcinogen. Without evidence of any actual injuries, vigilant attorneys brought suit on behalf of purchasers unaware of their "victimhood." The settlement gave several hundred known buyers $7 and some twenty-eight hundred undocumented buyers the opportunity to fill out forms and receive a package of discount coupons. Lawyers' fees and expenses totaled almost a million dollars. As Barry acknowledged, this may seem like "a lot of money. . . . [But] it cannot be easy, taking a case wherein it appears to the naked untrained layperson eye that nobody has suffered any observable harm, and using legal skills, turning it into a financial transaction that involves thousands of people and a million dollars! Plus coupons!" In other "phantom plaintiff" cases, it is equally unclear that anyone suffered significant injuries: The real parties in interest are lawyers. One such attorney is known for representing his mother in suits involving products that fell slightly short of advertised specifications, such as a child's wading pool that was a few inches short in diameter. Other enterprising lawyers willingly sue for *de minimis* damages, such as claims that would yield each class member 28 cents; the lawyers themselves expect to do considerably better. Where identifying injured parties has appeared too costly, some attorneys have negotiated a convenient alternative. They take their own fees in cash, and the defendant satisfies the remainder of the judgment by charitable donations. If legal work exceeds the value of the recovery, some plaintiffs can even end up in the situation described in one appellate opinion: "A class action in Alabama cost Dexter Kamilewicz $91.33 in attorneys' fees to recover $2.19 on the merits."[83]

Of course, the value of these cases cannot be measured solely in economic terms. Much of their function is deterrence. A primary rationale for class actions is to discourage misconduct where none of the injured parties suffers sufficient individual damages to justify legal challenge. Generous awards in successful cases also help compensate attorneys for cases that are not. Some plaintiffs' lawyers incur large risks in subsidizing litigation that serves crucial societal interests. And at least some evidence suggests that, outside the large metropolitan areas where high stakes litigation centers, the average earnings of contingent fee attorneys are not significantly higher than those of counsel who bill hourly. But in too many cases, lawyers' windfall recoveries far exceed a reasonable return or a necessary incentive to bring socially useful lawsuits. The magazine *American Lawyer* had it right in its chronicle of one class attorney who represented some eighty thousand clients with the same basic claim for leaky plumbing. Despite the minimal work required for duplicative actions, he sought over a hundred million dollars in fees and expenses, totaling about two-thirds of the class settlement fund. The story's headline came to the point: "Greedy, Greedy, Greedy."[84]

The cost of excessive fees is not simply absorbed by businesses with deep pockets. It often is diverted from the funds for compensating seriously injured plaintiffs or passed on to consumers in the form of higher prices. Nowhere is the price more apparent than in mass disaster product liability torts. In many of these contexts, the risks of sweetheart settlements are especially acute because the plaintiff class includes future claimants. These individuals have not yet filed claims, typically because their injuries have not yet materialized, and they may be unaware of the litigation or its implications for their own circumstances. All too often, these claimants' concerns remain out of sight and out of mind. Recent asbestos litigation offers a case in point. There, counsel representing some fourteen hundred current claimants negotiated a deal with twenty asbestos manufacturers. It provided generous fees for the attorneys and an attractive compensation package for their current clients in exchange for far less favorable terms for a much larger class of unidentified future claimants. This conflict of interest was sufficiently obvious and its impact sufficiently important to trigger review by the Supreme Court and disapproval of the settlement. But other similarly collusive agreements often pass muster.[85]

Even in the absence of such conflicts of interest, mass tort cases can be bonanzas for lawyers at the expense of everyone else. Tobacco litigation is a leading example. Here again, press headlines speak volumes: "First Thing We Do, Let's Pay All the Lawyers"; "[Tobacco] Defense Firms: No Need to

Kick the Habit"; "Will Legal Ethics Go Up in Smoke?" Defense lawyers for firms representing the major tobacco companies collect an estimated $750 million in annual fees. And plaintiffs' lawyers are doing considerably better. In the Texas settlement alone, class counsel pocketed $2.3 billion, for a return on their time estimated at $92,000 an hour. By comparison, the hourly rate caps in some proposed congressional legislation look modest: a mere $4,000 in one 1998 Senate bill.[86]

The problem in these contexts is, of course, not simply lawyers' fees. Law professor Carrie Menkel-Meadow notes that mass torts pose the broader challenge of "how our legal system can provide justice for all when there may not be enough justice to go around." Legislative remedies, alternative dispute resolution procedures, or expanded social insurance programs could provide more cost-effective remedies in many cases that now generate excessive fees. In addition, some of the regulatory functions of private lawsuits could be accomplished more cheaply if administrative agencies and law enforcement officials had adequate resources. But whatever the prospects for such reforms, it also makes sense to address fee-related problems directly. When it now comes to preventing excessive charges, many "clients can't, lawyers won't, and courts don't." Efforts should focus on strengthening bar ethical requirements, increasing clients' oversight capacity, and improving remedial processes.[87]

A crucial first step is for courts, bar associations, and ethics committees to adopt more demanding standards governing lawyers' billing practices. Sophisticated clients increasingly bargain for many of those protections, and unsophisticated clients would benefit from similar safeguards. Written fee agreements should be required and consumers should receive a standardized "client's bill of rights" detailing improper billing practices and complaint procedures. Certain practices, such as double billing, nonrefundable retainers, and unit billing above ten-minute intervals, should be presumed unethical unless a client gives explicit informed consent. Disclosure should be required for surcharges on expenses, the size of referral fees, and the services provided by referring attorneys. Before clients sign contingency agreements, they should receive information concerning the effort anticipated, the likelihood of recovery, and the costs and benefits of an alternative fee arrangement. Their final statement should indicate the hourly rate of return for work performed and their right to challenge an excessive fee.[88]

Courts, bar associations, and legislatures also should adopt stricter billing standards. Judicially approved guidelines for class actions and statutory fee awards could establish policies governing reasonable expenses.

Courts could base contingent fees on the amount of damages actually claimed, not the theoretical value of unredeemed awards or coupons. Such fees should not exceed a reasonable return for the work performed and risk assumed. Of course, what is, in fact, reasonable may often be subject to dispute. But the complexity of formulating appropriate guidelines should not deter efforts to curb clearly excessive recoveries. Better means of regulating contingency agreements are also necessary for the vast majority of cases where judicial oversight is not readily available. In theory, clients can appeal contingency arrangements that yield unreasonable fees. In practice, few individuals do so because litigation costs are substantial and the judiciary has been unreceptive. Courts lack the capacity to monitor even a small fraction of the approximately one million new contingent fee cases filed each year. Under these constraints, more categorical restrictions make sense.[89]

One such strategy, adopted by some states, is to require advancing percentage formulas. Under this approach, lawyers receive a larger portion of the total recovery as the case progresses and becomes more time-consuming. So, for example, in a matter settled without filing suit, the attorney is entitled to 25 percent of the recovery; in a case settled after filing, 33 percent; in a case that goes to trial, 40 percent; and in a case that wins on appeal, 50 percent. An obvious problem with such a formula is that it may encourage lawyers to prolong proceedings where the stakes are sufficiently high, and may still permit overcompensation where little work occurs before settlement. Research on how such percentages operate in practice is necessary to determine whether they are the reform strategy of choice.

An alternative approach, developed at the Manhattan Institute and endorsed by some prominent bar leaders, also would help prevent windfall fees. Under this proposal, a defendant would have an opportunity to make an early settlement offer, and if that offer were accepted, the plaintiff's attorney could recover only a reasonable hourly rate or a modest share of the recovery, for instance, 10 percent. If a defendant chose not to make an offer, the plaintiff's attorney would be free to negotiate a higher percentage contingent fee, subject to current ethical rules on reasonableness. Opponents of this approach claim that it would prove both under- and overinclusive; it would offer no protection in the absence of a settlement offer, and it could deny lawyers a reasonable recovery in some settled cases. The ultimate effect might be to reduce attorneys' willingness to take contingent cases, restrict clients' access to legal services, and decrease the deterrent value of liability claims. But only through experience with such a formula can these concerns be accurately assessed. The effects may differ across different categories of cases. However, the limited evidence now available indicates that some lawyers already take lower contingent fees in cases that settle early and nonetheless manage a reasonable return. Even if restrictions on windfall fees somewhat diminished other attorneys' ability to subsidize speculative cases, the trade-off might still be worthwhile.[90]

A second set of reform strategies should aim at increasing clients' capacity to negotiate and monitor fee arrangements. Not only should bar associations require disclosure of crucial fee-related information. They also should do more to help consumers evaluate alternative billing arrangements. Many sophisticated corporate clients are turning to options other than straight hourly billing or contingent fees in an effort to encourage efficiency and reduce costs. These organizations have found that fixed rates can be appropriate for routine tasks requiring relatively predictable amounts of time. For other services, where flat fees might encourage lawyers to compromise quality, some form of multistage or value billing can make sense. The first of these approaches breaks projects into discrete stages using different billing arrangements. For example, trial preparation requiring unpredictable amounts of time is billed under hourly rates, while courtroom advocacy is handled on a contingency basis. By contrast, value billing ties compensation to the worth of the lawyers' work to the client, measured by mutually accepted factors including the time required and results obtained. In some variations on this model, charges reflect discounted hourly rates with a bonus based on the quality of the outcome and the efficiency of lawyers in attaining it. Bar associations could help clients experiment with such arrangements by providing information and sponsoring research on their relative cost-effectiveness for particular work.[91]

Consumer groups and audit firms also could help clients better evaluate fee arrangements. The unsophisticated consumer "typically is looking for a bargain, but has no idea what a bargain would be." More efforts should build on the experience of unions, community organizations, and retirement associations that have assisted such clients negotiate fees. Audit organizations could develop procedures to certify law firms that satisfied appropriate billing standards. Certified firms would receive the equivalent of a "Good Housekeeping" seal of approval, which could prove useful to business as well as individual purchasers of legal services.[92]

Courts could also do much more to protect clients and enable clients to protect themselves in class action proceedings. Steering committees representative of the entire class can help select attorneys and negotiate competitive fee arrangements. Trial judges can require that lawyers document their efforts to address conflicting interests within a plaintiff class and can make those efforts relevant in setting attorneys' fees. Greater reliance on separate counsel for subclasses and on special masters to review fee agreements could reduce abuses, particularly those involving future claimants or awards of little monetary value.[93]

A final group of reforms should focus on improving fee-related remedies. More effective dispute resolution procedures should be a key priority. Over a third of all states have no fee arbitration programs, and only a few make lawyers' participation mandatory. Many of these programs are insufficiently responsive to clients' concerns. Little effort is made to publicize arbitration opportunities or to assist unsophisticated claimants. In some states, clients obtain fee reduction in less than a third of the cases. In others, although most complainants get at least some relief, 30 to 40 percent are unsatisfied with the process. Clients are significantly less satisfied than attorneys, who generally feel well served by arbitration programs. Part of the reason for these different evaluations is that many programs exclude issues concerning the quality of legal assistance, which often underlie clients' fee-related complaints. Another problem may have to do with who serves on arbitration panels. At most, nonlawyers constitute one out of three members, and all arbiters are selected and trained by the bar. No published research has attempted to evaluate the outcomes of these processes or the sources of clients' discontent. Nor has any state attempted to provide low-cost dispute resolution opportunities independent of the organized bar. More evaluation of current programs and more experimentation with alternatives is necessary to structure effective remedial processes.[94]

Not only do we need better remedies for consumers. We also need better responses from law firms. Studies such as law professor Lisa Lerman's profile of attorneys convicted of billing fraud illustrate common patterns of institutional indifference. When the issue is padding or meter running, supervising lawyers often look the other way or fail to look at all. And when significant misconduct comes to light, significant responses too seldom follow. In less than half of Lerman's surveyed cases did law firms report criminal conduct to bar disciplinary authorities or prosecutors. Some in-house counsel for corporate clients were equally reluctant to expose fraudulent billing that they had failed to detect. In one instance where partners learned of $120,000 in falsified expenses, their response was a discreet request (ultimately ineffectual) to their colleague to go forth and sin no more. Other firms have penalized junior attorneys who brought unwelcome tidings of unethical billing. As one juror noted in a case involving some $2 million in inappropriate charges by a high-billing partner, none of his colleagues "gave a shit as long as they were getting their money."[95]

To alter such attitudes, it will first be necessary to alter the incentive structure that underlies them. In Lerman's study, a majority of the firms that informed the bar of misconduct were from Illinois. Not coincidentally, Illinois is the only state that has disciplined a lawyer for failure to report violations of bar ethical rules. If other jurisdictions began holding attorneys accountable for nondisclosure of serious billing abuses, they might become less common. More firms could also establish internal audit procedures, develop formal reporting channels, and modify the unrealistic billable hour quotas that invite inflated charges. Courts and bar disciplinary authorities could encourage such preventive strategies by imposing more stringent sanctions for fee abuses. In most cases, the only penalty for excessive billing is a reduction of charges or reimbursement for overpayments, coupled with a potential loss of future business from the client. Given the low probability of detection, such sanctions provide inadequate deterrence, particularly where the clients are one-shot purchasers or the lawyers are junior associates more concerned with meeting billable hour quotas than maximizing repeat business. To change those incentive structures, sanctions must be more severe. A few courts have recognized as much and have required attorneys who charged grossly excessive contingency fees to forfeit all payment for their work. Such penalties should become far more common. So should structural remedies. All law firms should be required to develop appropriate oversight procedures, and those found responsible for billing abuses should have to satisfy random billing audits.[96]

Courts and arbiters should routinely refer any case involving serious fee-related misconduct to bar disciplinary agencies and, where appropriate, to government prosecutors. For such cases, significant sanctions should become the rule rather than the exception. It should not take twenty-three instances of fee-related misconduct, coupled with over one hundred other ethical violations, finally to result in disbarment, as was true in a recent Arizona case. Nor should prosecutors pass up opportunities to send clearer messages about the personal risks of fraudulent billing. As several studies indicate, understaffed law enforcement offices too often refrain from prosecuting prominent lawyers who can be expected to invest substantial resources in their defense. Deterring serious fee-related misconduct will require more sanctions like Webster Hubbell's twenty-one-month prison sentence. Other strategies could assist in that deterrent effort. Courts in malpractice suits can hold partners liable for knowing failure to address billing abuses. More states should permit fraudulent billing claims under consumer protection statutes. These statutes authorize punitive damages and attorneys' fees, which are not available in malpractice claims. If insurance and car salesmen can be statutorily liable for fraudulent charges, surely lawyers with fiduciary obligations should be subject to no lesser standards.[97]

Lawrence Fox, former chair of the ABA Litigation Section, prefaced his recent analysis of fee-related abuses with a view widely shared within the profession: "The solution to our problems is not to take vows of poverty. Indeed, in an era when script writers for TV sitcoms can command $13 million contracts and athletes earn eight figures per year, there is nothing wrong with talented lawyers earning very high incomes for their difficult labors." Yet that sense of entitlement is also what fuels billing abuses. All the lawyers in Lerman's study were a far distance from vows of poverty, and many lived as if they did earn eight figures a year. Their fraud funded Cartier jewelry, European travel, private planes, and expensive cars (one lawyer had six). As Lerman notes, "not the slightest hint of altruism" surfaced in any of these case histories. These lawyers wanted to believe that they deserved the lifestyle they desired, and they met too little resistance along the way.[98]

The reforms that this chapter identifies can reinforce that resistance, but they too are not the full "solution to our problems." As the title of an op-ed on fee abuses reminds us, no regulatory structure can fully compensate for "What Lawyers Didn't Learn in Kindergarten." The underlying problems are deeply rooted in a culture that values money as a way of keeping score and a profession that jealously (and for the most part successfully) guards its regulatory autonomy. Lawyers feel entitled not just to substantial income but also to substantial independence. They are convinced that they alone should decide who can be admitted to the bar, who can be ousted, and who can be liable to whom for what. That independence carries a cost. It is paid mainly by consumers in the form of excessive fees, inadequate discipline, and insufficient malpractice remedies. Lawyers have paid a price as well, as polls on their public image reflect.[99]

Yet those costs have not been sufficiently visible or substantial to trigger major reform efforts. And the profession's power in legislative and judicial arenas has created substantial barriers to external oversight. That needs to change. The public needs to become sufficiently informed and mobilized to demand it. In the interim, we can at least aim at incremental adjustments. The ones this chapter identifies are a start, offered in the spirit of Wallace Stevens's poem, *The Man with the Blue Guitar*: "I cannot make the world quite round / I patch it as I can."

CHAPTER 7

LEGAL EDUCATION

"All that is necessary for a [law] student is access to a library and directions in what order the books are to be read." That was Thomas Jefferson's view, and during the American bar's formative years, it was widely shared. Most legal education occurred through apprenticeships with practicing lawyers, and many provided more drudgery than instruction. Alternatively, students could enroll in one of the few for-profit law schools, where quality varied considerably. Toward the end of the nineteenth century, training for law, like other professions, grew more formal and academic. By the close of the twentieth century, about 180 law schools had three-year programs that met the American Bar Association's accreditation standards and that graduated some fifty thousand students each year.[1]

To many observers, the migration of legal education into these standardized academic programs seems a mixed blessing. Certainly, the overall quality of instruction has greatly increased. But so has the expense. And despite some recent improvements, the disjuncture between legal education and legal needs remains substantial. America offers the world's most expensive system of legal education, yet fails to address routine legal problems at a price most low- and middle-income Americans can afford. Today's law students can graduate well versed in postmodern literary theory but ill equipped to draft a document. They may have learned to "think like a lawyer" but not how to make a living at it.

These concerns are by no means a recent phenomenon, and some criticisms are inherent in the enterprise. Legal education has multiple constituencies with competing agendas and demanding expectations. Law schools are expected to produce both "Pericles and plumbers"—lawyer statesmen and legal scriveners. Faculty, students, clients, consumers, and central university administrators all have priorities that push schools in different directions. But it is by no means clear that legal education has developed the most effective structure for accommodating these varied concerns. As in other contexts involving professional regulation, the public has the least influence over institutions that profoundly affect its interests. Key decisions are controlled by legal academics, who have the greatest expertise but also the greatest self-interest in educational policy.[2]

Any serious commitment to improvements in the practice of law and the regulation of lawyers must start in law school. The foundations of the legal culture are laid there, and significant reforms will be impossible unless we change how entering lawyers think about their professional roles and responsibilities. Both the profession and the public need to give more searching scrutiny to the effectiveness of legal education. Although there is widespread agreement about educational objectives, there is considerable room for improvement in meeting those goals. At the abstract level, the educational mission is straightforward. Law schools should equip their graduates with legal knowledge, legal skills, and above all, legal judgment. Students should acquire the habits of mind and ethical values that will serve the public in the pursuit of justice. To realize those objectives, law schools should reflect the diversity in backgrounds and perspectives of the broader culture, and their curricula should address the diversity in American legal needs. By these standards, legal education falls short. For too many students, it does not provide an effective or efficient way of acquiring essential skills. In too many institutions, diversity remains an aspiration, not an achievement. For too many faculty, professional responsibility remains someone else's responsibility.

Just after the turn of this century, Thorsten Veblen declared that a law school "belongs in the modern university no more than a school of fencing or dancing." In subsequent efforts to establish its place and its pedigree, legal education lost touch with part of its mission. Legal academics have long sought to cast law as a "science," through the case method of instruction and rigorous doctrinal analysis. That legacy has proven inadequate.

Meeting the needs of the profession and the public will require fundamental changes in law school structures, curricula, and priorities.[3]

THE STRUCTURE OF LEGAL EDUCATION

The structure of legal education reflects a complex mix of public policy, professional oversight, market pressures, and academic self-interest. The U.S. Department of Education recognizes the American Bar Association's Council of the Section on Legal Education and Admission to the Bar as the accrediting authority for law schools. Under that authority, the Council has developed detailed standards governing matters such as classroom hours, student-faculty ratios, library resources, and so forth. About four-fifths of the states admit only lawyers who have graduated from an ABA-accredited law school and have passed a bar exam. A few of the others have developed their own accreditation systems, and some, like California, admit graduates of unaccredited schools who pass the exam.

The rationale for a system of accreditation parallels the rationale for other forms of professional regulation: a totally free market for legal education would not provide sufficient quality control to protect the public interest. Students, the most direct consumers of legal education, have limited information on which to compare law schools and limited capacity to assess the information that is available. Seldom do they have a basis for judging how characteristics like faculty teaching loads, library services, or reliance on adjunct professors will affect their educational experience.

Many students rely heavily on aggregate rankings, particularly the *U.S. News and World Report* survey. Yet the factors that most affect a school's position in such rankings are highly incomplete and often unreliable. For example, about two-thirds of a school's *U.S. News* score is based on the selectivity of its admissions, measured by LSAT scores, and on its general reputation among surveyed academics, lawyers, and judges. As discussion below suggests, test scores are an inadequate measure of applicant qualifications. And reputational rankings are a similarly inadequate proxy for educational quality. Few of those surveyed possess enough systematic knowledge about a sufficient number of institutions to make accurate comparative judgments. Many participants rely on the word-of-mouth reputation of the university, which explains why Princeton law and professional schools do so well even when they do not exist. Moreover, the ranking system excludes many factors that materially affect a student's educational experience, such as access to clinical courses, pro bono opportunities, and a diverse faculty and student body.[4]

That does not mean, as some law school deans have suggested, that all ratings are inherently flawed and that the enterprise is comparable to ranking religions. Some characteristics can be objectively assessed, and schools should be held accountable for their performance. Students also have a legitimate interest in subjective factors like reputation, however fuzzy the measures; prestige is, after all, part of what they are purchasing. Ratings can supply a useful counterweight to complacency and a check on puffing. In their absence, applicants might well encounter an educational Lake Wobegon, where all institutions are above average. But the problem with rankings like the *U.S. News* report is that they assign arbitrary weights to an incomplete set of relevant characteristics, rely on inadequate measures of those characteristics, and offer a single final score. That score establishes a pecking order for the top fifty schools and determines which tier the remainder occupy. These rankings have assumed an importance out of all proportion to their reliability, not only with prospective students but also with administrators, faculty, and alumni. Such ratings often distort law schools' priorities; the temptation is to underinvest in features that *U.S. News* editors find unimportant, like diversity or public service, and to divert scarce resources to promotional campaigns showcasing measures that could influence rankings.

A second problem in the market for legal education is that the most direct consumers—students—have interests that are not necessarily consistent with those of the ultimate consumers—clients and the public. Education is one of the rare contexts where buyers often want less for their money. Some students would like to earn a degree with the minimal effort required to pass a bar examination and land a job. In the absence of accreditation standards, law schools would need to compete for applicants who viewed "less as more." The problem would be compounded by the similar attitudes among central university administrations. Many institutions already view law schools as "cash cows." Much legal instruction can occur in relatively inexpensive large-lecture formats, and tuition can be set at comparatively high levels that reflect students' future earning potential. Without accreditation requirements, many universities would face even greater temptations to make law schools get by with less and to use more of their revenues for subsidizing other programs.

These concerns justify some regulatory standards, but it by no means follows that the current ones make sense. A threshold problem arises from conflicts of interest. As a practical matter, control of the accreditation process rests largely with the ABA Council on Legal Education. In theory, its members are responsible for protecting the public. In fact, they are also representatives of, and accountable to, a profession with its own interests to protect. Lawyers have an obvious stake in limiting competition, preserving status, and preventing what many bar leaders perceive as "overcrowding." From their perspective, "less is more" in legal education, but in a different sense than for applicants or administrators; less rigorous educational standards mean more new lawyers, more hungry mouths to feed, and more competitive pressures.[5]

Legal educators have an even greater stake in the educational structure. In a *New York Times* magazine profile, one faculty member put the point bluntly: Whatever its other faults, "law school works pretty well for us." On average, legal academics earn the highest salaries of all university faculty. And the accreditation process protects key aspects of their quality of life, such as tenure, teaching loads, and research support.[6]

Yet whether those standards protect the public as well as the profession is another matter. To be sure, the government makes some effort to ensure that the accreditation process is not narrowly self-serving. During the mid-1990s, the Justice Department's Antitrust Division forced changes in some plainly protectionist standards involving matters such as faculty salaries and competition from nonaccredited schools. Under recently revised regulations, the Department of Education also has authority to ensure that accreditation standards are "valid and reliable indicators of the quality of the education or training provided" and are "relevant to the needs of affected students." A departmental review of law school standards is in process, and it is not yet clear how demanding government scrutiny will be. Traditionally, the views of legal academics have been given great deference in the accreditation process, largely due to concerns about academic freedom and difficulties in measuring educational quality. But the price of that deference has been a structure that inadequately serves the public interest.[7]

Accreditation requirements substitute detailed regulation of educational inputs—such as facilities, resources, and faculty-student contact—for more direct measurement of educational outputs. Yet no evidence suggests that greater variation in these characteristics would significantly affect performance in practice. The limited data available reflect no correlation between the quality of a law school by conventional measures and the frequency of malpractice among its graduates. And considerable research suggests that the current educational structure leaves many students both underprepared and overprepared to meet societal needs. They typically are overqualified to offer routine assistance at affordable costs. And they frequently are underqualified in practical and interdisciplinary skills in areas such as finance, management, counseling, and information technology. On the infrequent occasions when attorneys are asked to evaluate their legal education, most report considerable dissatisfaction with skills preparation. For example, between two-thirds and four-fifths of surveyed graduates believe that negotiation, fact gathering, and document preparation could be taught effectively, but only about a quarter feel that those subjects receive sufficient attention. Similar disparities are reported for problem solving, oral communication, counseling, and litigation.[8]

This mismatch between what law schools supply and what law practice requires argues for a different approach. The diversity in America's legal needs demands corresponding diversity in its legal education. Accreditation frameworks should recognize in form what is true in fact. Legal practice is becoming increasingly specialized. It makes little sense to require the same training for the Wall Street securities specialist and the small town matrimonial lawyer. While some students may want a generalist degree, others could benefit from a more specialized advanced curriculum or from shorter, more affordable programs that would prepare graduates for limited practice areas. A similar point was made some seventy-five years ago in a prominent Carnegie Foundation report by Alfred Reed, *Training for the Public Profession of Law*. And since then, the variation across substantive fields has grown more pronounced. For some routine services, most law schools' current three-year program is neither necessary nor sufficient. Almost no institutions require students to be proficient in areas where unmet legal needs are greatest, such as bankruptcy, immigration, uncontested divorces, and landlord-tenant matters. Other nations permit nonlawyers with legal training to provide these services without demonstrable adverse effects. American law schools could offer such training and help design licensing structures that would increase access to affordable assistance from paralegal specialists.[9]

The profession as well as the public would benefit from an educational system that served more diverse audiences in more diverse ways. As costs escalate, applicant pools decline, and placement markets tighten, law schools have much to gain from broadening their mission and potential student body. Abandoning a one-size-fits-all accreditation framework would open a range of possibilities. Some schools could offer less expensive two- or three-year programs. A few states have accredited such programs, which cut tuition by strategies such as increased reliance on adjuncts and on-line library resources. Other institutions could supplement their standard curriculum with courses for paralegals, undergraduates, and professionals in law-related occupations. Many schools could develop advanced interdisciplinary opportunities for law students and practitioners, or shortened degree programs for individuals who would be licensed to practice in limited fields. More Internet-based distance learning could help decrease costs and increase access to specialized instruction that cannot be efficiently provided at all institutions. Each of these initiatives would, of course, present complicated cost-quality trade-offs, and not all of them might ultimately prove desirable. But we have no way of assessing the potential benefits without more innovation than the current structure permits.

Greater diversity in legal education also would permit greater diversity in the legal profession and in the career paths available to its members. Many individuals from disadvantaged backgrounds are deterred from applying to law school by the expense of current programs. Others who obtain legal degrees acquire such substantial debt burdens that they cannot afford to pursue the public-interest or public-sector career choices that led them to choose law in the first instance. A growing number of law school graduates are unable to find any jobs that pay enough to meet their loan obligations. Law school graduates have the highest default rate on student loans of all professionals, and almost a fifth declare bankruptcy. Although some schools have developed loan forgiveness programs for graduates who accept poorly paid public service positions, these programs address only a small part of the demand. More varied and affordable educational opportunities could increase access for applicants from disadvantaged backgrounds. Shorter, limited degrees could also enable more graduates to take jobs that address unmet legal needs.[10]

Not only should there be more choices in legal education but applicants also should have more reliable information about the choices available. That need is not met by rankings like those of *U.S. News* and its competitors or by the limited standardized information that the ABA supplies. Prospective students need more comparative data, and schools need more incentives to compete across a broader range of characteristics than current ratings address. So, for example, applicants might benefit from approaches adapted from undergraduate education that evaluate schools by reference to "good practices" on teaching. Such approaches can provide comparative information on students' experiences on matters such as faculty contact, effective feedback, skills instruction, and collaborative projects.[11]

That is not to suggest that a totally unregulated market in legal education with complete deference to consumer choices would be desirable. The public has an interest in maintaining threshold quality standards, and some students lack sufficient judgment, experience, or incentives to choose effective programs. But given the inadequacies of the current educational structure, more variation, experimentation, and research are justified. To make intelligent policy decisions, both the profession and the public need to know more about how different educational approaches affect performance in practice. Whether or not legal education should let a thousand flowers bloom, it should at least permit choices between delphiniums and dahlias.

DIVERSITY

Not only has legal education provided too little diversity across institutions, but it has also provided too little assurance of diversity within institutions. To be sure, the last quarter century has brought impressive progress. Until the 1960s, American lawyers received their training in institutions that were almost entirely white and male. When I attended law school a decade later, I had no course taught by or about women. And when I joined the Stanford faculty and expressed a desire to teach a class on gender discrimination, the dean was horrified. It would, as he put it, "type you as a woman." With what I hoped was faint irony, I noted that this probably would not come as a shock to most observers. And what, after all, were my alternatives? But that was, of course, beside the point. The point was academic credibility, and to establish that, I needed a "real subject." Negotiable instruments was the dean's suggestion.

On today's law school landscape, much has changed but much has remained the same. Women and courses on women's issues are now well represented. About 45 percent of entering law students are female, and about 20 percent are from racial and ethnic minorities. But too many of these individuals still feel uncomfortable in the educational environment, and too few have advanced to positions where they can significantly affect it. Women and men of color are still overrepresented at the bottom of academic pecking orders and underrepresented in the upper ranks of tenured faculty and senior administrative positions. Only 20 percent of full professors and 10 percent of law school deans are female, and only 10 percent of those in either position are faculty of color. These racial and gender disparities in promotion cannot be explained solely by disparities in objective qualifications, such as academic credentials or experience. Women and minority students also are more likely to be silenced in the classroom and harassed outside it. Issues concerning race, gender, and sexual orientation are often missing or marginal in core curricula. Given these patterns, it is scarcely surprising that women and minority men report higher levels of dissatisfaction and disengagement with the law school experience. If our goal is to create an educational community, and ultimately a profession, of equal opportunity and mutual respect, we have a significant distance yet to travel.[12]

At the same time, efforts to narrow that distance are under siege. California's Proposition 209 and a federal court of appeals ruling in *Hopwood v. Texas* have prohibited reliance on race at universities within their jurisdictions. Similar prohibitions are under consideration in other states as part of a national campaign against affirmative action. Opponents believe that policies based on race, ethnicity, or gender perpetuate a kind of preferential treatment that society should be seeking to eliminate. In critics' view, such treatment implies that women and men of color require special advantages, which reinforces the very assumptions of inferiority that our nation needs to counteract.[13]

Yet while the stigma associated with affirmative action is clearly a problem, opponents mistake its most fundamental causes and plausible solutions. Assumptions of inferiority predated affirmative action and would persist without it. The absence of women and men of color in key legal roles is also stigmatizing. Moreover, we are unlikely to achieve truly equal opportunity by pretending that we already have it or that all forms of preferential treatment are equally objectionable. Disfavoring women or men of color stigmatizes and subordinates the entire group. Disfavoring white males does not. Contrary to critics' assertions, the measures necessary for diversity do not undermine educational quality but rather enhance it. The Supreme Court's landmark 1978 decision, *Regents of the University of California v. Bakke*, recognized as much and upheld the narrowly tailored use of racial considerations in admissions as long as they did not impose rigid quotas. In his controlling opinion in *Bakke*, Justice Powell emphasized the crucial role that diversity plays in advancing intellectual inquiry and in exposing future leaders to different perspectives and values.[14]

Experience with affirmative action since *Bakke* has underscored the importance of those contributions. The value of diversity is widely acknowledged, as is clear from recent position papers by the Association of American Law Schools (AALS) and a coalition of virtually every other major organization in higher education. Empirical research consistently finds that students who experience racial diversity in education show less prejudice, more ability to deal with conflict, better cognitive skills, clearer understanding of multiple perspectives, and greater satisfaction with their academic experience. In a 1999 survey of some eighteen hundred students at two leading law schools, 90 percent reported positive effects of diversity on their educational experience. As the AALS statement recognizes, "Different backgrounds enrich learning, scholarship, public service, and institutional governance. They promote informed classroom interchanges and keep academic communities responsive to the needs of a changing profession and a changing world." A commitment to diversity is socially necessary, constitutionally justified, and morally imperative. In legal education, that commitment requires initiatives aimed at restructuring admission processes and fostering law school environments of mutual respect.[15]

To ensure adequate representation of students of color, law schools need admission criteria that more adequately reflect the range of talents required in legal practice. Most schools place undue reliance on LSAT scores and undergraduate grade point averages, a practice encouraged by *U.S. News* and similar rankings. Ironically enough, these quantitative criteria that were once introduced to limit biases and equalize opportunities are now having the opposite effect. Yet such ostensibly "merit"-based criteria fail adequately to assess it. Grades and test scores together predict only about a quarter of the variation in law school performance. And we have no idea how well they predict performance in practice. The few attempts to follow students after graduation have not found significant relationships between law school grades and later achievements. In one of the most systematic studies to date, by Michigan Law School, LSATs and GPAs did not correlate with its graduates' earned income, career satisfaction, or pro bono contributions. And minorities admitted under affirmative action criteria did as well on these measures as other graduates. Although national studies find that minorities have lower bar pass rates than whites, about 85 percent are successful. Without affirmative action, the vast majority of these attorneys would never have had the opportunity to attend law school.[16]

A serious commitment to diversity as well as educational quality argues both for maintaining affirmative action programs and for developing more inclusive, less quantitative admission standards. As experience in some California law schools indicates, reliance on economic class alone as a substitute for race and ethnicity will neither ensure diversity nor capture the range of qualities likely to ensure professional success. Rather, schools should follow the approach of a growing number of institutions that are experimenting with additional characteristics such as leadership ability, employment experience, community service, and perseverance in the face of economic disadvantage or other hardships. Consideration of such factors does, of course, carry a cost. More time is required for review of applications, and more room is created for idiosyncratic bias. But the costs of overreliance on quantitative factors are far greater. Merit is an inescapably value-laden concept. There is no neutral, objective basis on which to weigh relevant characteristics. Nor is there any such foundation for determining which groups deserve special consideration and how much representation from different constituencies is appropriate. However, some evaluation processes are more defensible than others. And both the public and the profession have a stake in ensuring judgments that consider applicants' full potential and that foster diverse learning environments. As with other issues of educational structure, questions about how best to pursue these goals should be subjects of continuing experimentation and evaluation.[17]

Similar diversity-related initiatives are necessary in other educational contexts. One area of concern involves women's underrepresentation in tenured faculty and administrative positions and minorities' underrepresentation at all academic levels. The inability to explain these disparities by objective factors should come as no surprise. As chapter 2 indicated, racial, ethnic, and gender biases persist within the legal profession generally, and there is no reason to expect legal education to be different. But there *is* reason to expect law schools to address the issue. Without a critical mass of similar colleagues, women and minorities bear disproportionate burdens of counseling and committee assignments, and they lack adequate mentoring and support networks. Institutions also lose valuable guidance, and students lose valuable role models. A true commitment to diversity will require more sustained recruitment and retention efforts.[18]

Law schools also need more effective treatment of issues related to race, gender, ethnicity, and sexual orientation throughout the educational experience. Too often, such topics are tacked on as curricular afterthoughts—as brief digressions from the "real" subject. Some teachers exclude issues of obvious importance, such as domestic violence, same-sex marriage, or racist speech, because the discussion may become too volatile. When such issues do arise, students who express strong views are frequently dismissed or demeaned. Most institutions have experienced racist, sexist, and homophobic backlash in E-mails, graffiti, or anonymous flyers. Law School Admission Council surveys find that discrimination is reported by about two-thirds of gay and lesbian students, a majority of African American students, and a third of women, Asian American, and Hispanic students. Less systematic surveys suggest that harassment of vocal conservative students is also common.[19]

What is especially disturbing about such patterns is the tendency among some faculty to dismiss their significance. For example, when one law school published guidelines endorsing gender-neutral language in class discussions, a male professor responded by changing all "man" endings to "person," as in "Doberperson Pinsher." A more common faculty response is simply to ignore inappropriate comments or rely on other students to respond. Yet such tolerance of intolerance falls short of ensuring the equal opportunity and mutual respect that professionally responsible professional schools should demand. Sustaining these values requires active efforts to promote diversity, civility, and empathy.[20]

These efforts should invite rethinking other classroom structures as well. A wide variety of studies have found that female students participate less in class than their male colleagues and that women of color are most likely to feel alienated and unsupported by their law school experience. Much of the problem lies in the hypercompetitive culture of many law school courses, which undermines self-esteem and discourages participation by less confident or less assertive students.[21]

A critical first step in addressing these problems is for more educators to recognize that there are, in fact, serious problems. To that end, law faculties should gather information from their own institutions about the experience of women and minorities and the effectiveness of diversity-related initiatives. Such initiatives could include affirmative action, workshops, lectures, and curricular integration. Faculty should be encouraged to develop supplemental readings, case studies, and role-playing exercises that effectively engage students on sensitive subjects. Such efforts will be effective only if legal education rearranges its reward structures. Valuing diversity must become a central mission, not just in theory but in practice.[22]

EDUCATIONAL METHODS AND PRIORITIES

To paraphrase former Yale Law School professor Fred Rodell, there are only two things wrong with conventional law school teaching. One is style; the other is content. The dominant classroom approach is a combination of lecture and Socratic dialogue, with a focus on doctrinal analysis. Although abusive questioning styles that once were associated with Socratic methods have largely vanished, the increase in civility has deflected attention from more fundamental questions about educational effectiveness. Part of the problem is that we do not ask law school professors to ask those questions. We do not effectively educate legal educators. Most law professors get no formal training in teaching. Nor have legal academics shown much interest in building on broader educational research about how students learn. That research underscores a number of inadequacies in traditional law school teaching.[23]

The first involves the overly authoritarian and competitive dynamics of many classrooms. Under conventional Socratic approaches, the professor controls the dialogue, invites the student to "guess what I'm thinking," and then inevitably finds the response lacking. The result is a climate in which "never is heard an encouraging word and . . . thoughts remain cloudy all day." For too many students, the clouds never really lift until after graduation, when a commercial bar review cram course supplies what legal education missed or mystified. Highly competitive classroom environments can compound the confusion. All too often, the search for knowledge becomes a scramble for status in which participants vie with each other to impress rather than inform. Combative classroom styles also work against cooperative collaborative approaches that can be essential in practice. That is not to suggest that Socratic techniques are entirely without educational value. In the hands of an adept professor, they cultivate useful professional skills, such as careful preparation, reasoned analysis, and fluent oral presentations. But large-class Socratic formats have inherent limits. They discourage participation from too many students, particularly women and minorities, and they fail to supply enough opportunities for individual feedback and interaction, which are crucial to effective education.[24]

These inadequacies exact a personal price as well. A growing body of research suggests that the highly competitive atmosphere of law schools, coupled with the inadequacy of feedback and personal support structures, leaves many students with personal difficulties that set the stage for problems in their future practice. Although the psychological profile of entering law school students matches that of the public generally, an estimated 20 to 40 percent leave with some psychological dysfunction including depression, substance abuse, and various stress-related disorders. These problems are not inherent by-products of a demanding professional education; medical students do not experience similar difficulties.[25]

The law school experience shortchanges graduates in other respects as well. Despite recent improvements, most institutions do not focus sufficient attention on practical skills such as interviewing, counseling, negotiation, drafting, and problem solving. The dominant texts are appellate cases, which present disputes in highly selective and neatly digested formats. Under this approach, students never encounter a "fact in the wild," buried in documents or obscured by conflicting recollections. The standard casebook approach offers no sense of how problems unfolded for the lawyers or ultimately affected the parties. Nor does it adequately situate formal doctrine in social, historical, and political context. Much classroom discussion is both too theoretical and not theoretical enough; it neither probes the social context of legal doctrine nor offers practical skills for using that doctrine in particular cases. Students get what Stanford professor Lawrence Friedman aptly characterizes as the legal equivalent of "geology without the rocks . . . dry arid logic, divorced from society." Missing from this picture is the background needed to understand how law interacts with life.[26]

Also absent is any sustained effort to address the interpersonal dimensions of legal practice. Law schools claim, above all else, that they teach students how to "think like a lawyer." In fact, they often teach how to think like a law professor, in a form distanced and detached from human contexts. The psychological dimensions of lawyering are largely relegated to clinical courses. And despite recent improvements, clinical training still is treated as a poor relation in most law schools. Without adequate resources, status, or class hours, clinical courses cannot compensate for the neglect of practical and interpersonal skills in the rest of the curricula. It is thinking about thinking—Grand Theory and doctrinal analysis—that earns greatest academic respect. As UCLA professor Gerald Lopez notes, law school is "still almost entirely about law and . . . only incidentally and superficially about lawyering."[27]

It is, moreover, about law from too insular a perspective. Despite growing recognition of the importance of cross-cultural and cross-disciplinary perspectives, the core curriculum stubbornly resists intruders. With the exception of law and economics, which has managed a fair amount of infiltration, these perspectives generally remain on the margins. To many faculty, students, and legal employers, such "law and society" courses seem like "law and bananas": esoteric fluff largely irrelevant to the needs of practice. At most schools, a bit of borrowed intellectual finery dresses up the standard legal wardrobe, but the fashion remains the same. The consequence is to deprive students of approaches that could prove highly useful in their future practice. An obvious example involves problem solving, which most lawyers find central to their daily work and which only a small number of schools have begun to address directly. Adequate preparation for this role could offer background in counseling, risk analysis, game theory, and organizational behavior. Similar interdisciplinary approaches could enrich understanding of other equally critical roles. Students planning to specialize in corporate law should have more exposure to economics and finance. Future matrimonial lawyers would benefit from a better background in psychology. And almost all graduates, whatever their substantive interests, would be well served by more grounding in information technology, alternative dispute resolution, international law, social science research methodology, and managerial strategies. More sequenced programs would better prepare students for many specialized practice areas.[28]

Similar benefits would emerge from expanding clinical offerings and integrating more skills training into the core curriculum. Capacities for collaboration, legal judgment, and ethical analysis are most likely to develop through experiential learning. Simulation exercises and supervised practice offer opportunities to develop a more diverse range of skills than is possible in conventional Socratic or lecture formats. Clinics serving low-income clients offer especially valuable opportunities for students to learn how the law functions, or fails to function, for the have-nots.

In principle, most law school administrators agree. They would like to offer more clinical opportunities, skills training, interdisciplinary approaches, and international perspectives. But talk is cheap, and many educationally desirable initiatives are not. There are obvious limits to how much time-intensive or specialized training law schools can provide without increasing tuition, which may further restrict access and raise student debt burdens to intolerable levels. Yet not all curricular initiatives require extensive additional resources or unreasonably burdensome faculty involvement. Much could be accomplished through greater use of interdisciplinary collaboration, on-line technology, case histories, role-playing exercises, and cooperative out-of-class projects. The problem with these strategies is generally not that they are unaffordable but rather that they are insufficiently rewarded. Improvements in the curriculum usually are not well reflected in law school rankings. Nor is excellence in teaching the path to greatest recognition for individual faculty.

Significant changes in law school curricula will require equally significant changes in law school incentive structures. A crucial first step is to develop more systematic ways of assessing educational effectiveness and of holding institutions and individuals accountable. At a minimum, more information needs to be available comparing law schools on curricular issues and monitoring their efforts to ensure quality. And educators need more prodding to educate themselves about effective teaching and to support curricular reforms.

PROFESSIONAL RESPONSIBILITY

Law schools have always played a pivotal role in shaping professional values. But until quite recently, legal ethics education seldom rose above one early commentator's apt characterization: "general piffle." Few institutions offered any basic course in professional responsibility, and many made do with brief, ungraded lectures. Bar exams, if they addressed the topic at all, invited reflection on undemanding topics like "What the Code of Ethics means to me." In the late 1960s and early 1970s, the rise of progressive social movements brought new attention to long-standing issues of professional responsibility. Lawyers' involvement in the Watergate scandal pushed the profession's public image to new lows and prodded the ABA into action. Its primary initiative was to require law schools to provide instruction on professional responsibility. State bar examiners felt similar pressure, and most added multiple choice ethics tests to their admission processes. Such ethics requirements were not, of course, an obvious answer to the criminal conduct involved in Watergate. Their focus was on ensuring familiarity with bar ethical codes. Yet ignorance of those codes was not an obvious factor in the felonies committed by White House lawyers. Nor did the superficiality of the bar's response escape notice. As Gary Trudeau put it in one Doonesbury cartoon, the ethics requirements seemed largely cosmetic: "Trendy lip service to our better selves."[29]

Yet despite their inauspicious beginnings, these requirements produced at least some of their intended effects. They put professional responsibility on the educational agenda and laid the foundations for a respectable academic field. But progress has been uneven, and the bar ethics exam has been a mixed blessing at best. Its multiple choice format trivializes many issues and puts pressure on law school courses to focus on ABA disciplinary rules. Professors with more ambitious agendas bump up against resistance. In one all too typical case, a student was overheard advising a friend to avoid taking professional responsibility with a certain faculty member, who "asks a lot of uncomfortable questions about what you think is right and never spends any time teaching you the rules for the exam."[30]

The result has been to discourage the kind of searching inquiry that professional roles and regulation demand. Most schools offer little attention to the subject apart from a single required course that focuses primarily on bar codes of conduct. The result is too often "legal ethics without the ethics." Students learn the disciplinary rules but lack the foundations for critical analysis. The inadequacy of this approach is of particular concern in bar regulatory contexts where codes are ambiguous or self-serving. For example, students may learn that the ABA's rules prohibit unauthorized practice of law by nonlawyers but not whether less restrictive licensing structures for paralegal specialists might better serve the public interest. Doctrinal frameworks also leave out many of the crucial issues facing the American legal profession: inadequate access to justice for low- and moderate-income citizens; disciplinary processes that fail to provide effective remedies for most complaints; excessively adversarial norms that impose undue costs; and workplace pressures that compromise pro bono commitments. Less than a fifth of surveyed lawyers feel that legal practice has met their expectations about contributing to the social good. Yet code-oriented courses fail to address the structural reasons why legal practice so often falls short.[31]

Neither these problems nor other common ethical dilemmas receive significant attention outside of professional responsibility courses. This curricular irresponsibility toward professional responsibility is well captured in a favorite story of Supreme Court Justice Ruth Bader Ginsburg. The professor in a core first-year course was discussing a lawyer's tactic that left a student "bothered and bewildered." "But what about ethics?" the student asked. "Ethics," the professor informed him frostily, "is taught in the second year." Few law schools make systematic efforts to integrate legal ethics into the core first-year or upper-level curriculum, and few casebooks outside the field provide significant coverage. In one survey, less than 2 percent of the total pages in leading texts touched on issues of professional responsibility. The classroom treatment that does occur outside the standard course is often superficial or ad hoc, with no assigned reading and no questions on exams. Here again, students get too little theory and too little practice; classroom discussions are too uninformed by interdisciplinary frameworks and too far removed from lawyers' day-to-day experience. This minimalist approach to legal ethics marginalizes its significance. Educational priorities are apparent in subtexts as well as texts. What the core curriculum leaves unsaid sends a powerful message that no single required course can counteract.[32]

The failure of legal education to make professional responsibility a professional priority has multiple causes. For nonexperts in ethics, a little knowledge feels like a dangerous thing and more is not readily accessible in standard textbooks. These problems, however, are not as imposing as faculty often assume. A substantial range of material has been developed for integrating ethical issues into the core curricula. With modest effort, most faculty could readily incorporate relevant topics of professional responsibility in their substantive fields. The real problem is that most prefer not to. Some doubt the value of discussing values in professional schools. From their perspective, postgraduate ethics instruction promises too little too late. A common assumption is that moral conduct is primarily a matter of moral character. Students either have it or they don't. As NAACP lawyer Eric Schnapper once put it, legal ethics, "like politeness on subways . . . and fidelity in marriage," cannot be acquired through classroom moralizing. Even if legal education can have some effect on students' attitudes, skeptics doubt that it will significantly influence their later practice. Moral conduct is highly situational, and many educators assume that contextual pressures are likely to dwarf anything learned in law school.[33]

Such concerns are not without force, but they suggest reasons to avoid overstating law schools' influence, not to undervalue their efforts. Skeptics are, of course, correct that values do not of themselves determine conduct. One particularly sobering study found no significant differences between the moral beliefs of Illinois ministers and those of prison inmates. Ethical behavior reflects both situational constraints and personal capacities: the ability to recognize and analyze moral issues, the motivation to act morally, and the strength to withstand external pressures. Although not all of these characteristics can be effectively developed in law school, some are open to influence. Research on ethics education finds that moral views and strategies change significantly during early adulthood and that well-designed courses can improve capacities for ethical reasoning. Despite the importance of situational pressures, moral judgment does affect moral conduct. And education can assist that judgment. Students can benefit from exploring dilemmas of legal practice before they have a vested interest in the outcomes. Law school courses have an important role in helping future lawyers evaluate the consequences of their decisions and respond to the economic and organizational incentives underlying ethical problems.[34]

Moreover, many crucial issues of professional responsibility are not matters on which students already have fixed views. These issues often involve complex trade-offs among competing values, and professional standards that depart from personal intuitions. Future practitioners need to learn where the bar draws the line before they are at risk of crossing one. Since some students eventually will help determine where future lines are drawn, legal education should also provide adequate background on the policy considerations at stake. Most surveyed attorneys agree. They report that the ethics instruction they received in law school has been helpful in practice and that coverage should be maintained or expanded.[35]

For some faculty, however, the greatest concerns regarding legal ethics material involve doubts not about its effectiveness but about their own. Many are wary about turning podiums into pulpits or inviting "touchy feely" digressions from "real" law. But while many ethical questions yield no objectively valid answers, not all answers are equally valid; some are more consistent, coherent, and respectful of available evidence. The risks of proselytizing are by no means unique to issues of professional responsibility. Faculty can abuse their prerogatives by self-righteous or peremptory pronouncements on any subject. They do not avoid the difficulty by avoiding ethics. The answer, rather, is to educate educators. Law professors cannot be value-neutral on matters of value. What they choose to discuss itself conveys a moral message, and silence is a powerful subtext. All too often, legal educators have substituted unimportant questions they can answer for important ones they cannot. When they decline to put ethical issues on the educational agenda, they suggest that professional responsibility is someone else's responsibility. And they encourage future practitioners to do the same.

To make professional values central in professional schools requires a significant institutional commitment. The conventional approach—add an ethics class and stir—is inadequate to the task. Professional responsibility needs to be integrated into the core curriculum, not isolated in a specialized course or trotted out on ceremonial occasions. Strategies for institutionalizing ethics are not in short supply. Law schools should support course development and special programs related to professionalism, as well as monitor their effectiveness. More attention should focus on the messages that are implicitly as well as explicitly reinforced throughout the law school culture, messages about the relative value of money, status, and social justice. And more institutions need to follow the model of schools of public health and focus attention on broader issues concerning the profession's responsibility for effective regulation and delivery of professional services. Without such efforts, a wide distance will remain between the bar's rhetorical commitments and educational priorities. Students recognize this gap. Law schools should as well.

PROFESSIONAL VALUES AND PRO BONO OPPORTUNITIES

In 1996, the American Bar Association amended its accreditation standards to call on schools to "encourage students to participate in pro bono activities and to provide opportunities for them to do so." The revised ABA standards also encourage schools to address the obligations of faculty to the public, including participation in pro bono activities. Although a growing number of schools have made efforts to increase public service, substantial challenges remain. Only about 10 percent of schools require pro bono participation by students, and fewer still impose specific requirements on faculty. Even at these schools, the amounts demanded are sometimes quite minimal: less than eight hours per year. Although most institutions offer voluntary public service programs, only a minority of students are involved. About a third of schools have no law-related pro bono projects, or they have programs involving fewer than fifty participants per year. In short, most law students graduate without pro bono legal work as part of their educational experience. As a 1999 report by the AALS Commission on Public Service and Pro Bono Opportunities concluded, "Law schools can and should do more."[36]

The rationale for pro bono service by law students and faculty depends partly on the rationale for pro bono service by lawyers, discussed in chapter 2. Such assistance rests on two premises: first, that access to legal services is a fundamental need, and second, that lawyers have a responsibility to help make those services available. Although many legal educators agree, they question whether requiring pro bono contributions is a cost-effective way of addressing unmet needs. Having corporate law professors or unwilling students dabble in poverty law seems like an inefficient way to assist the poor. Yet we lack adequate experience and research to assess that objection. Many law schools have developed pro bono training and placement strategies that accommodate a wide range of interests. And some mandatory pro bono proposals allow overburdened faculty as well as lawyers to substitute financial support for direct service. In any event, the question is always, "Compared to what?" The current political climate offers little hope of meeting legal needs through more efficient strategies, such as adequate government funding for specialists in poverty law and public interest causes. Particularly among low-income communities, some access to legal assistance is preferable to no access at all, which is their current situation.

Pro bono work also offers law professors and students a range of practical benefits, such as training, trial experience, and professional contacts. For many participants, this work provides their only direct exposure to what passes for justice among the poor and to the need for legal reforms. Involvement in public service is a way for individuals to expand their perspectives, enhance their reputations, and build problem-solving skills. And for law schools themselves, pro bono programs can be a way to generate goodwill with alumni and with the broader community.[37]

In addition to these educational and practical benefits, law school pro bono programs serve an equally significant purpose: to inspire long-term commitments among students that will "trickle up" to the profession generally. In surveys at several schools with required programs, most students report that participation has increased their willingness to provide pro bono contributions after graduation. Although systematic research is needed to determine whether law school experiences in fact make future service more likely, related studies of American volunteer activity point in this direction. Involvement in public service as a student increases the likelihood of later participation.[38]

Given this range of benefits, it is hard to find anyone who opposes law school pro bono programs, at least in principle. But in practice, there is considerably less consensus about the form that these programs should take and the priority that they should assume in a world of scarce institutional resources. According to some educators, if the law school's goal is to maximize future pro bono contributions by lawyers, then it should maximize contributions by students through required service. Such requirements send the message that pro bono work is a professional obligation, and convert some individuals who would not have participated voluntarily. Yet we lack sufficient research to determine whether mandatory programs in fact yield greater long-term pro bono contributions than well-supported optional alternatives. Some law school administrators worry that required participation may produce incompetent service by unmotivated students and may undermine the voluntary ethic that is necessary to sustain commitment after graduation. Particularly for schools outside urban areas, it can also be difficult to find sufficient public interest legal opportunities to accommodate the skills, schedules, and time constraints of all graduating students. But voluntary pro bono programs have limitations as well. At most schools they attract relatively small numbers of participants, inadequate institutional resources, and few efforts at quality control.[39]

Creating a culture of commitment to public service will require more sustained efforts. At a minimum, law schools should follow the primary recommendation of the AALS Commission: They should "seek to make available for every law student at least one well supervised law-related pro bono opportunity and either require student participation or find ways to attract the great majority of students to volunteer." Schools should also establish policies that encourage professors to meet the ABA standard of fifty hours a year of pro bono service or the financial equivalent. Research on volunteer activity finds that students learn better by example than by exhortation. If faculty are unwilling to practice the pro bono that they preach, they again reinforce the message that professional responsibility is everyone else's responsibility. Mark Twain was, of course, correct when he said, "To do right is noble. To advise others to do right is also noble and much less trouble to yourself." But law schools could do more to reduce the obstacles and increase the incentives associated with public service. More adequate resources and recognition are obvious strategies. Legal education has a unique opportunity and a corresponding responsibility to make pro bono involvement a rewarding and rewarded opportunity.[40]

Finally, and most important, pro bono strategies need to be part of broader efforts to encourage a sense of professional responsibility for the public interest. Research on legal education suggests that the "latent curriculum" at most law schools works against that sense of responsibility. Traditional teaching methods leave many students skeptical at best and cynical at worst about issues of public interest: There is "always an argument the other way and the devil often has a very good case." At most institutions, the standard curriculum fails to engage students in any searching scrutiny of what they want to be doing in the world. Legal coursework often seems largely a matter of technical craft, divorced from the broader social concerns that led many students to law school. Individuals who enter talking about justice often leave talking about jobs.[41]

Countering these forces will require a substantial commitment. But there is much to gain and little to lose from the effort. Enlarging students' sense of professional responsibility reinforces their best instincts and aspirations. By making professionalism a priority, law school faculty can reinforce the same aspirations in themselves.

CHAPTER 8

PROFESSIONAL REFORM

The concerns about professional responsibility and the public interest that inspired this book began a quarter century ago, during my first year in law school. I was a student intern in a New Haven legal aid office that was overwhelmed with routine divorce cases. The office's triage strategy was to accept new family law cases only one morning a month. As a consequence, only a tiny fraction of poor clients seeking a legal aid divorce ever got one, no matter how compelling their circumstances. Nor did they have any good alternatives. For a routine uncontested case, private practitioners generally charged the equivalent of $1,500 to $2,000 in today's dollars. No do-it-yourself kits or services were then available for individuals who wanted to represent themselves. When my office proposed to distribute one, the local bar threatened to sue for unauthorized practice of law. It was not the profession's most selfless hour.

The bar eventually lost that skirmish, but its anticompetitive efforts persist, and millions of Americans pay the price. Although self-help kits and typing services have gained acceptance, lawyers have blocked efforts to simplify procedures and increase access to nonlawyer providers. The result has been a shameful mismatch between what the public requires and what the profession supplies. America has the world's highest concentration of lawyers and the most thoroughly legalized culture. Yet it meets less than a fifth of the legal needs of the poor and routinely leaves middle-income households without a remedy they can afford. Law is least available to those who most need help. Equal access to justice is a ceremonial platitude, not a plausible description of the legal process in action.

Ordinary Americans are not only priced out of the justice system. They are also locked out of the regulatory decisions that affect it. Control over legal processes and legal ethics has often been left to the organized bar, the very group least capable of disinterested decision making. Although lawyers' regulatory codes claim to protect the public, the public has had almost no voice in their content or enforcement. The result is an oversight structure that is unresponsive to consumer concerns. Less than a fifth of Americans have confidence in the integrity of lawyers or in their disciplinary system— and with reason. The bar dismisses about 90 percent of complaints about attorneys; less than 2 percent result in public sanctions. Most litigation misconduct goes unreported and unchallenged. Obstruction, obfuscation, and delay are chronic features of the legal landscape, and money often matters more than merits. In short, the current system offers overly zealous representation for those who can afford it and inadequate representation for everyone else.

At the root of these problems is the profession's reluctance to come to terms with what the problems are. Much of the reason involves the lack of public accountability. The organized bar has far outmatched consumers on issues involving the regulation of legal services and the administration of justice. And as William Ralph Inge once observed, "It is useless for the sheep to pass resolutions in favor of vegetarianism while the wolf remains of a different opinion." Although many lawyers and judges are genuinely committed to reform, they have been hobbled by the bar's own political and economic interests, which often push in the opposite direction. Regulation of the legal profession has been designed primarily by and for the profession, and too often protects its concerns at the public's expense. Although a cottage industry of bar conferences, commissions, committees, and centers have focused on a "crisis in professionalism," they have failed to produce the reforms necessary to address it.

Bar efforts have also failed to respond to lawyers' own dissatisfaction with their professional lives. Commercialism and incivility are increasing; collegiality and collective responsibility are in decline. The priority of profits and the resulting sweatshop schedules have squeezed out time for public service and family commitments. Equal opportunity remains an aspiration, not an achievement. Race and gender bias are condemned in principle but often overlooked in practice. No occupation offers greater opportunities for power, money, and status. But lawyers pay the price in other ways: in disproportionate rates of stress, depression, and substance abuse. Many have lost connection with the ideals of social justice that led them to law in the first instance. Most attorneys would choose another career; few would encourage law for their children.

Addressing these problems will require structural reforms far beyond the largely aspirational appeals of the bar's current professionalism campaign. Any adequate agenda would start from different premises. The public deserves reasonable access to legal assistance and to legal processes that satisfy basic standards of fairness, integrity, and efficiency. It also deserves a regulatory system that can enforce those principles and ensure accountability for the results. Lawyers deserve conditions of practice that will reinforce ethical values in the service of social justice. And they deserve workplaces that encourage equal opportunity, public service, and a decent quality of life. Meeting these challenges will require reforms on several levels. First, we need to harness market forces to promote more and better choices in legal services, legal workplaces, and legal education. Second, we need to provide more effective responses to market failures, which, in turn, means giving the public a greater voice in oversight structures. And finally, we need to socialize lawyers to accept more personal responsibility for their professional actions, their working conditions, and their regulatory processes.

One cluster of reforms should focus on markets for legal services. Although there is much to dislike in the way that market values have influenced professional life, the appropriate response is to harness and learn from competition, not to suppress it. Increasing consumer choice has often promoted more cost-effective service. Millions of Americans now benefit from self-help alternatives to lawyers and from the resulting drop in lawyers' prices that competition has promoted. Both the profession and the public have much to gain by further expanding consumer choices. Clients choosing lawyers, litigants choosing dispute resolution processes, attorneys choosing law firms, and students choosing law schools all should have more options and more reliable information about the options available. This, in turn, will require increased flexibility in bar regulatory policies as well as increased research and disclosure concerning legal services, legal workplaces, and legal education.

An obvious starting point is to take a less restrictive approach to licensing lawyers and nonlawyer specialists. The diversity in American legal needs argues for greater diversity in educational and regulatory structures. Law schools should offer a broader range of degree programs, including shorter training for limited practice specialties. Graduates of these limited degree programs, along with other qualified nonlawyers, should be permitted to offer routine services, subject to ethical requirements regarding competence, conflicts of interest, confidentiality, malpractice insurance, and so forth.

The public should also have more opportunities for alternative dispute resolution procedures and more information about the effectiveness of these alternatives. For too many Americans, law is inaccessible, unintelligible, and unaffordable. Processes that are simpler and less adversarial could better address a wide range of disputes and enable individuals to meet more of their own needs directly, without expensive representation. More disputes could be prevented if individuals had better access to information about their legal rights and their lawyers' performance. Promising strategies include requiring attorneys to provide clients with a "bill of rights" about their representation and establishing centralized ethics clearinghouses with information about the disciplinary process and the ethical records of particular attorneys.

Lawyers as well as clients also need fuller information about law firms and other legal employers. Bar and public interest organizations should help develop best practice standards and ways to assess compliance. Such standards could require procedures concerning ethical training, supervision, diversity, pro bono service, and related concerns. The point should be to reward lawyers for socially responsible behavior and to encourage individuals to select practitioners with strong ethical reputations. By the same token, law school accreditation requirements and ranking systems could do more to hold educators accountable for their performance along dimensions such as diversity, professional responsibility instruction, pro bono programs, skills training, and interdisciplinary opportunities.

The bar also needs to develop better regulatory responses in areas where market forces are inadequate or counterproductive. Comprehensive information on the quality of legal services, legal education, and legal processes is inevitably difficult and expensive to acquire. Even with full information, not everyone makes socially desirable choices; clients intent on maximizing the costs for their adversaries often prefer lawyers willing to do the same. To prevent a race to the bottom by these lawyers, the bar needs more effective regulatory structures. And those structures can only develop if public interests play a more central role in the process. All too often, the bar's own concerns have dominated decisions about admission, discipline, competition, confidentiality, and malpractice. Significant progress will require more significant involvement by judges, legislatures, administrative agencies, and consumer organizations. Professional conduct implicates public values, and they should figure more prominently in the formulation and enforcement of professional standards.

To that end, lawyers' ethical rules should be recast in more socially responsible directions. Many bar standards are insufficiently demanding or overly self-protective. They do too little to prevent overrepresentation for clients who can afford it and underrepresentation for those who cannot. Curbing adversarial excesses will require more effective prohibitions on delay, distortion, and deception. For example, lawyers should have obligations to disclose material evidence and confidential information necessary to prevent significant physical or financial injury. Ensuring adequate representation of vulnerable clients, such as indigent criminal defendants or members of class actions, will require additional resources and judicial oversight. In jurisdictions that fail to provide the necessary financial support for appointed counsel, courts need to find constitutional violations and to develop appropriate remedies. In other contexts, where lawyers lack excuses for inadequate advocacy, they should become more accountable through disciplinary proceedings, malpractice actions, and denials of legal fees.

Ethical rules on competition also require rethinking. Regulations concerning advertising, solicitation, and nonlawyer practice need to focus more on protecting the public and less on protecting the profession. Categorical prohibitions on undignified marketing and direct client contact should be replaced with more targeted regulations aimed at fraud, exploitation, and invasions of privacy. The goal should be to promote consumer choice, not attorneys' public image. Rules concerning "unauthorized practice" by out-of-state lawyers and nonlawyer competitors should reflect clients' interests in cost-effective services, not local practitioners' interests in preserving their monopoly. Nonlawyer specialists and multidisciplinary collaborations should be regulated rather than repressed, and their regulatory framework should be designed by a more disinterested decision maker than the organized bar.

The profession also needs to develop more effective and accountable disciplinary structures. At a minimum, lawyer complaint records should be open to the public, and disciplinary agencies should have expanded resources, jurisdiction, and remedial options. For minor grievances involving neglect, delay, and overcharging, the bar should develop alternative dispute resolution systems that satisfy the public, not just the profession. More efforts should be made to identify and deter misconduct through strategies such as random financial audits, free assistance with complaints, and enforcement of rules requiring lawyers to report serious ethical violations. A wider range of sanctions and a greater willingness to impose them are critical, as are better internal ethics procedures and reward structures in organizations that employ lawyers. As officers of justice, lawyers should assume greater obligations to pursue it.

This is, of course, not a modest agenda and substantial obstacles stand in its way. Any regulatory structure risks being captured and co-opted by the group to be regulated. Such risks are compounded for the legal profession, given the prevalence of lawyers and former lawyers among the officials normally expected to provide oversight. These judicial, administrative, and legislative officials often encounter significant disincentives to enforce professional standards or to challenge the bar's own enforcement system. Judges, particularly those who are elected, depend on lawyers' support for their reputation, advancement, and campaign contributions. Constraints of time and resources often work against adequate review of lawyers' fees or performance. Most elected officials see little to gain from challenging an interest group as powerful as the organized bar on issues of regulatory reform, especially since consumers have not mobilized around these concerns. The same is true of disciplinary agencies, which depend directly or indirectly on bar support.

Countering these disincentives is no small challenge, and significant progress will require building more structural checks and public accountability into the process. One promising proposal would be to place authority for the development and enforcement of ethical standards in an independent regulatory commission. Such a commission could strike a better balance between professional autonomy and accountability than the current system if its members were selected from diverse constituencies by diverse legislative, judicial, and executive officials. Consumer regulation experts, public interest organizations, and competing occupations, as well as bar associations, should have representation in that process.

All of these strategies for reform could benefit from greater law school involvement. Specialized educational programs, analogous to those in public health, should focus more attention on the cost, regulation, and distribution of legal services. Law schools, together with bar associations and public interest organizations, also must create more opportunities to rethink and reinforce professional responsibilities. The current ethics curriculum is inadequate, and occasions for systematic reflection during practice are all too rare. Neither market nor regulatory structures alone can fill the gap or cope with all the opportunities for lawyers to favor their own interests over those of the public.

The central challenge for the legal profession is how to strengthen a sense of ethical obligations and to inspire a richer sense of what they demand in practice. In essence, lawyers need to assume greater moral responsibility for the consequences of their professional conduct and for the adequacy of their own regulatory processes and working conditions. That will, in turn, require attorneys to consider all the societal values at issue in particular practice settings. Such considerations will inevitably be contextual, but the results should be defensible under disinterested and generalizable principles. Individual clients' concerns are entitled to deference, but not to the exalted position they now occupy in the profession's moral universe. Lawyers' primary responsibility should run to the system of justice and to the core values of honesty, fairness, and good faith that sustain it. The independence of the profession from governmental domination similarly deserves protection, but not at the cost of preempting public accountability. Lawyers' financial needs and law firms' profits should carry weight, but they should not trump other workplace values more central to personal fulfillment and public service.

Such a vision of professionalism is much easier to defend in principle than to realize in practice. As then ABA President Jerome Shestack noted, professionalism "is no sport for the shortwinded." Getting from here to there is difficult enough. But a still greater challenge lies in convincing lawyers that significant progress is in fact possible, that there is a "there" beyond the ceremonial rhetoric of professionalism campaigns. Despite their considerable influence in American life, many lawyers perceive themselves as uncharacteristically powerless in the face of the profession's own problems.

Yet the obstacles to reform are by no means insurmountable. Lawyers have been at the forefront of every major movement for social justice in American history, and their efforts have been a model throughout the world. The bar has made dramatic progress in addressing many issues of professional responsibility that were not even acknowledged as serious issues when I was in law school: issues such as access to justice, diversity, work/family conflicts, and less adversarial methods of dispute resolution. At a time of widespread dissatisfaction with many aspects of lawyers' work, it does not seem unrealistic to hope that some of the bar's best instincts could be rechanneled toward more fundamental change. The greatest source of discontent among today's lawyers is their perceived lack of contribution to social justice. The challenge now is to enlist both the public and the profession in reforms that will reconnect the ideals and institutions of legal practice.

NOTES

1. THE PROFESSION AND THE PUBLIC INTEREST

1. *American Lawyer,* quoted in Marc Galanter and Thomas Paly, in *The Law Firm and the Public Good,* ed. Robert A. Katzmann (Washington, D.C.: Brookings Institution, 1995), 19, 38–39; Seneca, quoted in "Special Law Firm Report: Quality of Life," Online Exchange, *Legal Times,* April 1, 1996, S39–40; Plato, *Theatetus* in *The Dialogues of Plato,* 2 vols., trans. Benjamin Jowett (New York: Random House, 1937), 2:143.

2. Lunz Research Companies, *The Language of the Twenty-first Century* (Arlington: Lunz Research Companies, 1999), 128.

3. Gary A. Hengstler, "Vox Populi," *ABA Journal,* September 1993, 60; "New Mexico's Legal System Reviewed," *Legal Reformer,* fall 1997, 5; Deborah L. Rhode, " The Delivery of Legal Services by Nonlawyers," *Georgetown Journal of Legal Ethics* 4 (1990): 209.

4. Hengstler, "Vox Populi," 62; Randall Samborn, "Anti-Lawyer Attitude Up," *National Law Journal,* August 9, 1993, 20; Stephen Budiansky, Ted Gest, and David Fisher, "How Lawyers Abuse the Law," *U.S. News and World Report,* January 30, 1995, 50; Leslie McArney and David W. Moore, "Annual Honesty and Ethics Poll," *Gallup Poll Monthly,* October 1994, 2; Leslie McArney, "Gallup Poll Releases," (November, 1999), http://www.gallup.

5. Hengstler, "Vox Populi," 62; Janet Stidman Eveleth, "Perception Is Reality," *Maryland Bar Journal* (July/August 1994): 7; Roy B. Fleming, "Client Games: Defense Attorney Perspectives on Their Relations with Criminal Clients," *American Bar Foundation Research Journal* (1986): 25; Paul M. Barret, "Poll Finds New York Law Firms Cost Too Much and Are Arrogant," *Wall Street Journal,* November 11, 1996, interactive ed.; Samborn, "Anti-Lawyer Sentiment Up," 20.

6. Thomas Macaulay, *The Works of Lord Macaulay,* 6 vols., ed. Lady Travelyan (Boston: Houghton, 1900), 6:135, 163; Hengstler, "Vox Populi," 60; Samborn, "Anti-Lawyer

Sentiment Up," 1; American Bar Association (ABA), *Perceptions of the United States Justice System* (Chicago: American Bar Association, 1999).

7. Buchwald, quoted in Frances Zemans and Victor Rosenblum, *The Making of a Public Profession* (Chicago: American Bar Foundation, 1981), 3, 5; ABA, *Perceptions,* 59; "Confidence Game," *ABA Journal,* July 1999, 86.

8. Tony Mauro, "Lawyers' Top Topic: Public's Perception," *USA Today,* August 10, 1993, 3A.

9. Amy C. Black and Stanley Rothman, "Shall We Kill All the Lawyers First? Insider and Outsider Views of the Legal Profession," *Harvard Journal of Law and Public Policy* 21 (1999): 835, 856 ; "Law Poll: Lawyers Concerned about Their Image and Credibility," *ABA Journal,* April 1983, 440; Wes Hanson, "Lawyers, Lawyers, Lawyers," *Ethics: Easier Said than Done* (Josephson Institute newsletter), 1993, 23–24, 38; Robert L. Haig, "Lawyer Bashing: Have We Earned It?" *New York Law Journal,* November 19, 1993, 2; Laurence Gerber quoted in Chris Klein, "Poll: Lawyers Not Liked," *National Law Journal,* August 25, 1997, A6; Ed Garland, quoted in Bill Rankin, "Nation's Lawyers Seeking to Polish Tarnished Image," *Atlantic Journal and Constitution,* August 9, 1993, 4; Haig, "Lawyer Bashing," 2. See also Jerome J. Shestack, "Respecting Our Profession," *ABA Journal,* December 1997, 8.

10. See Deborah L. Rhode, "Cultures of Commitment: Pro Bono for Lawyers and Law Students," *Fordham Law Review* 67 (1999): 2415; Administrative Board of The Unified Court System, *Report on the Pro Bono Activities of the New York State Bar* (New York: 1999); Richard L. Abel, "Revisioning Lawyers," in *Lawyers in Society: An Overview,* ed. Richard L. Abel and Philip S. C. Lewis (Berkeley: University of California Press, 1995), 14; ABA, *Lawyer Advertising at the Crossroads* (Chicago: ABA, 1995), 51; Saundra Torry, "A Million Dollar Campaign to Love the Lawyers," *Washington Post,* May 24, 1993, F7.

11. Hengstler, "Vox Populi," 62; Black and Rothman, "Shall We Kill the Lawyers?" 854; Jerome Shestack, "Respecting Our Profession," *ABA Journal,* Dec 1997 p. 8. Only about two-thirds of surveyed corporate clients felt lawyers deserved to be called "professional." ABA, Commission on Professionalism, ". . . *In the Spirit of Public Service": A Blueprint for the Rekindling of Lawyer Professionalism* (Chicago: ABA, 1986), 3.

12. Hengstler, "Vox Populi," 61; Samborn, "Anti-Lawyer Sentiment Up," 24; ABA, *Perceptions,* 59; John Hou, quoted in *San Francisco Chronicle,* May 29, 1995.

13. ABA, *Perceptions,* 59; Robert Post, "On the Popular Image of the Lawyer: Reflections in a Dark Glass," *California Law Review* 75 (1987): 379, 380.

14. Rhode, "Cultures of Commitment," 2420–21; Legal Serivces Corporation, *Serving the Civil Legal Needs of Low Income Americans,* (Washington, D.C.: Legal Services Corporation, 2000), 12; Roy W. Resse and Carolyn A. Eldred; Jonathan Asher, quoted in Brian Sullivan, Chris Zombory, and Kali Sabins, "So They Say," *ABA Journal,* November 1995, 37.

15. Deborah L. Rhode and David Luban, *Legal Ethics* (Westbury, N.Y.: Foundation Press, 1995), 673–81, 691–703, 855–63.

16. Norman Redlich, quoted in the Committee on the Profession, Association of the Bar of the City of New York, "Is Professionalism Declining?" *Record* 47 (1992): 129.

17. Nancy McCarthy, "Pessimism for the Future," *California Bar Journal,* November 1994, 1; Mary Ann Glendon, *A Nation under Lawyers* (New York: Farrar, Straus and Giroux, 1994), 85–87.

18. Hanson, "Lawyers," 35; Anthony T. Kronman, *The Lost Lawyer* (Cambridge: Harvard University Press, 1993).

19. Richard Posner, quoted in Glendon, *A Nation under Lawyers,* 91.

20. Lorraine Dusky, *Still Unequal* (New York: Crown, 1996); Nancy D. Holt, "Are Longer Hours Here to Stay?" *ABA Journal,* February 1993, 62, 64; Benjamin Sells, "Stressed Out Attorneys," *San Francisco Daily Journal,* May 25, 1994, 3A; Carl T. Bogus, "The Death of an Honorable Profession," *Indiana Law Review* 71 (1996): 911, 925–26, note 129; Kronman, *The Lost Lawyer,* 281, 303.

21. Bogus, "Death of an Honorable Profession," 926; Deborah L. Rhode, *Speaking of Sex: The Denial of Gender Equality* (Cambridge: Harvard University Press, 1997), 6–7, 149–53; "Women in the Law Survey: Analyzing Job Dissatisfaction," *California Lawyer,* January 1990, 84–85; ABA, report of At the Breaking Point, a national conference on the emerging crisis in the quality of lawyers' health and lives, Airlie House, Airlie, Va., April 5–6, 1991; Suzanne Nossel and Elizabeth Westfall, *Presumed Equal: What America's Top Women Lawyers Really Think about Their Firms* (Franklin Lakes, N.J.: Career Press, 1998), 68, 138–39, 160; Cynthia Fuchs Epstein et al., "Glass Ceilings and Open Doors: Women's Advancement in the Legal Profession," *Fordham Law Review* 64 (1996): 291, 387–88, 391–99, 411.

22. ABA Young Lawyers Division, *The State of the Legal Profession 1990* (Chicago: ABA, 1991), 55; Stephen Gillers, "Great Expectations: Conceptions of Lawyers at the Angle of Entry," *Journal of Legal Education* 33 (1983): 662, 669; ABA, Young Lawyers Division Survey, *Career Satisfaction* (Chicago: ABA, 1995), 11.

23. Walt Bachman, *Law v. Life: What Lawyers Are Afraid to Say about the Legal Profession* (Rhinebeck, N.Y.: Four Directions Press, 1995); Deborah L. Arron, *Running from the Law: Why Good Lawyers Are Getting Out of the Legal Profession* (Seattle: Niche Press, 1989), 25; McCarthy "Pessimism for the Future," 6; Bruce A. Ackerman, "Commencement Remarks," *Yale Law Report,* spring/summer 1987, 6.

24. Marc Galanter, "Lawyers in the Mist: The Golden Age of Legal Nostalgia," *Dickenson Law Review* 100 (1996): 561; Glendon, *A Nation under Lawyers,* 57.

25. Harlan Fiske Stone, "The Public Influence of the Bar," *Harvard Law Review* 48 (1934): 1, 5–7; Arthur C. Train, *Ambition* (New York: Scribner's, 1928), quoted in Maxwell Bloomfield, *Law and Lawyers in American Popular Culture* (Chicago: Commission on Undergraduate Education in Law and the Humanities, 1980), 47–48.

26. Committee on the Profession, "Is Professionalism Declining?" 139; Galanter, "Lawyers in the Mist," 558.

27. Sol M. Linowitz with Martin Mayer, *The Betrayed Profession* (New York: Charles Scribner's Sons, 1994), 6.

28. See sources cited in Deborah L. Rhode, "Why the ABA Bothers? A Functional Perspective on Professional Codes," *Texas Law Review* 59 (1980): 689, 699.

29. Warren E. Burger, "The Decline of Professionalism," *Fordham Law Review* 63 (1995): 949; Warren E. Burger, "The Law Suffers When Lawyers Ignore Professional Ethics," *Los Angeles Daily Journal,* July 28, 1988, 4; McCarthy, "Pessimism for the Future," 1; Benjamin Sells, "Lawyers Aren't as Trapped as They Think," *San Francisco Daily Journal,* September 12, 1994, 5.

30. ABA Commission on Professionalism, *Spirit of Public Service,* 1; Stanley Fish, "Antiprofessionalism," *Cardozo Law Review* 7 (1986): 645, 647; Commission on the Future of the Legal Profession and the State Bar of California, *The Future of the California Bar:*

Final Report (San Francisco: California Bar Association, 1995), 52; Glendon, *A Nation under Lawyers,* 31.

31. Robert E. Lane, "The Road Not Taken: Friendship, Consumerism, and Happiness," *Critical Review* 8 (1994): 521, 527; Robert E. Lane, "Does Money Buy Happiness?" *Public Interest* 113 (fall 1993): 56, 57; Daniel Goleman, "Forget Money: Nothing Can Buy Happiness, Some Researchers Say," *New York Times,* July 16, 1996, B5; James Q. Wilson, "Wealth and Happiness," *Critical Review* 8 (1994): 555, 560, 563.

32. Mark J. Osiel, "Lawyers as Monopolists, Aristocrats, and Entrepreneurs," *Harvard Law Review* 103 (1990): 2009, 2047–48.

33. ABA, *Model Code of Professional Responsibility* (Chicago: American Bar Foundation, 1979); Ethical Consideration 7–1. For requirements of confidentiality see ABA Code, DR4-101 and ABA, *Model Rules of Professional Conduct* (Chicago: ABA Center for Professional Responsibility, 1996), Rule 1.6; See Eugene R. Gaetke, "Lawyers as Officers of the Court," *Vanderbilt Law Review* 42 (1989): 39. For general critiques, see David Luban, *Lawyers and Justice: An Ethical Study* (Princeton: Princeton University Press, 1988); and William H. Simon, *The Practice of Justice* (Cambridge: Harvard University Press, 1998).

34. See sources cited in Deborah L. Rhode, "Ethical Perspectives on Legal Practice," *Stanford Law Review* 37 (1985): 589, 592.

35. Preamble, *Model Rules of Professional Conduct.*

36. Association of the Bar of the City of New York, quoted in Committee on the Profession, "Is Professionalism Declining?" 133; Roscoe Pound, *The Lawyer from Antiquity to Modern Times* (St. Paul: West, 1953), 7; Michael Bayles, *Professional Ethics* (Belmont, Calif.: Wadsworth, 1981), 138; David Young, *The Rule of Experts* (Washington, D.C.: Cato Institute, 1987); Jonathan Ris, "Professional Regulation," *Law and Human Behavior* 7 (1983): 103; Eliot Freidson, *The Profession of Medicine* (New York: Dodd, Mead, 1970), 370.

37. Sylvia Ostrey, "Competition Policy and the Self-Regulating Professions," in *The Professions and Public Policy,* ed. Philip Slayton and Michael Trebilcock (Toronto: University of Toronto Press, 1978), 17; Rhode, "Institutionalizing Ethics," *Case Western Law Review* 44 (1994): 665, 687.

38. See sources cited in Rhode and Luban, *Legal Ethics,* 855–57; ABA, Commission on Evaluation of Disciplinary Enforcement, *Lawyer Regulation for a New Century* (Chicago: ABA, 1992); McCarthy, "Pessimism for the Future," 1.

39. The Working Group on Lawyer Conduct and Professionalism, *A National Action Plan on Lawyer Conduct and Professionalism* (Chicago: ABA, 1999), 15; Robert L. Nelson and David M. Trubek, "Arenas of Professionalism: The Professional Ideologies of Lawyers in Context," in *Lawyers' Ideals/Lawyers' Practices,* ed. Robert L. Nelson, David M. Trubek, and Rayman L. Solomon (Ithaca: Cornell University Press, 1992), 177.

40. Model Rule 1.2; Robert W. Gordon, "Corporate Law Practice as a Public Calling," *Maryland Law Review* 49 (1990): 255, 258; Anthony T. Kronman, "The Future in Legal Ethics," *Dickenson Law Review* 100 (1996): 489, 498.

41. Roger Cramton, "The Delivery of Legal Services to Ordinary Americans," *Case Western Law Review* 44 (1994): 531, 562–63. See the sources cited in Deborah L. Rhode, "Professionalism in Perspective: Alternative Approaches to Nonlawyer Practice," *New York University Review of Law and Social Change* 22 (1996): 701; ABA, "Report of the

Committee on Multidistrict Practice to the House of Delegates," *Professional Lawyer* 10 (1999): 1.

42. Cramton, "Delivery of Services," 581–90; Jim Towry, "Addressing the Needs of the Poor," *California Bar Journal,* August 1996, 4.

43. See chapter 5 and Deborah L. Rhode, "Too Much Law, Too Little Justice: Too Much Rhetoric, Too Little Reform," *Georgetown Journal of Legal Ethics* 11 (1999): 989, 1009–1112.

44. Americans for Legal Reform, *Attorney Discipline: National Survey and Report* (Washington D.C. : Americans for Legal Reform, 1990); Rhode and Luban, *Legal Ethics*, 863–75.

45. ABA Commission on Professionalism, *Spirit of Public Service,* 11.

46. See Ted Schneyer, "Professionalism as Politics: The Making of a Modern Legal Ethics Code," in *Lawyers' Ideals/Lawyers' Practices*, ed. Robert L. Nelson, David M. Trubek, and Rayman L. Solomon (Ithaca: Cornell University Press, 1992), 95, 132–35; Rhode, "Ethical Perspectives," 616.

47. See Ronald Gilson and Robert H. Mnookin, "Disputing Through Agents: Cooperation and Conflict Between Lawyers in Litigation," *Columbia Law Review* 194 (1994): 509; Robert Gordon and William Simon, "The Redemption of Professionalism," in *Lawyers' Ideals/Lawyers' Practices*, ed. Robert L. Nelson, David M. Trubek, and Rayman L. Solomon (Ithaca: Cornell University Press, 1992), 230.

48. See sources cited in Rhode, "Gender and Professional Roles," *Fordham Law Review* 63 (1994): 39, 70.

2. LAWYERS AND THEIR DISCONTENT

1. See Deborah R. Hensler and Marisa E. Reddy, *California Lawyers View the Future* (Santa Monica, Calif.: RAND Institute for Social Justice, 1995).

2. "Lawyers in Profile," *Researching Law* 10 (Chicago: American Bar Foundation Research Newsletter, 1999), 8; American Bar Association, *Lawyer Populations in 1980 and 1991* (Chicago: American Bar Foundation, 1994), 7; Samuel R. Ogden, *America the Vanishing: Rural Life and the Price of Progress* (Brattleboro, Vt.: Stephen Green Press, 1969), vii (quoting Ogden Nash).

3. Maura Dolan, "Miserable with the Legal Life," *Los Angeles Times*, June 27, 1995, A1; Tom Locke, "Running from the Law," *Denver Business Journal*, April 22, 1994, 3; Kate Muir, "Counsel for the Depressed and the Stressed," *Times*, July 13, 1995.

4. ABA, Young Lawyers Division, *Career Satisfaction* (Chicago: ABA, 1995), 53; John P. Heinz, Kathleen E. Hull, and Ava H. Harter, "Lawyers and Their Discontents: Findings from a Survey of the Chicago Bar," *Indiana Law Journal* 74 (1999): 735, 736; Glenn Firebaugh and Brian Harley, "Trends in Job Satisfaction in the United States by Race, Gender, and Type of Occupation," *Research in the Sociology of Work* (1995): 87. Slightly over half of surveyed lawyers felt that law had only somewhat met their expectations concerning positive social contributions, and about half felt that it had not met their expectations at all. (ABA, *Career Satisfaction*, 11.) For career changes and preferences for children, see Hensler and Reddy, *California Lawyers View the Future*, 8; Shelly Phillips, "Lawyers Who Want Out: Nearly Half Say They Would Change Jobs If They Felt There Was a

Reasonable Alternative," *Philadelphia Inquirer*, June 8, 1993, F1; Dolan, "Miserable with the Legal Life," A1.

5. David G. Myers, *The Pursuit of Happiness* (New York: W. Morrow, 1992), 27; personal interview, Deborah Hensler, Stanford, California, August 14, 1998. For competing accounts, see Symposium, "Attorney Well-Being in Large Firms," *Vanderbilt Law Review* 52 (1999): 869–1050.

6. Michael J. Sweeny, "The Devastations of Depression," *Bar Leader*, March/April 1998, 11; Benjamin Sells, "Counsel on the Verge of a Nervous Breakdown," *San Francisco Daily Journal*, May 25, 1994; Don P. J. Jones and Michael J. Crowley, "Depression and Suicide," *Bar Leader*, March/April 1997; Laura Gatland, "Dangerous Dedication," *ABA Journal*, December 1997, 28–30; R. Lynn Pregenzer, "Substance Abuse in the Legal Profession: A Symptom of Malaise," *Notre Dame Journal of Law and Ethics* 7 (1993): 305, 306.

7. Stephen Brent, *In an Age of Experts* (Princeton: Princeton University Press, 1994), 42; Robert N. Bellah et al., eds., *Habits of the Heart: Individualism and Commitment in American Life* (Berkeley: University of California Press, 1996); Rebecca Fowler, "Lawyers Sentenced to a Life of Misery," *Independent*, May 6, 1996, 1; "Working Your Nerves: The Toughest Job," *Newsweek*, March 6, 1995, 60.

8. Myers, *The Pursuit of Happiness*, 32–38, 63; Robert E. Lane, "The Road Not Taken: Friendship, Consumerism, and Happiness," *Critical Review* 8 (1994): 521; Robert E. Lane, "Does Money Buy Happiness?" *Public Interest* 113 (fall 1993): 56, 58–59; Robert H. Frank, *Luxury Fever* (New York: Free Press, 1999), 133; Mihaly Csikszentmihalyi, *Beyond Boredom and Anxiety* (San Francisco: Jossey-Bass, 1975), 182–99; Daniel Goleman, "Forget Money: Nothing Can Buy Happiness, Some Researchers Say," *New York Times*, July 16, 1996, B5; David G. Myers and Ed Diener, "Who Is Happy?" *Psychological Science* 6 (1995): 13; Lawrence S. Krieger, "What We're Not Telling Law Students—and Lawyers," *Journal of Law and Health* 13 (1999): 1, 7.

9. Mary Ann Glendon, *A Nation under Lawyers* (New York: Farrar, Straus and Giroux, 1994), 201 (quoting Patrick Griffin); Michael Trotter, *Profit and the Practice of Law* (Athens: University of Georgia Press, 1997), 60.

10. Stephen Gillers, "Great Expectations: Conceptions of Lawyers at the Angle of Entry," *Journal of Legal Education* 33 (1983): 662, 667; William R. Keates, *Proceed with Caution* (Chicago: Harcourt Brace Legal and Professional Publications, 1997), 119; Jerry Van Hoy, *Franchise Law Firms and the Transformation of Personal Legal Services* (Westport, Conn.: Quorum, 1997), 38, 69, 85–88; Davis, "Debtor Class," *National Law Journal*, May 22, 1995, 24.

11. Walt Bachman, *Law v. Life: What Lawyers Are Afraid to Say about the Legal Profession* (Rhinebeck, N.Y.: Four Directions Press, 1995), 117; Eve Spangler, *Lawyers for Hire: Professionals as Salaried Employees* (New Haven: Yale University Press, 1986), 167, 203; Carroll Seron, *The Business of Practicing Law* (Philadelphia: Temple University Press, 1996), 117; "As We See It . . . A Roundtable Discussion among Solo/Small Firm Practitioners," *Houston Lawyer* 35 (1998): 10.

12. Spangler, *Lawyers for Hire*, 77, 208 (resentment and deal breaking); Seron, *The Business of Practicing Law* (divorce), 107–13; Austin Sarat, "Lawyers and Clients: Putting Professional Service on the Agenda of Legal Education," *Journal of Legal Education* 41 (1991): 43, 46

(divorce); Randy Bellows, "Notes of a Public Defender," in *The Social Responsibility of Lawyers,* ed. Philip B. Heymann and Lance Liebman (Westbury, N.Y.: Foundation Press, 1988), 69, 78–99 (criminal).

13. Deborah L. Arron, *Running from the Law* (Seattle: Niche Press, 1989), 10; ABA, report of At the Breaking Point, a national conference on the emerging crisis in the quality of lawyers' health and lives, Airlie House, Airlie, Va., April 5–6, 1991, 4; Sherri Kimmel, "Alone and on Your Own: The Growing Allure of Solo Practice," *Pennsylvania Lawyer* 19 (1997): 12 ; Van Hoy, *Franchise Law Firms,* 21, 131.

14. Nancy Dart and Marilyn Tucker, "Workaholic Lawyers," *Washington Lawyer,* January/February 1998, 36, 39; Seron, *The Business of Practicing Law,* 124. For delivery rooms, see Meredith K. Wadman, "Family and Work," *Washington Lawyer,* November/December 1998, 28; Cameron Stracher, *Double Billing* (New York: William Morrow, 1998), 32, 42.

15. Tom Wells, "The Technological Arms Race, *Washington Lawyer,* March/April 1997; Charles Ogletree, "Beyond Justification: Seeking Motivations to Sustain Public Defenders, *Harvard Law Review* 106 (1993): 1239, 1240; Boston Bar Association, Task Force on Professional Fulfillment, *Expectations, Reality, and Recommendations for Change* (Boston: Boston Bar Association, 1997), 2, 15.

16. Clara N. Carson, *The Lawyer Statistical Report* (Chicago: American Bar Foundation, 1999), 1; John E. Morris, "Five Questions to Ask Yourself Between Crises," *American Lawyer,* June 1996, 5; Richard A. Posner, *Overcoming Law* (Cambridge: Harvard University Press, 1995), 65. For under- and unemployed, see National Association of Law Placement (NALP), *Class of 1995: Employment Report and Salary Survey* (Washington, D.C.: NALP, 1996), 14.

17. Jill Schachner Chanen, "A Wake-up Call," *ABA Journal,* June 1997, 68–72; Ward Bowman, "Law Firm Economics and Professionalism," *Dickenson Law Review* 100 (1996): 515, 520–22.

18. Anthony T. Kronman, *The Lost Lawyer* (Cambridge: Harvard University Press, 1993), 277; California State Bar, Commission on the Future of the Legal Profession and the State Bar of California, *Final Report* (San Francisco: State Bar of California 1995), 53; Dale H. Seamans, "In 1996, Big Firms Must be 'Lean and Mean,'" *Massachusetts Lawyer Weekly,* March 11, 1996, B3.

19. Cartoon by Robert Weber, *New Yorker,* June 6, 1998, 5.

20. Bureau of the Census, *Census of Population and Housing* (Washington, D.C.: Bureau of the Census, 1992) (http://igovinfo.library.orst.edu/stateis); Patrick Schlitz, "On Being a Happy, Healthy and Ethical Member of an Unhappy, Unhealthy, and Unethical Profession," *Vanderbilt Law Review* 58 (1999): 871, 881–89; Boston Bar Association, *Expectations, Reality, and Recommendations,* 4.

21. Myers and Diener, "Who is Happy?" 12–13; Juliet B. Schor, *The Overspent American* (New York: Basic Books, 1998), 7; Frank, *Luxury Fever,* 72, 112–13.

22. Schor, *The Overspent American,* 7; Mike Papantonio, "Legal Egos on the Loose," *ABA Journal,* September 1999, 108; see generally Frank, *Luxury Fever.*

23. Schor, *The Overspent American,* 12, 145; Susan Orenstein, "Down and Out on $100,000," *American Lawyer,* October 1998; Michael D. Goldhaber, "Greedy Associates Envy I-Bankers," *National Law Journal,* December 21, 1998, A17; Stracher, *Double Billing,* 28, 74;

Denis Diderot, "Regrets on Parting with My Old Dressing Gown," in *Rameau's Nephew*, trans. Jacques Barzun and Ralph H. Bowen (New York: Bobbs-Merrill, 1964), 311.

24. Lane, "Does Money Buy Happiness?" 61, 63; Frank, *Luxury Fever*; Keates, *Proceed with Caution*, 126; Jim Shroder, "Midlevels' Money and Myths," *American Lawyer*, October 1999, 67.

25. Robert H. Frank and Philip J. Cook, *The Winner-Take-All Society* (New York: Free Press, 1995), 41, 66; Keates, *Proceed with Caution*, 144; Schor, *The Overspent American*, 5–12; Steven Brill, "'Ruining' the Profession," *American Lawyer*, July/August 1996, 5; David Leonhardt, "I Am Lawyer, Hear Me Whine," *New York Times*, February 6, 2000, E2; Karen Hall and P. Hann Livingston, "Perking Up," *American Lawyer*, February 2000, 60; Papantonio, "Legal Egos," 108; Debra Baker, "Show Me the Money.Com," *ABA Journal*, June 2000, 20.

26. Marc Galanter and Thomas Palay, *Tournament of Lawyers* (Chicago: University of Chicago Press, 1991), 128–29; Trotter, *Profit and the Practice of Law*, 136.

27. Galanter and Palay, *Tournament of Lawyers*, 94–100; Seron, *The Business of Practicing Law*, 12; Carl T. Bogus, "The Death of an Honorable Profession," *Indiana Law Journal* 71 (1996): 911, 923.

28. Galanter and Palay, *Tournament of Lawyers*, 103–7 ; Seron, *The Business of Practicing Law*, 71; Carson, *The Lawyer Statistical Report*, 8; Van Hoy, *Franchise Law Firms*, 90–108.

29. Jim Schroeder, "Slowing the Revolving Door," *American Lawyer*, October 1998, S7.

30. Larry Fox, "Money Didn't Buy Happiness," *Dickenson Law Review* 100 (1996): 531, 535; Jill Schachner Chanen, "A Wake-up Call," *ABA Journal*, June 1997, 68–70; David B. Wilkins and G. Mitu Gulati, "Reconceiving the 'Tournament of Lawyers': Tracking, Secrets, and Information Control in Internal Labor Markets of Elite Firms," *Virginia Law Review* 84 (1998): 1581, 1663; Chris Klein, "Big Firm Partners: Profession Sinking," *National Law Journal*, May 26, 1997.

31. See studies cited in Schlitz, "On Being a Happy Member," 888–95.

32. Cynthia Fuchs Epstein, Carroll Seron, Bonnie Oglensky, and Robert Saute, *The Part-Time Paradox: Time Norms, Professional Lives, Family, and Gender* (New York: Routledge, 1998), 14–25; Renee M. Landers, James B. Ribtzer, and Lowell J. Taylor, "Rat Race Redux: Adverse Selection in the Determination of Work Hours," *American Economic Review* 86 (1996): 329.

33. John E. Morris, "The New Seller's Market," *American Lawyer*, October 1996, 7; Bachman, *Law v. Life*, 106; Boston Bar; Boston Bar Association Task Force, *Facing the Grail: Confronting the Cost of Work-Family Imbalance* (Boston: Boston Bar Association, 1999), 12, 14.

34. Renee M. Landers, James B. Rebitzer, and Lowell J. Taylor, "Rat Race Redux: The Adverse Selection in the Determination of Work Hours in Law Firms," *American Economic Review* 86 (1996): 329.

35. ABA, *Model Rules of Professional Conduct*, Rule 6.1; Carroll Seron, *The Business of Practicing Law*, 129–35 (Philadelphia: Temple University Press, 1996); sources cited in Deborah L. Rhode, "Cultures of Commitment: Pro Bono for Lawyers and Law Students," *Fordham Law Review* 67 (1999). For inadequacies among firms and corporate law departments, see David E. Rovella, "Can the Bar Fill the LSC's Shoes?" *National Law Journal*, August 5, 1996, A1; Harvey Berkman, "Past Struggles Echo as Clinton Makes a Pitch for Pro Bono Work," *National Law Journal*, August 2, 1999, A8.

36. Donald W. Hoagland, "Community Service Makes Better Lawyers," in *The Law Firm and the Public Good*, ed. Robert A. Katzmann (Washington, D.C.: Brookings Institution, 1995), 104, 109; ABA, Young Lawyers Division Survey, *Career Satisfaction* (Chicago: ABA, 1995), 11.

37. Fleming, *Lawyers, Money, and Success* (Westport, Conn.: Quorum, 1997), 94; Joel F. Henning, *Maximizing Law Firm Profitability* (New York: Law Journal Seminars Press, 1997), secs. 1.06–1.08; Wilkins and Gulati, "Reconceiving the 'Tournament of Lawyers,'" 138; National Association for Law Placement Foundation, *Keeping the Keepers: Strategies for Associate Retention in Times of Attrition* (Washington, D.C.: National Association for Law Placement Foundation, 1998), 53–57; Debra Baker, "Cash-and-Carry Associates," *ABA Journal*, May 1999, 41; "Waging a War of Attrition," *National Law Journal*, December 13, 1999, 1; Boston Bar Association Task Force, *Facing the Grail*, 17.

38. "Los Angeles County Bar Association Report on Sexual Orientation Bias," *Southern California Review of Law and Women's Studies* (1995): 295, 305.

39. ABA Commission on Women in the Profession, *Unfinished Business: Overcoming the Sisyphus Factor* (Chicago: ABA, 1995); Douglas McCallum, "Taking It to the Street," *American Lawyer*, March 1999, 125; Deborah L. Rhode, "Myths of Meritocracy," *Fordham Law Review* 65 (1996): 585, 587; interview, Richard White, Association of American Law Schools, July 13, 1999; Melody Patterson, "Her Partners Call Her Ms. Chairman," *New York Times*, October 9, 1999, B1; ABA Commission on Opportunities for Minorities in the Profession, *Miles to Go: Progress of Minorities in the Legal Profession* (Chicago: ABA, 1999); David B. Wilkins and G. Mitu Gulati, "Why Are There So Few Black Lawyers in Corporate Law Firms? An Institutional Analysis," *California Law Review* 94 (1996): 501, 570; Darryl Van Duch, "Minority GCs Are Few, Far Between," *National Law Journal*, October 18, 1999, 1; "Study Shows Inequalities in Pay, Partnership," *San Francisco Daily Journal*, August 25, 1998, 31; Kathleen E. Hull and Robert L. Nelson, "Divergent Patterns: Gender Differences in the Careers of Urban Lawyers," *Researching Law* 10 (1999): 1, 5; California Bar Association, *Report and Recommendations Regarding Sexual Orientation, Discrimination in the California Legal Profession* (San Francisco: California Bar Association, 1996), 2.

40. State Bar of Texas Gender Bias Task Force of Texas, *Final Report* (1994), 20, 25; Diane F. Norwood and Arlette Molina, "Sex Discrimination in the Profession," *Texas Bar Journal*, January 1992, 50, 51; Bar Association of San Francisco Committee on Minority Employment, *Interim Report on Goals and Timetables for Minority Hiring and Advancement* (San Francisco: San Francisco Bar Association, 2000), 18–19.

41. Rhode, "Myths" 586; Arthur S. Hayes, "Color-Coded Hurdle," *ABA Journal*, February 1999, 56; National Association for Law Placement Foundation for Research and Education, *Perceptions of Partnership: The Allure and Accesssibility of the Glass Ring* (Washington, D.C.: National Association for Law Placement, 1999), 33.

42. Judith Lichtenberg, "Racism in the Head, Racism in the World," *Report from the Institution for Philosophy and Public Policy* 12 (1992): 1; Multicultural Women Attorneys Network of the ABA, *The Burdens of Both, the Privileges of Neither* (Chicago: ABA, 1994) [hereinafter Multicultural Women Attorneys Network]; San Francisco Bar, *Interim Report*, 18–19.

43. Jacob Herring, *The Everyday Realities of Minority Professional Life in the Majority Workplace*, quoted in San Francisco Bar, *Interim Report*, 28; Wilkins and Gulati, "Why Are There So Few Black Lawyers?" 557, 571; Michael Fix and Raymond J. Struyk, eds., *Clear and Convincing Evidence: Measurement of Discrimination in America* (Washington, D.C.: Urban Institute Press, 1993); Kathleen E. Hall and Robert L. Nelson, "Gender Inequality in Law: Problems of Structure and Agency in Recent Studies of Gender in Anglo-American Legal Professions," *Law and Social*

Inquiry 23 (1998): 688–91; NALP, *Perceptions of Partnership,* 37; David A. Thomas and Karen L. Proudford, "Making Sense of Race Relations in Organizations," in *Addressing Cultural Issues in Organizations: Theory for Practice,* ed. Robert T. Carter (Los Angeles: Sage, 2000).

44. Cameron Strather, "All Aboard the Mommy Track," *American Lawyer,* March 1991, 126; Rhode, "Myths," 592–93; Boston Bar Association Task Force, *Facing the Grail,* 17. Meredith K. Wadman, "Family and Work," *Washington Lawyer,* November/December 1998, 33; NALP, *Perceptions of Partnership,* 99; Cynthia Fuchs Epstein et al., "Glass Ceilings," 291, 391–99.

45. Epstein, "Glass Ceilings," 409; Rhode, "Myths," 592; Boston Bar Association Task Force, *Facing the Grail,* 17.

46. Federal Glass Ceiling Commission, *Good for Business: Making Full Use of the Nation's Human Capital* (Washington, D.C.: Government Printing Office, 1995), 26–28, 64–72, 93–96 104–6, 123–25; NALP, *Perceptions of Partnership,* 37, 93; Melvin Lerner, *The Belief in a Just World* (New York: Plenum, 1980), vii–viii.

47. Lichtenberg, "Racism"; Judith Lorber, *Paradoxes of Gender* (New Haven: Yale University Press, 1994), 237–38; Federal Glass Ceiling Commission, 552; NALP, *Perceptions of Partnership,* 54–58.

48. Epstein, "Glass Ceilings," 343–46; ABA Commission on Minorities, *Miles to Go,* 6–7, 14–15; Committee on Minority Employment, *Goals,* 17, 25; William B. Rubenstein, "Queer Studies II: Some Reflections on the Study of Sexual Orientation Bias in the Legal Practice," *UCLA Women's Law Journal* (1998): 379, 394; Wilkins and Gulati, "Why Are There So Few Black Lawyers?" 570; David Wilkins, "Do Clients Have Ethical Obligations to Lawyers? Some Lessons from the Diversity Wars," *Georgetown Journal of Legal Ethics* 11 (1998): 855, 863; Thomas and Proudford, "Making Sense of Race"; NALP, *Perceptions of Partnership.*

49. ABA Commission on the Status of Women, "Green Pastures," *Perspectives,* summer 1995, 3; Association of the Bar for the City of New York, Committee on Lesbians and Gay Men in the Legal Profession, "Report of Findings from the Survey on Barriers and Opportunities Related to Sexual Orientation," *Record* 51 (1996): 130; Los Angeles County Bar, "Report on Sexual Orientation," 355; Thomas and Proudford, "Making Sense of Race Relations; Paul M. Barrett, *The Good Black* (New York: Dutton, 1998), 59.

50. Barrett, *The Good Black,* 42–48, 97–104.

51. Barrett, *The Good Black,* 280; David Wilkins, "On Being Good and Black," *Harvard Law Review* 112 (1999): 1924; Walter Lagrande, "Getting There, Staying There," *ABA Journal,* February 1999, 54.

52. ABA Commission on Minorities, *Miles to Go,* 5–8; San Francisco Bar, *Interim Report,* 48.

53. Harry Frankfurt, "The Importance of What We Care About," *Synthesis* 53 (1982): 257, 262; Krieger, "What We're Not Telling Law Students," 2–12.

54. J. P. Ogilvie, Leah Wetheimer, and Lisa F. Lerman, *Learning from Practice* (Eagan, Minn.: West Group, 1998), 239–40; Myers, *Pursuit of Happiness,* 133; National Association for Law Placement Foundation, *Keeping the Keepers;* Henning, *Maximizing Law Firm Profitability,* §§ 1.08 and 1.17; Boston Bar Association Task Force, *Facing the Grail,* 13.

55. For a fuller discussion, see Rhode, "Cultures of Commitment," 2421–25.

56. NALP, *Perceptions of Partnership,* 38, 44; Boston Bar Association Task Force, *Facing the Grail,* 24–25.

57. Rubenstein, "Sexual Orientation Bias," 394–96; Stephanie Francis Cahill and Pearl J. Platt,

"Bringing Diversity to Partnerships Continues to Be an Elusive Goal," *San Francisco Daily Journal,* July 28, 1997, 1, 2.

58. ABA, *Promoting Professionalism* (Chicago: ABA, 1998), 61–62; ABA Commission on Minorities, *Miles to Go,* 15; Wilkins, "Do Clients Have Ethical Obligations?" 864–65; Cahill and Platt, "Diversity," 2; Lawyers for One American, *Action is the Difference We Make* (San Francisco: Lawyers for One America, 2000).

59. Ritchenya A. Shepherd, "ABA Position May Boost Solos and Small Firms," *New York Law Journal,* June 14, 1999, 1; James H. Johnston, "Old-Fashioned Bars Should Support Solos," *Texas Lawyer,* June 28, 1999, 42.

3. THE ADVOCATE'S ROLE IN THE ADVERSARY SYSTEM

1. Roscoe Pound–American Trial Lawyers Foundation, *The American Lawyer's Code of Conduct* (Washington, D.C.: American Trial Lawyers' Foundation, 1981), 202.

2. David Hoffman, "Resolutions in Regard to Professional Deportment," in *A Course of Legal Study,* 2d ed. (Baltimore: J. Neal, 1836), 755; George Sharswood, *An Essay on Professional Ethics,* 3d ed. (Philadelphia: T. & J. W. Johnson, 1869), 84–85.

3. American Bar Association, Model Rules of Professional Conduct, Rule 1.2, and Comment.

4. ABA, Model Code of Professional Responsibility, EC 2-27, EC 7-9; Model Rules Commentary 1.2; Model Rules, Rule 1.2; Model Code, DR 7-101; Model Rule 13; Model Rules, Rule 1.6; Selected State Variations, in Stephen Gillers and Roy P. Simon, eds. *Regulation of Lawyers: Statutory Supplement* (New York: Aspen Law and Business, 1998), 74–78.

5. Erving Goffman, *Encounters* (Indianapolis: Bobbs-Merrill, 1961), 105–10, 132–52.

6. David Luban, *Lawyers and Justice: An Ethical Study* (Princeton: Princeton University Press, 1988).

7. American Bar Association and Association of American Law Schools, *Report of the Joint Conference on Professional Responsibility,* reprinted in *ABA Journal* 44 (1958): 1161; Robert J. Kutak, "The Adversary System and the Practice of Law," in *The Good Lawyer: Lawyers' Roles and Lawyers' Ethics,* ed. David Luban (Totowa, N.J.: Rowman and Allanheld, 1983), 172, 174.

8. Kutak, "The Adversary System," 174; Stephen L. Pepper, "The Lawyer's Amoral Ethical Role: A Defense, a Problem, and Some Possibilities," *American Bar Foundation Research Journal* (1986): 613, 617 (oligarchy); Samuel Bowles, quoted in Michael Schudson, "Public, Private, and Professional Lives: The Correspondence of David Field and Samuel Bowles," *American Journal of Legal History* 21 (1977): 191, 199. See sources cited in Deborah L. Rhode, "Ethical Perspectives on Legal Practice," *Stanford Law Review* 37 (1985): 589, 621.

9. See Jerold Auerbach, *Unequal Justice: Lawyers and Social Change in Modern America* (New York: Oxford University Press, 1976), 254; Richard Kluger, *Simple Justice* (New York: Knopf, 1976).

10. Ma Rongjie, quoted in Monroe Freedman, "Our Constitutionalized Adversary System," *Chapman Law Review* 1 (1998): 57, 59. See John Kaplan, Jerome H. Skolnick, and Malcolm M. Feeley, eds., *Criminal Justice: Introductory Cases and Materials,* 5th ed. (Westbury, N.Y.: Foundation Press, 1991), 323–24.

11. For American examples, see Dan T. Carter, *Scottsboro: A Tragedy of the American South* (Baton Rouge: Louisiana State University Press, 1969); Daniel H. Pollitt, "Counsel for the Unpopular Cause: The Hazard of Being Undone," *North Carolina Law Review* 43 (1964):

9. For racial bias, see Clem Turner, "What's The Story? An Analysis of Juror Discrimination and a Plea for Affirmative Jury Selection," *American Criminal Law Review* 34 (1996): 289; ABA, *Perceptions of the United States Justice System* (Chicago: ABA, 1999), chap. 2. For law enforcement misconduct, see Jim Dwyer, Peter Neufield, and Barry Scheck, *Actual Innocence* (New York: Doubleday, 2000), 175; Myron W. Orfield, "Deterrence, Perjury, and the Heater Factor: An Exclusionary Rule in the Chicago Criminal Courts," *University of Colorado Law Review* 67 (1996): 75; Christopher Slobogin, "Testifying: Police Perjury and What to Do about It," *University of Colorado Law Review* 67 (1996): 1037. For the conduct of the Independent Counsel, see Deborah L. Rhode, "Conflicts of Commitment: Legal Ethics in the Impeachment Proceedings," *Stanford Law Review* 52 (1999): 269, 328–42.

12. ABA, General Practice Section, "Proposed Revisions of Model Rules of Professional Conduct," *American Bar Association Materials on Model Rules of Professional Conduct* (Chicago: ABA, 1982), Item 519, 4.

13. Franklin Strier, *Reconstructing Justice* (Chicago: University of Chicago Press, 1996), 78; Marc Galanter, "Why the Haves Come Out Ahead: Speculations on the Limits of Legal Change," *Law and Society* 9 (1974): 95. For discussion of inadequate access to legal services, see chapter 5.

14. Model Rules of Professional Conduct, preamble; Abe Krash, "Professional Responsibility to Clients and the Public Interest: Is There a Conflict?" *Chicago Bar Record* 55 (1974): 31, 37. See also Stephen L. Pepper, "A Rejoinder to Professors Kaufman and Luban," *American Bar Foundation Research Journal* (1987): 657.

15. David Luban, "The Adversary System Excuse," in *The Good Lawyer: Lawyers' Roles and Lawyers' Ethics,* ed. David Luban (Totowa, N.J.: Rowman and Allanheld, 1983), 83; Marvin E. Frankel, "The Search for Truth: An Umpireal View," *University of Pennsylvania Law Review* 123 (1975): 1031, 1036.

16. See Paul Brodeur, *Outrageous Misconduct: The Asbestos Industry on Trial* (New York: Pantheon, 1985); Susan Perry and Jim Dawson, *Nightmare: Women and the Dalkon Shield* (New York: Macmillan, 1985), 208; David Margolick, "'Tobacco' Its Middle Name, Law Firm Thrives, for Now," *New York Times*, November 20, 1992, A1; *Lincoln Savings and Loan Association v. Wall,* 743 F. Supp. 901 (D.D.C. 1990).

17. David Luban, "The Lysistratian Prerogative: A Response to Stephen Pepper," *American Bar Foundation Research Journal* (1986): 637, 639. See also Joseph Raz, *The Morality of Freedom* (New York: Oxford University Press, 1986), 381.

18. John Laylin, partner at Covington and Burling, quoted in Joseph C. Goulden, *The Super-lawyers* (New York: Weybright and Tally, 1972), 52; ABA Comments, vol. 2, Rule 1.13, 24. For similar views, see the sources cited in Rhode, "Ethical Perspectives," 620.

19. Felix Frankfurter, quoted in Auerbach, *Unequal Justice*, 254; Pollitt, "Counsel for the Unpopular Cause"; Rhode, "Ethical Perspectives," 630; Ted Schneyer, "Moral Philosophy's Standard Misconception of Legal Ethics," *Wisconsin Law Review* (1984): 1529, 1545; cases cited in Deborah L. Rhode, *Professional Responsibility: Ethics by the Pervasive Method* (New York: Aspen, 1998), 26.

20. ECS 2-29, 2-30, 7-8; DR 2-110; Model Rules 1.2, 6.2; DR 2-110; EC 7-8; EC 2-30; Model Rule 6.2; and Commentary. See sources cited in Rhode, *Professional Responsibility*, 26.

21. Karl N. Llewellyn, *The Bramble Bush* (New York: Oceana, 1951) 150; Jack Hitt, "Who Will Do Abortions Here?" *New York Times Magazine*, January 18, 1998, 20.

22. See the Washington lawyers quoted in Goulden, *The Super-lawyers*, 132, and in Richard Zitrin and Carol M. Langford, *The Moral Compass of the American Lawyer* (New York: Ballantine, 1999), 155.

23. John Basten, "Control and the Lawyer-Client Relationship," *Journal of the Legal Profession* 6 (1981): 7, 34.

24. For general discussion of individual strategies for reducing conflict, Leon Festinger, *A Theory of Cognitive Dissonance* (Evanston, Ill.: Row, Peterson, 1957), 128–34; Eliot Aronson, *The Social Animal*, 6th ed. (New York: W. H. Freeman, 1992), 202–3.

25. ABA, *Perceptions of the U.S. Justice System*, 66; Report of the Commission to Review the Criminal Justice Act, reprinted in *Criminal Law Reporter* 52 (March 10, 1993): 2265, 2284–85. The phrase about justice in the halls is commonly attributed to Lenny Bruce.

26. Chester Mersky, "Quality Legal Aid: Going, Going, Gone," *National Law Journal*, December 4, 1995, A19; Alan Bellow, "Requiem for a Public Defender," *The American Prospect*, June 5, 2000, 28; Stephen B. Bright, "Keep the Dream Alive," excerpted in *Yale Law School Report*, fall 1999, 22.

27. For private practitioners, see Dwyer, Neufield, and Scheck, *Actual Innocence*, 204; David Cole, *No Equal Justice* (New York: New Press, 1999), 83–85; Marcia Coyle, "Hoping for $75 an Hour," *National Law Journal*, June 7, 1999, 1, 18: Bob Herbert, "Cheap Justice," *New York Times*, March 3, 1998, 15. For public defenders, see Cole, *No Equal Justice*, 83; Stephen B. Bright, "Counsel for the Poor: The Death Sentence Not for the Worst Crime but for the Worst Lawyer," *Yale Law Journal* 103 (1994): 1835, 1850–54; J. Michael McWilliams, "The Erosion of Indigent Rights: Excessive Caseloads Resulting in Ineffective Counsel for Poor," *ABA Journal*, March 1993, 8. For the Missouri state senator, see Ron Ostroff, "Missouri Remains Unable to Pay Indigents Counsel," *National Law Journal*, May 11, 1981, 2.

28. Stephen J. Schulhofer, "Plea Bargaining as Disaster," *Yale Law Journal* 101 (1992): 1979, 1988; Kenneth B. Mann, "The Trial as Text: Allegory, Myth, and Symbol in the Adversarial Criminal Process: A Critique of the Role of Public Defender and a Proposal for Reform," *American Criminal Law Review* 32 (1995): 743, 803–12; Paul Craig Roberts and Lawrence M. Stratton, *The Tyranny of Good Intentions* (Roseville, CA: Prima Publishing, 2000), 88.

29. McWilliams, "Erosion of Individual Rights," 219, 224; Schulhofer, "Plea Bargaining," 1990–92; Robert E. Scott and William J. Stuntz, "Plea Bargaining as Contract," *Yale Law Journal* 101 (1992): 1909, 1959; Roberts and Stratton, *Tyranny*, 89.

30. Cole, *No Equal Justice*, 87; Bright, "Keep the Dream Alive;" Stephen J. Schulhofer, "Effective Assistance on the Assembly Line," *New York University Review of Law and Social Change* 14 (1986): 137; Scott and Stuntz, "Plea Bargaining," 1957–58; Bruce A. Green, "Lethal Fiction: The Meaning of 'Counsel' in the Sixth Amendment," *Iowa Law Review* 78 (1993): 433, 499–501; Victor E. Flango and Patricia McKenna, "Federal Habeas Corpus Review of State Court Convictions," *California Western Law Review* 31 (1995): 237, 259–60.

31. *McFarland v. State*, 928 S.W. 2d 482, 505 n. 20 (Tex. 1996); Herbert, "Cheap Justice," 15; Bruce Shapiro, "Sleeping Lawyer Syndrome," *Nation*, April 7, 1997, 27–29 (quoting Judge Doug Shaver); *Tippins v. Walker*, 77 F.2d 682, 687 (2d Cir. 1996); *Burdine v. Texas*, 66 F. Supp. 854 (S.D. Tex. 1999).

32. Fox Butterfield, "Death Sentence Being Overturned in 2 of 3 Appeals," *New York Times*, June 12, 1, 21; Margaret L. Steiner, "Adequacy of Fact Investigation in Criminal Lawyer's

Trial Preparation," *Arizona State Law Journal* (1981): 523, 538; Mike McConville and Chester Mirsky, "Guilty Plea Courts: A Social Disciplinary Model of Criminal Justice," *Social Problems* 42 (1995): 216; William A. Mintz, "Lawyer Wouldn't Go to 'Sleazy Bar,' Client Wins Freedom from Life Term," *National Law Journal*, November 24, 1980, 7; Bright, "Keep the Dream Alive."

33. Donald D. Landon, *Country Lawyers: The Impact of Context on Professional Practice* (New York: Praeger, 1990); 136, 142; Richard Abel, "Revisioning Lawyers," in *Lawyers in Society: An Overview*, ed. Richard Abel and Philip Lewis (Berkeley: University of California Press, 1995), 6; Karen Winner, *Divorced from Justice* (New York: HarperCollins/Regan Books, 1996); Paul E. Lee and Mary M. Lee, "Reflections from the Bottom of the Wall: Racial Bias in the Provision of Legal Services to the Poor," *Clearinghouse Review* 27 (1993): 311.

34. See sources cited in Deborah L. Rhode, "Institutionalizing Ethics," *Case Western Reserve Law Review* 44 (1993): 665, 715–17; letter to the Standing Committee on Ethics and Professional Responsibility, reprinted in *Fordham Law Review* 65 (1996): 229; Lester Brickman, "Contingency Fee Abuses, Ethical Mandates, and the Disciplinary System: The Case Against Case-by-Case Enforcement," *Washington and Lee Law Review* 53 (1996): 1339; Rhode, *Professional Responsibility*, 803.

35. Richard Wasserstrom, "Lawyers as Professionals: Some Moral Questions," *Human Rights* 5 (1975): 1, 9.

36. Wasserstrom, "Lawyers as Professionals," 9; Gerald Postema, "Moral Responsibility in Professional Ethics," *New York University Law Review* 55 (1980): 63; Donald Nicolson and Julian Webb, *Professional Legal Ethics: Critical Interrogations* (New York: Oxford University Press, 1999), 176.

37. Robert Gordon, "The Independence of Lawyers," *Boston University Law Review* 68 (1988): 1, 26–28, 71–74, 78.

38. See lawyers quoted in Rhode, *Professional Responsibility*, 682; Raoul Felder, *Divorce* (New York: World, 1971), 2–7. For the costs of partisanship, see Standards 2.27 and 3.6 of the Standards of Conduct of the American Academy of Matrimonial Lawyers (1992).

39. Gordon, "The Independence of Lawyers," 72.

40. ABA and AALS, *Report of the Joint Conference*, 1159; Robert Gordon, "Why Lawyers Can't Just Be Hired Guns," in *Ethics in Practice*, ed. Deborah L. Rhode (New York: Oxford University Press, 2000), 42.

41. For objections, see Krash, "Professional Responsibility," 33–34, 37; Alan Donagan, "Justifying Legal Practice in the Adversary System," in *The Good Lawyer: Lawyer's Roles and Lawyers' Ethics*, ed. David Luban (Totowa, N.J.: Rowman and Allanheld, 1983), 123, 132; Rhode, "Ethical Perspectives," 620. For responses, see William H. Simon, *The Practice of Justice* (Cambridge: Harvard University Press, 1998), 2; William H. Simon, "Ethical Discretion in Lawyering," *Harvard Law Review* 101 (1988): 1083.

42. Clarence Darrow, quoted in John Basten, "Control and the Lawyer Client Relationship," *Journal of the Legal Profession* 6 (1981): 15.

43. Thomas D. Morgan and Robert W. Tuttle, "Legal Representation in a Pluralist Society," *George Washington Law Review* 63 (1995): 984, 997; Goulden, *The Superlawyers*, 561–62; sources cited in Rhode, "Ethical Perspectives," 620.

44. Marvin Frankel, "The Search for Truth," 1031, 1056; Geoffrey C. Hazard Jr., *Ethics in the Practice of Law* (New Haven: Yale University Press, 1978), 145.

45. Donald Langevoort, "Where Were the Lawyers? A Behavioral Inquiry into Lawyers' Responsibility for Clients' Fraud," *Vanderbilt Law Review* 46 (1993): 75, 98–99; Robert Nelson, "Ideology, Practice, and Professional Autonomy: Social Values and Client Relationships in the Large Law Firm," *Stanford Law Review* 37 (1985): 503, 535–37. As chapter 1 notes, less than a fifth of attorneys feel law has lived up to their expectations concerning justice. ABA, Young Lawyers Division, *Survey: Career Satisfaction* (Chicago: ABA, 1995), 11.

46. Hoffman, "Resolutions in Regard to Professional Deportment," 754–55; Sharswood, *Essay on Professional Ethics,* 26–35, 42; David Margolick, "Like Sex Acts, Lawyer's Job Is a Matter of Definition," *New York Times,* September 26, 1998, B7; William Safire, "Kill the Lawyers," *New York Times,* December 7, 1998, 27; Maureen Dowd, "Power of Attorney," *New York Times,* September 20, 1998, E5.

47. Simon, *The Practice of Justice,* 33; Luban, *Lawyers and Justice,* 47–48.

48. Model Rule 1.2 requires that lawyers "abide by a client's decision concerning the objectives of representation and . . . consult with the client as to the means by which they are to be pursued."

49. Kenneth Starr, remarks before the Mecklenburg Bar Foundation, June 1, 1998; Harry I. Subin, " The Criminal Defense Lawyer's 'Different Mission': Reflections on the 'Right' to Present a False Case," *Georgetown Journal of Legal Ethics* 1 (1987): 125, 148; William Simon, "The Ethics of Criminal Defense," *Michigan Law Review* 91 (1993): 1703.

50. See the research summarized in David Luban, "Are Criminal Defenders Different?" *Michigan Law Review* 91 (1993): 1729.

51. John Monahan and Henry J. Steadman, *Violence and Mental Disorder: Developments in Risk Assessment* (Chicago: University of Chicago Press, 1994); John B. Mitchell, "The Ethics of the Criminal Defense Attorney: New Answers to Old Questions," *Stanford Law Review* 37 (1980): 293, 332–33; Barbara Allen Babcock, "Defending the Guilty," *Cleveland State Law Review* 32 (1983): 175, 177–78.

52. Rhode, "Conflicts of Commitment," 331–41.

53. *United States v. DeCoster,* 624 F.2d 196, 264 (D.C. Cir. 1979)(en banc)(Bazelon, J., dissenting); David E. Rovella, "Unclogging Gideon's Trumpet," *National Law Journal,* January 20, 2000, A1.

54. Hazard, *Ethics in the Practice of Law,* 144.

55. Jules Feiffer, quoted in Anthony Lukas, "The ACLU Against Itself," *New York Times Magazine,* July 9, 1978, 9; "The High Cost of Free Speech," *Time,* June 26, 1978, 63 (paraphrasing William Kunstler).

56. David B. Wilkins, "Race, Ethics, and the First Amendment: Should a Black Lawyer Represent the Ku Klux Klan?" *George Washington Law Review* 63 (1995): 1030; Sue Anne Presley, "Klan Leader and NAACP Counsel Make an Odd Couple on Civil Rights," *Washington Post,* September 29, 1993, A3.

57. Luban, *Lawyers and Justice,* 161; Wilkins, "Race, Ethics, and the First Amendment."

58. Justice M. Steinbrink, "Testimony before the New York Legislative Committee on Matrimonial and Family Law," *New York Herald Tribune,* October 1, 1965, A19.

59. See sources cited in Deborah L. Rhode, *Speaking of Sex: The Denial of Gender Equality* (Cambridge: Harvard University Press, 1997), 199; Ruth Sidel, *Keeping Women and Children Last* (New York: Penguin, 1996), 88; Jason de Parle, "Learning Poverty Firsthand," *New York Magazine,* April 27, 1997, 32.

60. Simon, "Ethical Discretion in Lawyering," 1116; Andrew Kaufman, "Book Review

of Alan Goldman, *The Moral Foundations of Professional Ethics*," *Harvard Law Review* 94 (1981): 1504, 1514; Geoffrey C. Hazard Jr., "Panel Discussion: Professional Responsibility and Professional Conduct," *University of Miami Law Review* 35 (1981): 639, 654.

61. Lawyers who receive funding from the federal Legal Services Corporation may not assist political activities and may not engage, or encourage others to engage, in public demonstrations, boycotts, or other related activities. 42 U.S.C. § 2996e (1997). Nor may they engage in welfare reform lobbying. Omnibus Consolidated Recessions and Appropriation Act of 1996, Public Law No. 104-134, Section 504(16).

62. William Kunstler, quoted in Wilkins, "Race, Ethics, and the First Amendment," 1036n. 34.

63. William Herndon and Jesse Weik, *Herndon's Lincoln* (Chicago: Belford Charter, 1989), 2n. 345.

4. AMERICA'S SPORTING THEORY OF JUSTICE

1. S. F. C. Milsom, *Historical Foundations of the Common Law* (London: Buttersworth, 1969), 28; Marion Neef and Stuart Nagel, "The Adversary Nature of the American Legal System: A Historical Perspective," in *Lawyers' Ethics*, ed. Allan Gerson (New Brunswick, N.J.: Transaction Books, 1980).

2. Roscoe Pound, "The Causes of Popular Dissatisfaction with the Administration of Justice," *American Bar Association Report* 29 (1906): 395; Donald Nicolson and Julian Webb, *Professional Legal Ethics: Critical Interrogations* (New York: Oxford University Press, 1999), 161. surveys cited in chapter 1.

3. Oscar Wilde, quoted in Jonathan and Andrew Roth, *Poetic Justice* (Berkeley, Calif.: Nolo Press, 1988), 88; Evelle J. Younger, quoted in Brian Nash and Allan Zuto, *Lawyer's Wit and Wisdom* (Philadelphia: Running Press, 1995), 189.

4. N. Lee Cooper, "Courtesy Call," *ABA Journal,* March 1997, 8; ABA, *Promoting Professionalism* (Chicago: ABA, 1998), 66.

5. John Marks, "The American Uncivil War," *U.S. News and World Report,* April 22, 1996, 66; Virginia Bar Section on Litigation, "Principles of Professional Courtesy," *Virginia Lawyer,* July, 1989, 29.

6. Frank F. Flegal, "Discovery Abuse: Causes, Effects, and Reform," *Review of Litigation* 3 (1982): 21, 22; Austin Sarat, "Ethics in Litigation," in *Ethics in Practice,* ed. Deborah L. Rhode (New York: Oxford University Press, 2000); Robert F. Nagel, "Lies and Law," *Harvard Journal of Law and Public Policy* 22 (1999): 605n. 1; Mark A. Cohen, "Courts Cracking Down on Discovery Abuse by Attorneys," *Massachusetts Lawyers Weekly,* September 2, 1996; Peter Pringle, *Cornered: Big Tobacco at the Bar of Justice* (New York: Henry Holt, 1998), 5, 153; Nicolson and Webb, *Professional Legal Ethics,* 171–91.

7. John S. Beckerman, "Confronting Civil Discovery's Fatal Flaws," *Minnesota Law Review* 84 (2000): 505, 507–9; James S. Kakalik et al., *Discovery Management: Further Analysis of the Civil Justice Reform Act Evaluation Data* (Santa Monica, Calif.: RAND Institute for Civil Justice, 1998), xx, 55; Susan Keilitz, Roger Hanson, and Richard Semiatin, "Attorneys' Views of Civil Discovery," *Judges Journal* (winter 1993): 2–6, 34–35. For large cases, see Flegal, "Discovery Abuse," 23; Wayne D. Brazil, "Views from the Front Lines: Observations by Chicago Lawyers about the System of Civil Discovery," *American Bar Foundation Research Journal* (1980), 219; Sarat, "Ethics in Litigation," 150–51.

8. Sarat, "Ethics in Litigation," 54; Brazil, "Views from the Front Lines," 219; James B. Stewart, *The Partners* (New York: Simon and Schuster, 1983), 327; Steven Brill, "When a Lawyer Lies," *Esquire,* December 19, 1978, 23; *Haines v. Ligget Group, Inc.,* 814 F. Supp. 414, 421 (D.N.J. 1993) (quoting memo).

9. Laura Pappano, "The Crusade for Civility," *Boston Globe Magazine,* May 4, 1997, 39; Susan Getzendanner, quoted in "Overheard," *Newsweek,* November 18, 1991, 23.

10. Robert N. Saylor, "Rambo Litigator: Why Hardball Tactics Don't Work," *ABA Journal,* March 1988, 79; Bartlett H. McGuire, "Rambo Litigation: A Losing Proposition," *American Lawyer,* May 1996, 39–40.

11. Maurice Franks, *Winning Custody* (Englewood Cliffs, N.J.: Prentice Hall, 1983), 32, 34; Raoul Felder, *Divorce* (New York: World, 1971), 2; "Roy Cohn's Tips to Men on the Divorce Game," *People,* January 24, 1983, 17; American Academy of Matrimonial Lawyers, Standards of Conduct, Standard 2.25 (Chicago: ABA, 1992); Pauline H. Tesler, "Collaborative Law: What It Is and Why Family Law Attorneys Need to Know about It," *American Journal of Family Law* 13 (1999): 215. The term *matrimonial mafia* comes from Michael Gross, "Trouble in Splitsville," *New York Magazine,* December 13, 1999, 39.

12. Deborah L. Rhode, *Professional Responsibility: Ethics by the Pervasive Method* (Boston: Aspen, 1998), 185–95; Jerome Braunn, "Increasing SLAPP Protection," *University of California, Davis Law Review* 32 (1999): 965.

13. *Washington State Physicians Insurance and Exchange Association v. Fisons Corporation,* 858 P.2d 1054 (Wash. Sup. Ct. 1993).

14. David Boerner, Jerry McNaul, and Payton Smith, quoted in Stuart Taylor, "Sleazy in Seattle," *American Lawyer,* April 1994, 74, 78.

15. Monroe Freedman, "Masking the Truth to Resolve Competing Duties," *Legal Times,* September 11, 1996, 22; Robert Aronson, quoted in Ralph Nader and Wesley J. Smith, *No Contest: Corporate Lawyers and the Perversion of Justice in America* (New York: Random House, 1996), 126.

16. Sarat, "Ethics in Litigation," 150; Thomas E. Willging et al., "An Empirical Study of Discovery and Disclosure Practice under the 1995 Federal Rules Amendments," *Boston College Law Review* 39 (1998): 525, 540; Brazil, "Views from the Front Line," 225.

17. Paul Brodeur, *Outrageous Misconduct: The Asbestos Industry on Trial* (New York: Pantheon Books, 1985); Susan Perry and Jim Dawson, *Nightmare: Women and the Dalkon Shield* (New York: Macmillan, 1985), 208; Ralph Nader and Wesley Smith, *No Contest,* 70–93, 194–218; Karen Donovan, "Ex-Texaco Execs Say the Lawyers Were to Blame," *National Law Journal,* March 4, 1998, A1, A24.

18. For lawyers' views, see Sarat, "Ethics in Litigation," 148–50; Willging et al., "Empirical Study," 542; Brazil, "View from the Front Lines," 245–51; and Keilitz, Hanson, and Semiatin, "Attorneys' Views," 38.

19. Federal Rules of Civil Procedure, Rule 11; Saul M. Kassin, *An Empirical Study of Rule 11 Sanctions* (Washington, D.C., Federal Judicial Center, 1985). Some but not all studies find disproportionate punishment of civil rights claims. See David Wilkins, "Who Should Regulate Lawyers?" *Harvard Law Review* 102 (1989): 799, 869.

20. Beckerman, "Confronting Civil Discovery," 584 (quoting Judge Keeton); Sarat, "Ethics in Litigation," 159; Council of the Chief Justices Committee on Professionalism and Lawyer

Competence, *A National Action Plan on Lawyer Conduct and Professionalism* (Chicago: ABA, 1998), 49.

21. The reference to contact sports is David Luban's, and the *Fisons* comment is Richard Zitrin's at ABA Annual Conference on Professional Responsibility, Montreal, May 30, 1998. See generally Charles Sorenson, "Disclosure under Federal Rule of Civil Procedure 26(a)— 'Much Ado about Nothing?'" *Hastings Law Review* 46 (1995): 679, 705–9; Brazil, "Views from the Front Lines," 246–48.

22. Peter Appleton, quoted in Craig Anderson, "State Bar Revamps Project to Encourage Reporting of Nasty Lawyers," *San Francisco Daily Journal,* October 10, 1997, 1; Shawn Collins, "Be Civil? I'm a Litigator," *National Law Journal,* September 20, 1999, A21. For Jamail's conduct and income, see Roger E. Schechter, "Changing Law Schools to Make Less Nasty Lawyers," *Georgetown Journal of Legal Ethics* 10 (1997): 367, 379n. 43; "The Forbes 400," *Fortune,* October 13, 1997, 418.

23. Oregon State Bar Statement of Professionalism; State Bar of Arizona, A Lawyer's Creed of Professionalism; Kentucky Bar Association, Code of Professional Courtesy; Virginia State Bar, Principles of Courtesy.

24. *Sprung v. Negwer Materials,* 775 S.W. 2d 97, 109 (Mo. 1989) (Blackmore, J., dissenting).

25. John B. Harris, "Should New York Adopt a Code of Civility: No," *New York Law Journal,* August 11, 1997, 2.

26. Los Angeles Superior Court Rules, Rule 7.12; James E. Moliterno, "Lawyer Creeds and Moral Seismography," *Wake Forest Law Review* 32 (1997): 781, 797–800; Craig Anderson, "In Search of Civility," *San Francisco Daily Journal,* October 10, 1997, 19.

27. "Civility Conference Draws Record Attendance," *Professional Lawyer,* August 1996, 22.

28. ABA Discussion Draft, Rules 3.3 and 3.1; Carrie Menkel-Meadow, "The Limits of Adversarial Ethics," in *Ethics in Practice,* 123; *Brady v. Maryland,* 373 U.S. 83 (1963), ABA Model Rules, Rule 3.8, and ABA Model Code, DR 7-103(B).

29. See surveys cited in Kakalik, *Discovery Management,* 71–72; Franklin Strier, *Reconstructing Justice* (Chicago: University of Chicago Press, 1996), 213–15, 265–68. Andrew Boon and Jennifer Levin, *The Ethics and Conduct of Lawyers in England and Wales* (Oxford: Hart, 1999), 203–4 (quoting Justice Robert Walker).

30. Robert W. Gordon, "The Ethical World of Large Law Firm Litigators: Preliminary Observations," *Fordham Law Review* 67 (1998): 709, 734.

31. Jerome Shapiro, quoted in Steven Brill, "Roy Cohn Rides Again," *American Lawyer,* March 1980, 5.

32. Patrick E. Murphy, "Creating Ethical Corporate Structures," *Sloan Management Review* (winter 1989): 81; Peter A. French, Publicity and the Control of Corporate Conduct: Hester Prynne's New Image," in *Corrigible Corporations and Unruly Law,* ed. Brente Fisse and Peter French (San Antonio, Tex.: Trinity University Press, 1985), 159; Robert L. Nelson, "The Discovery Process as a Circle of Blame," *Fordham Law Review* 67 (1998): 773, 807.

33. Gordon, "The Ethical World," 729; Nelson, "The Discovery Process," 790–92.

34. ABA Model Rules, Rule 3.3; Model Code, DR 7-102. See E. Allan Lind and Tom R. Tyler, *The Social Psychology of Procedural Justice* (New York: Plenum, 1988), 115–16; Richard C. Wydick, "The Ethics of Witness Coaching," *Cardozo Law Review* 17 (1995): 1, 9; Michael Owen Miller, "Working with Memory," *Litigation,* (summer 1993): 10, 12.

35. Marvin E. Frankel, *Partisan Justice* (New York: Hill and Wang, 1980), 15.

36. Lester Brickman, "When Witnesses Are Told What to Say," *Washington Post,* January 13, 1998; Michael Higgins, "Fine Line," *ABA Journal,* May 1998, 52, 54.

37. Higgins, "Fine Line," 52–54.

38. Jane Berentson, "Integrity Test: Five of Thirteen Lawyers Fail," *American Lawyer,* May 1980, 15–18.

39. Monroe H. Freedman, "Professional Responsibility of the Criminal Defense Lawyer: The Three Hardest Questions," *Michigan Law Review* 64 (1966): 1460, 1479, 1481; "How about a Tony for Best Asbestos-Related Script?" *Wall Street Journal,* October 7, 1997, 23.

40. Monroe H. Freedman, "Counseling the Client: Refreshing Recollection or Prompting Perjury?" *Litigation* 2 (spring 1976): 35, 46.

41. John Steel, "The Ethics of Witness Preparation," unpublished paper, Palo Alto, 1996.

42. Steel, "Witness Preparation"; Higgins, "Fine Line," 58; "I Honestly Don't Recall," *American Enterprise,* May/June 1999, 34.

43. John H. Langbein, "The German Advantage in Civil Procedure," *University of Chicago Law Review* 52 (1985): 823, 824; Frankel, *Partisan Justice,* 115–17.

44. Anthony Trollope, quoted in Jerome Frank, *Courts on Trial* (Princeton: Princeton University Press, 1949), 83; Model Code DR 7-106(c); Model Rules, Rule 4.4; ABA Standards for Criminal Justice, Defense Standard 7.6(b) (Chicago: ABA, 1971); Flyer for *Cross-Examination: Evidence and Tactics* (Menlo Park: Practicing Law Institute, 1999); Irving Younger's "Ten Commandments of Cross-Examination," quoted in David Luban, *Lawyers and Justice: An Ethical Study* (Princeton: Princeton University Press, 1988), 70.

45. Rhode, *Professional Responsibility,* 659; Gary LaFree, *Rape and Criminal Justice* (Belmont, Calif.: Wadsworth, 1989): 95–107; Nicolson and Webb, *Professional Legal Ethics,* 174–75.

46. Elizabeth Kessler, "Pattern of Sexual Conduct Evidence and Present Consent: Limiting the Admissibility of Sexual History Evidence in Rape Prosecutions," *Women's Rights Law Reporter* 14 (1992): 79; Peter Laufer, *A Question of Consent* (San Francisco: Mercury House, 1994), 64–70; sources cited in Deborah L. Rhode, *Speaking of Sex* (Cambridge: Harvard University Press, 1997), 126–27; Laura Mamsnerus, "When the Job Requires a Walk on the Ethical Line," *New York Times,* May 30, 1999, E10.

47. Federal Rules of Evidence 412(b); Ellen E. Schulz and Junda Woo, "Bedroom Ploy: Plaintiffs' Sex Lives Are Being Laid Bare in Harassment Cases," *Wall Street Journal,* September 19, 1994, A1; Andrea Bernstein, "Sex Harassment Suits: The Fight for Damages Gets Uglier," *Ms.,* July–August 1996, 18–19; *Jones v. Clinton,* 990 F. Supp. 657 (E.D. Ark. 1998); Jeffrey Rosen, *The Unwanted Gaze* (New York: Random House, 2000).

48. Rhode, *Speaking of Sex,* 102–4; Bob Wilson, quoted in Patricia Yancy Marlin and R. Marlene Powell, "Accounting for the 'Second Assault': Legal Organizations' Framing of Rape Victims," *Law and Social Inquiry* 19 (1994): 853, 854; Sharon Wolf and David A. Montgomery, "Effects of Inadmissible Evidence and Level of Judicial Admonishment to Disregard on the Judgments of Most Jurors," *Journal of Applied Social Psychology* (July–September 1997): 205.

49. For the hypothetical bar rule, see Albert Alschuler, "How to Win the Trial of the Century," *McGeorge Law Review* 29 (1998): 291, 299n. 34. For attorneys' views, see Timothy Beneke, *Men on Rape* (New York: St. Martin's Press, 1982): 104–5; Ronald M. Green, quoted in Schulz and Woo, "Bedroom Ploy," A1. For surveys comparing lawyers and nonlawyers, see

Wes Hanson, "Lawyers, Lawyers, Lawyers," *Ethics: Easier Said than Done* (Josephson Institute newsletter), 1993, 38.

50. *Chavik v. Volkswagen of America,* 808 F.2d 639, 644 (7th Cir. 1986) (Posner, J., dissenting).

51. Federal Rule of Evidence 702, *Daubert v. Merrell Dow Pharmaceuticals,* 509 U.S. 579 (1993); *Kunho Tire Co. v. Carmelaw,* 526 U.S. 137 (1999); Peter W. Huber, *Galileo's Revenge: Junk Science in the Courtroom* (New York: Basic Books, 1991); Ralph A. Cohen, "Dallas' Unreliable Expert Witness Testimony," *For the Defense,* April 1990, 8.

52. *Daubert v. Merrell Dow Pharmaceuticals,* 509 U.S. 579 at 596; Luban, *Lawyers and Justice,* 70.

53. *Jones v. Clinton,* 990 F. Supp. 657 (E.D. Ark. 1998).

54. See George Fisher, "The O. J. Simpson Corpus," *Stanford Law Review* 49 (1997): 971, 991n. 147.

55. ABA Model Code, DR 7-109; ABA Model Rules, Rule 3.4(b); Jeffrey Parker, "Contingent Expert Witness Fees: Access and Regulation," *University of Southern California Law Review* 64 (1991): 1363, 1387.

56. Marcia Angell, *Science on Trial* (New York: Norton, 1996), 6; Patrick R. Andersen and L. Thomas Winfree Jr., eds., *Expert Witnesses: Criminologists in the Courtroom* (Albany: State University of New York Press, 1987), 4; John H. Langbein, "The German Advantage in Civil Procedure," *University of Chicago Law Review* 52 (1985): 823.

57. E. M. Forster, *Two Cheers for Democracy* (London: E. Arnold, 1951), 68; Tom Coakley, "N.M. Rapists Free 10 Years in Court Foul-Up," *Denver Post,* March 23, 1983, 12A; "OPM Leasing Services, Inc.," in *The Social Responsibilities of Lawyers,* ed. Philip B. Heymann and Lance Liebman (Westbury, N.Y.: Foundation Press, 1988), 184 ; *Spaulding v. Zimmerman,* 116 N.W. 2d 704 (Minn. 1962); Arthur Powell, "Privilege of Counsel and Confidential Communications," *Georgia Bar Journal* 6 (1964): 334, 345; *Ballau;* Nader and Smith, *No Contest,* 347 (discussing Gambrell).

58. *Balla v. Gambro Inc.,* 584 N.E. 2d 104 (Ill. Gambro, Inc., 584 N.E. 2d 104 (Ill. 1991); 1991).

59. *Spaulding v. Zimmerman,* 263 Minn. 346 (1962); Roger C. Cramton and Laurie P. Knowles, "Professional Secrecy and Its Exceptions: *Spaulding v. Zimmerman* Revisited," *Minnesota Law Review* 83 (1998): 63, 126.

60. Coakley, "Rapists," 12A.

61. Powell, "Privilege of Counsel," 345.

62. David Kaplan, "Death Row Dilemma," *National Law Journal,* January 25, 1988, 35.

63. Paul Brodeur, *Outrageous Misconduct: The Asbestos Industry on Trial* (New York: Pantheon Books, 1985); Susan Perry and Jim Dawson, *Nightmare: Women and the Dalkon Shield* (New York: Macmillan, 1985), 208; John Schwartz and Saundra Torry, "Anti-Tobacco Activists Hope to Put Industry's Legal Tactics on Trial," *Washington Post,* September 26, 1995, A8; Martin Mayer, *The Greatest-Ever Bank Robbery* (New York: Charles Scribner's Sons, 1990), 2; Keith B. Bradsher, "S. & L.'s See New Threat, This Time from Banks," *New York Times,* October 20, 1994, D6; *Lincoln Savings and Loan Association v. Wall,* 743 F. Supp. 901 (D.D.C. 1990).

64. Mayer, *The Greatest-Ever Bank Robbery,* 20, 122–23.

65. ABA, Model Rules of Professional Conduct 3.3, 1.6.

66. Model Rules 1.6, 3.3.

67. William H. Simon, "Ethical Discretion in Lawyering," *Harvard Law Review* 101 (1988): 1083, 1142.

68. Fred C. Zacharias, "Rethinking Confidentiality," *Iowa Law Review* 74 (1989): 351, 382–83; Nicolson and Webb, *Professional Legal Ethics,* 257–260. Leslie C. Levin, Testing the Radical 1 Experiment: A Study of Lawyer Response to Clients Who Intend to Harm Others, *Rutgers L. Rev.* 47 (1994): 81, 122.

69. Deborah L. Rhode, "Ethical Perspectives on Legal Practice," *Stanford Law Review* 37 (1985): 589, 614; Steven Lubet and Cathryn Stewart, "A 'Public Assets' Theory of Lawyers' Pro Bono Obligations," *University of Pennsylvania Law Review* 145 (1997): 1245, 1280–81; Richard Zitrin, "Overprivileged," *Recorder,* March 17, 1999, 5; See also Canon 41 of the ABA Canons of Professional Ethics (Chicago: ABA, 1964); *Tarasoff v. Board of Regents of the University of California,* 551 P.2d 334 (Cal. 1976) (holding that psychiatrist had duty to warn victim of patient's threat).

70. Geoffrey C. Hazard Jr. and Susan P. Koniak, *The Law and Ethics of Lawyering* (Westbury, N.Y.: Foundation Press, 1990), 279.

71. Ted Schneyer, "Professionalism as Bar Politics: The Making of the Model Rules of Professional Conduct," *Law and Social Inquiry* 14 (1989): 677, 728; Rhode, "Ethical Perspectives," 612–15; Model Rules, Rule 1.6, Comment; Sissela Bok, *Lying: Moral Choice in Public and Private Life* (New York: Pantheon, 1978), 170–72.

72. Zacharias, "Rethinking Confidentiality," 362–63; Hansen, "Lawyers, Lawyers, Lawyers," 42.

73. John Rawls, *A Theory of Justice* (Cambridge: Harvard University Press, 1971).

74. Marvin E. Frankel, "The Search for Truth: An Umpireal View," *University of Pennsylvania Law Review* 123 (1975): 1057–58.

75. James J. White, "Machiavelli and the Bar: Ethical Limitations on Lying in Negotiations," *American Bar Foundation Research Journal* (1980): 926, 937–38; Michael D. Goldhaber, "Blowing a Whistle on Client Misdeeds," *National Law Journal,* October 25, 1999, A10; Levin, "Radical Experiment," 148.

76. See Rhode, *Professional Responsibility,* 575–82; Robert D. Boyle, "A Review of Whistle-blower Protections and Suggestions for Change," *Labor Law Journal* 41 (1990): 821; Terry M. Dworkin and Eletta S. Callahan, "Internal Whistle-blowing: Protecting the Interests of the Employee, the Organization, and Society," *American Business Law Journal* 29 (1991): 267, 306–7.

77. For gatekeeper rules see Rhode, *Professional Responsibility,* 576–87; Boon and Levin, *Ethics and Conduct,* 210–11. For whistle-blowing, see *GTE Products Corp. v. Stewart,* 653 N.E. 2d 161, 166–67 (Mass. 1995): *General Dynamics Corp. v. Superior Court,* 876 P.2d 487 (Cal. 1977); Rhode, *Professional Responsibility,* 281–85; Myron P. Glazer and Penina M. Glazer, *The Whistle-blowers: Exposing Corruption in Government and Industry* (New York: Basic Books, 1989), 210. For cases imposing liability, see *Petrillo v. Bachenberg,* 655 A.2d 1354 (N.J. 1995), and *Greyeas v. Provd.,* 826 F.2d 1560 (7th Cir.), cert. denied 484 U.S. 1043 (1987); *Schatz v. Weinberg and Green,* 943 F.2d 485 (4th Cir. 1991), cert. denied, 503 U.S. 936 (1992).

78. Ian Ayres and John Braithwaite, *Responsible Regulation: Transcending the Deregulation Debate* (New York: Oxford University Press, 1992); Toni Mikkai and Valerie Braithwaite, "Profession-alism, Organizations, and Compliance," *Law and Social Inquiry* 18 (1993): 33, 35–37.

79. E. Allen Lind, "Procedural Justice," in *Everyday Practices and Trouble Cases,* ed. Austin Sarat et al. (Evanston, Ill.: Northwestern University Press/ABA, 1998), 177, 181; Floyd Abrams, "Why Lawyers Lie," *New York Times Magazine,* October 9, 1994, 54.

5. TOO MUCH LAW/TOO LITTLE JUSTICE:
TOO MUCH RHETORIC/TOO LITTLE REFORM

1. Census Report, quoted in E. Norman Vesey, "The Role of Supreme Courts in Addressing Professionalism of Lawyers and Judges," *Professional Lawyer* (1997): 2, 8; American Bar Association, *Perceptions of the United States Justice System* (Chicago: ABA, 1999), 59; "Anti-Lawyer Attitude Up," *National Law Journal,* August 9, 1993; Amy C. Black and Stanley Rothman, "Shall We Kill All the Lawyers First? Insider and Outsider Views of the Legal Profession," *Harvard Journal of Law and Public Policy* 21 (1998): 835, 854; see also Gary A. Hengsler, "Vox Populi," *ABA Journal,* September 1993, 63. For a more extended treatment of issues raised in this chapter, see Deborah L. Rhode, "Too Much Law, Too Little Justice: Too Much Rhetoric, Too Little Reform," *Georgetown Journal of Legal Ethics* 11 (1998): 989.

2. For critiques, see Lawrence M. Friedman, *A History of American Law,* 2d ed. (New York: Simon and Schuster, 1985), 96; Jerold Auerbach, "A Plague of Lawyers," *Harper's,* October 1976, 37; Robert Dee, "Blood Bath," *Enterprise* 10 (March/April 1986), 23; Terry Carter, "A Lesson Learned," *ABA Journal,* May 1998 (quoting Thomas Donahue, president of the U.S. Chamber of Commerce); Paul W. McCracken, "The Big Domestic Issue: Slow Growth," *Wall Street Journal,* October 4, 1991, A14. For responsible research, see Marc Galanter, "News from Nowhere: The Debased Debate on Civil Justice," *Denver University Law Review* 71 (1993): 77, 79–80; Marc Galanter, "Pick a Number, Any Number," *Legal Times,* February 17, 1992, 26.

3. Kahei Rokumoto, "Issues of Lawyer Population in Japan," in *The Social Role of the Legal Profession,* ed. Kahei Rokumoto (Tokyo: International Center for Comparative Law and Politics, 1993), 206; Junjiro Tsubota, quoted in Marc Galanter, "The Day after the Litigation Explosion," *Maryland Law Review* 46 (1986): 3, 13n. 36.

4. Marc Galanter, "Predators and Parasites: Lawyer Bashing and Civil Justice," *Georgia Law Review* 28 (1994): 633, 677; Robert Kagan, "Do Lawyers Cause Adversarial Legalism? A Preliminary Inquiry," *Law and Social Inquiry* 9 (1994): 1, 8.

5. Derek Bok, "A Flawed System of Law Practice and Training," *Journal of Legal Education* 33 (1983): 570, 573–74; Robert Wills, *Lawyers Are Killing America* (Santa Barbara: Capra Press, 1990) 10, 57.

6. David Luban, "Tasseled Loafers," *Report from the Institute for Philosophy and Public Policy* 12 (summer/fall 1992): 9.

7. Roger Abrams, "Are There Too Many Lawyers?" *New Jersey Law Journal,* February 11, 1995, 23; Paul Tremblay, "A Very Moral Type of God: Triage among Poor Clients," *Fordham Law Review* 67 (1999): 2475; State Bar of California, Office of Legal Services, *And Justice for All: Fulfilling the Promise of Access to Civil Justice in California* (San Francisco: State Bar of California, 1996), 1–2, 17; Albert H. Cantrel, ABA Commission on Legal Service and the Public, *Agenda for Access: The American People and Civil Justice* (Chicago: ABA, 1996), 4, 26–27.

8. *U.S. News and World Report,* December 4, 1978, 50; Dee, "Blood Bath," 23; McCracken, "Domestic Issue," *Wall Street Journal,* October 4, 1991, A14; Dan Rather, quoted in W. Lance Bennett, *News: The Politics of Illusion,* 3d ed. (New York: Longman, 1996), 1; Deborah L. Rhode and David Luban, *Legal Ethics,* 2d ed. (Westbury, N.Y.: Foundation

Press, 1995), 722; Mary Ann Glendon, *A Nation under Lawyers* (New York: Farrar, Straus and Giroux, 1994), 263; "The Trouble with Lawyers," with John Stossel, ABC News special, January 2, 1996, transcript, 69; Roger Cramton, "What Do Lawyer Jokes Tell Us about Lawyers and Lawyering?" *Cornell Law Forum,* July 1996, 7.

9. Bennett, *News,* 39; "Ridiculous Unjustified Suits Are Bringing Down State's Economy," *San Jose and Silicon Valley Business Journal,* May 12–18, 1997, 43 (quoting Wilson); George Lardner Jr., "'Tort Reform': Mixed Verdict," *Washington Post,* February 10, 2000, A6 (quoting Bush); Dan Quayle, *Standing Firm: A Vice Presidential Memoir* (New York: HarperCollins, 1994), 283; *Congressional Record* S948–49 (daily ed., February 4, 1986).

10. Marc Galanter, "Reading the Landscape of Disputes: What We Know and Don't Know (and Think We Know) about Our Allegedly Contentious and Litigious Society," *University of California at Los Angeles Law Review* 31 (1983): 4, 56n. 238; Lawrence M. Friedman, "Access to Justice: Social and Historical Context," in *Access to Justice,* ed. Mauro Cappelletti and John Weisner (Milan: Giuffee, 1978), 2:3.

11. "Asides: The Office Bore," *Wall Street Journal,* July 21, 1997, 22; John Leo, "An Empty Ruling on Harassment," *U.S. News and World Report,* November 29, 1993, 20; John McLaughlin, quoted in Deborah Epstein, "Can a Dumb Ass Woman Achieve Equality in the Workplace? Running the Gauntlet of Hostile Environment Harassing Speech," *Georgetown Law Journal* 84 (1996): 399, 408; Deborah L. Rhode, *Speaking of Sex* (Cambridge: Harvard University Press, 1997), 97–98. For costs, see Kerry Segrave, *The Sexual Harassment of Women in the Workplace, 1600–1993* (Jefferson, N.C.: McFarland, 1994), 203.

12. Ralph Nader and Wesley J. Smith, *No Contest: Corporate Lawyers and the Perversion of Justice in America* (New York: Random House, 1996), 267.

13. Cindy Webb, "Boiling Mad," *Business Week,* August 21, 1995, 32. "Ridiculous" is the Chamber of Commerce's characterization. See Nader and Smith, *No Contest,* 267–73; Andrea Gerlin, "A Matter of Degree: How a Jury Decided That a Coffee Spill Is Worth $2.9 Million," *Wall Street Journal,* September 1, 1994, A1.

14. David L. Paletz and Robert M. Entman, *Media Power Politics* (New York: Free Press, 1981), 16. For examples, see Richard Lacayo, "Anecdotes Not Antidotes," *Time,* April 10, 1995, 40; Steven Brill and James Lyons, "The Not So Simple Crisis," *American Lawyer,* May 1986, 1, 12.

15. Michael J. Saks, "Do We Really Know Anything about the Behavior of the Tort Litigation System—and Why Not?," *University of Pennsylvania Law Review* 140 (1992): 1147, 1161.

16. John Leo, "The World's Most Litigious Nation," *U.S. News and World Report,* May 22, 1995, 24; Stephen Budiansky with Ted Gest and David Fischer, "How Lawyers Abuse the Law," *U.S. News and World Report,* January 30, 1995, 50, 56; Marc Galanter, "Real World Torts: An Antidote to Anecdote," *Maryland Law Review* 55 (1996): 1093, 1104–6; sources discussed in Galanter, "Litigation Explosion," 3; Michael H. Trotter, *Profit and the Practice of Law* (Athens: University of Georgia Press, 1997), 167; Galanter, "Pick a Number"; Glendon, *Nation under Lawyers,* 268; Galanter, "News from Nowhere," 79–80.

17. Ralph C. Cavanagh and Deborah L. Rhode, "The Unauthorized Practice of Law and Pro Se Divorce," *Yale Law Journal* 86 (1976): 104, 129.

18. Office of Legal Services, *And Justice for All,* 17; Cantrel, *Agenda for Access,* 4, 26–27.

19. Deborah R. Hensler et al., *Compensation for Accidental Injuries in the United States* (Santa Monica, Calif.: RAND Institute for Civil Justice, 1991), 110, 121–28; Peter A. Bell and Jeffrey O'Connell, *Accidental Justice: The Dilemmas of Tort Law* (New Haven: Yale University Press, 1997), 58; Harvard Medical Practice Study, *Patients, Doctors, and Lawyers: Medical Injury, Malpractice Litigation, and Patient Compensation in New York: The Report of the Harvard Medical Practice Study to the State of New York* (Cambridge: Harvard University Press, 1990) 6-9, 7-1; Saks, "Do We Really Know Anything," 1183–84.

20. Marc Galanter, "Law Abounding: Legislation Around the North Atlantic," *Modern Law Review* 55 (1992): 1; Thomas E. Baker, "Tyranneous Lex," *Iowa Law Review* 82 (1997): 689, 700–702; Adam Nosseter, "Six-Year-Old's Sex Crime: Innocent Peck on Cheek," *New York Times,* September 27, 1996, A9.

21. Lawrence M. Friedman, *Total Justice* (New York: Russell Sage Foundation, 1994).

22. Kagan, "Do Lawyers Cause Adversarial Legalism?" 8.

23. Dan Quayle, quoted in David Margolick, "Address by Dan Quayle on Justice Proposals Irks Bar Association," *New York Times,* August 14, 1991, A1; McCracken, "Domestic Issue," A14; Karen O'Conner, "Civil Justice Reform and Prospects for Change," *Brooklyn Law Review* 59 (1993): 917, 922; Samborn, "Anti-Lawyer Attitude Up," 1; Galanter, "The Regulatory Function of the Civil Jury," in *Verdict: Assessing the Civil Jury System,* ed. Robert E. Litan (Washington, D.C.: Brookings Institution Press, 1993), 61; Sullivan, "Ridiculous Suits," 43.

24. Robert E. Litan, "The Liability Explosion and American Trade Performance: Myths and Realities," in *Tort Law and the Public Interest: Competition, Innovation, and Consumer Welfare,* ed. Peter H. Schuck (New York: Norton, 1991), 127, 128; Nader and Smith, *No Contest,* 279; Nathan Weber, *Product Liability: The Corporate Response,* report no. 893 (New York: Conference Board, 1987), v.

25. Daniel S. Bailis and Robert J. MacCoun, "Estimating Liability Risks with the Media as Your Guide: A Content Analysis of Media Coverage of Tort Litigation," *Law and Human Behavior* 20 (1996): 419, 426; Marc Galanter, "The Regulatory Function of the Civil Jury," 85; Amos Tversky and Daniel Kahneman, "Availability: Heuristic for Judging Frequency Probability," *Cognitive Psychology* 5 (1977): 207; Donald R. Songer, "Tort Reform in South Carolina: The Effect of Empirical Research on Elite Perceptions Concerning Jury Verdicts," *South Carolina Law Review* 39 (1988): 5, 85; Galanter, "Civil Jury," 86; William Glaberson, "When the Verdict Is Just a Fantasy," *New York Times,* June 6, 1999, E1.

26. John Sullivan, "Ridiculous Unjustified Lawsuits Are Bringing Down State's Economy," *San Jose and Silicon Valley Business Journal,* May 12–18, 1997, 43; Marc Thompson, "Applying the Brakes to Punitives," *ABA Journal,* September 1997, 69; Nader and Smith, *No Contest,* 280–81; Erik Moller, *Trends in Civil Jury Verdicts since 1985* (Santa Monica, Calif.: RAND Institute for Social Justice, 1996), 35–36; Glaberson, "Verdict," E1; Andrew Blum, "Study Finds Punitives Are Small, Rare," *National Law Journal,* July 1, 1996, A6. For undercompensation see Frank A. Sloan and Stephen S. van Wert, "Cost and Compensation of Injuries in Medical Malpractice," *Law and Contemporary Problems* 54 (1991): 131, 155; W. Kip Viscusi, "Toward a Diminished Role for Tort Liability: Social Insurance, Government Regulation, and Contemporary Risks to Health and Safety," *Yale Journal on Regulation* 6 (1989): 65, 95–97; Saks, "Do We Really Know Anything?" 1286–87.

27. "The Trouble with Lawyers," transcript, 4.

28. "The Trouble with Lawyers," transcript, 6; John Stossel, "Protect Us from Legal Vultures," *Wall Street Journal,* January 2, 1996, A8.

29. Bell and O'Connell, *Accidental Justice,* 189; Linda Ranson, "Lawyers May Kill My Daughter," *Wall Street Journal,* March 29, 1996, A16; Andrew D. Dyer, Todd E. Hymstead, and N. Craig Smith, "Dow Corning Corporation: Product Stewardship," in *Cases on Leadership, Ethics, and Organizational Integrity: A Strategic Perspective,* ed. Lynn Sharp Paine (Chicago: Irwin, 1997), 298. For examples of positive effects, see Nader and Smith, *No Contest,* 315–17.

30. Leo, "Litigious Nation," 24; Bell and O'Connell, *Accidental Justice,* 92–93; Office of Technology Assessment, *Defensive Medicine and Medical Malpractice* 103 (1994): 56, 71, 74; "Health Plans Depict Lawyers as Threat," *New York Times,* October 8, 1999, A22.

31. See Glaberson, "Verdict," 1; Lardner, "'Tort Reform,'" 46; Common Sense Legal Reform Act, H.R. 10, 104th Cong., 1st sess. (1995); Lawsuit Reform Act of 1995, S. 300, 104th Cong., 1st sess. (1995); Attorney Accountability Act, H.R. 988, 104th Cong., 1st sess. (1995); Joanne Doroshow and J. Robert Hunter, *Premium Deceit—the Failure of Tort Reform to Cut Insurance Prices* (New York: Citizens for Corporate Accountability and Individual Rights, 1999); Herbert M. Kritzer, prepared statement, and Thomas D. Rowe Jr., prepared statement, Attorney Accountability, Hearings before the Subcommittee on Courts and Intellectual Property of the Committee on the Judiciary, House of Representatives, 104th Congress, 1st sess., February 6, 1995, 49–66, 42–47.

32. "The Trouble with Lawyers," transcript, 24; Werner Pfenningstorf and Donald G. Gifford, introduction to *A Comparative Study of Liability Law and Compensation Schemes in Ten Countries and the United States,* ed. Donald G. Gifford and William M. Richman (Oak Brook, Ill.: Insurance Research Council, 1991); Kagan, "Adversarial Legalism," 8; Kritzer, Hearings, 57; Rowe, Hearings, 70.

33. Budiansky, Gest, and Fisher, "How Lawyers Abuse the System," 53; Saks, "Do We Really Know Anything?"; Thompson, "Letting the Air Out of Tort Reform," 68–69; Galanter, "Civil Jury."

34. Peter Shuck, quoted in Hope Viner Samborn, "Public Discontent: The Debate Goes Beyond Tort Law: It's about Lawyers," *ABA Journal,* August 1995, 70, 73.

35. H. L. Mencken, quoted in Donna Woolfolk Cross, *Mediaspeak* (New York: Calvert-McCann, 1983), 49; Richard H. Tawney, *Equality,* 5th ed. (London: Unwin Books, 1964), 102–3.

36. ABA, *Perceptions of the United States Justice System,* 1, 4; James S. Kakalik and Nicholas M. Page, *Costs and Compensation Paid in Tort Litigation* (Santa Monica, Calif.: RAND, 1986) vi; see also Saks, "Do We Really Know Anything?" 1282; Wills, *Lawyers Are Killing America,* 10.

37. Nader and Smith, *No Contest,* 299–300; Robert Gnaizda, "Secret Justice for the Privileged Few," *Judicature* 66 (1987): 6, 11; Owen Fiss, "Against Settlement," *Yale Law Journal* 93 (1984): 1073.

38. Deborah R. Hensler, "In Search of Good Mediation: Rhetoric, Practice, and Empiricism," in *Handbook of Justice Research in Law,* ed. Joseph Sanders and V. Lee Hamilton (New York: Plenum, 2000); Marc Galanter and Mia Cahill, "Most Cases Settle: Judicial Promotion and Regulation of Settlements," *Stanford Law Review* 46 (1994): 1339; Richard C. Reuben, "The Lawyer Turns Peacemaker," *ABA Journal,* August 1996, 5; Judith Resnik, "Failing Faith: Adjudicatory Procedure in Decline," *University of Chicago Law Review* 53 (1986): 494, 553;

E. Allan Lind and Tom R. Tyler, *The Social Psychology of Procedural Justice* (New York: Plenum, 1988), 177. For imbalances, see Trina Grillo, "The Mediation Alternative: Process Dangers for Women," *Yale Law Journal* 100 (1991): 1545; Richard Delgado, "Fairness and Formality: Minimizing the Risk of Alternative Dispute Resolution," *Wisconsin Law Review* (1985): 135. For a study finding no significant differences in federal cases, see James S. Kakalik et al., "An Evaluation of Mediation and Early Neutral Evaluation under the Civil Justice Reform Act: A Summary," *Dispute Resolution Magazine,* summer 1997, 4–7. For mixed results, see studies cited in Reuben, "The Lawyer Turns Peacemaker," 56–59.

39. Deborah R. Hensler, "Puzzling over ADR: Drawing Meaning from the RAND Report," *Dispute Resolution Magazine,* summer 1997, 8, 9.

40. Grillo, " Mediation Alternative, 1599; Lisa Lerman, "Mediation of Wife Abuse Cases: The Adverse Impact of Informal Dispute Resolution on Women," *Harvard Womens Law Journal* 7 (1988): 53; Reuben, "The Lawyer Turns Peacemaker," 61; Jeffrey W. Stempel, "Reflections on Judicial ADR and the Multi-Door Courthouse at Twenty: Fait Accompli, Failed Overture, or Fledgling Adulthood?" *Ohio State Journal on Dispute Resolution* 11 (1996): 297, 319, 339, 351; Richard C. Reuben, "The Bias Factor," *California Lawyer,* November 1999, 25.

41. See Fiss, "Against Settlement"; David Luban, "Settlements and the Public Realm," *Georgetown Law Review* 83 (1995): 2619; Lind and Tyler, *Social Psychology,* 122.

42. Marc Galanter, "Why the Haves Come Out Ahead: Speculations on the Limits of Legal Change," *Law and Society Review* 9 (1974): 95.

43. Lind and Tyler, *Social Psychology,* 216–17; Judith Resnik, "Many Doors? Closing Doors? Alternative Dispute Resolution and Adjudication," *Ohio State Journal on Dispute Resolution* 10 (1995): 211. Frank E. A. Sander and Stephen B. Goldberg, "Fitting the Forum to the Fuss: A User-Friendly Guide to Selecting an ADR Procedure," *Negotiation Journal* 10 (January 1994): 49, 60. See also Grillo, "Mediation Alternative," and Federal Courts Pilot Project, Judicial Improvements and Access to Justice Act, 28 USC §§ 651–658 (permitting courts to require arbitrator for monetary disputes under $100,000).

44. Sander and Goldberg, "Fitting the Forum," 67 (crediting the phrase to Maurice Rosenberg); Resnik, "Many Doors," 216.

45. Sander and Goldberg, "Fitting the Forum," 60–61; Carrie Menkel-Meadow, "Whose Dispute Is It Anyway? A Philosophical and Democratic Defense of Settlement (in Some Cases)," *Georgetown Law Journal* 83 (1995): 2663, 2670; Stempel, "Reflections on Judicial ADR," 389; Katherine Van Wezel Stone," Rustic Justice: Community and Coercion under the Federal Arbitration Act," *North Carolina Law Review* 77 (1999): 931.

46. The procedures are administered by the District of Columbia Multi-Door Dispute Resolution Division. For an overview of other programs, see Susan Keilitz, ed., *National Symposium on Court-Connected Dispute Resolution Research: Research Findings; Implications for the Courts; Future Research Needs* (Williamsburg, Va.: National Center for State Courts, State Justice Institute, 1994).

47. Lind and Taylor, *Procedural Justice,* 64–67, 102–4; Stempel, "Reflections on Judicial ADR," 353–54.

48. For scholars' views, see the sources cited in Deborah L. Rhode, "Professionalism in Perspective: Alternative Approaches to Nonlawyer Practice," *New York University Review of Law and Social Change* 22 (1996): 701; Deborah L Rhode, "The Delivery of Legal Services

by Nonlawyers," *Georgetown Journal of Legal Ethics* 4 (1990): 209. For other experts, see Commission on Nonlawyer Practice, ABA, *Nonlawyer Activity in Law-Related Situations: A Report with Recommendations* (Chicago: ABA, 1995); *Report of the State Bar of California Commission on Legal Technicians* (San Francisco: State Bar of California, July 1990).

49. Rhode and Luban, *Legal Ethics,* 670–73; Debra Baker, "Is This Woman a Threat to Lawyers?" *ABA Journal,* June 1999, 5; Kentucky Bar Association, Opinion U-58 (1999); Resolution on Unauthorized Practice, ABA House of Delegates, February, 2000; ABA, Model Rules of Professional Conduct, Rule 5.5, Comment; In re Opinion No. 26, 654 A.2d 1344 (N.J. Sup. Ct. 1995).

50. Herbert Kritzer, *Legal Advocacy* (Ann Arbor: University of Michigan Press, 1998), 193–203; Rhode, "Delivery of Legal Services," 230–31; Mathew A. Melone, "Income Tax Practice and Certified Public Accountants: The Case for a Status Based Exemption from Unauthorized Practice of Law Rules," *Akron Tax Journal* 41 (1995); *California State Bar Commission Report,* 41; Geraldine Mund, "Paralegals: The Good, the Bad, and the Ugly," *American Bankruptcy Journal* 2 (1994): 337; Cameron Stracher, *Double Billing* (New York: William Morrow, 1998), 52.

51. Hal Lancaster, "Rating Lawyers: If Your Legal Problems Are Complex, a Clinic May Not Be the Answer," *Wall Street Journal,* July 31, 1980, 1, 8 (quoting Robert Ellickson); Richard L. Abel, "Comparative Sociology of Legal Professions: An Exploratory Essay," *American Bar Foundation Research Journal* (1985): 1, 29; Judith Citron, *The Citizens Advice Bureaux: For the Community, by the Community* (London: Pluto Press, 1989); Andrew Boon and Jennifer Levin, *The Ethics and Conduct of Lawyers in England and Wales* (Oxford: Hart, 1999), 55–59, 402; Kritzer, *Legal Advocacy.*

52. See ABA Commission on Nonlawyer Practice, *Nonlawyer Practice in the United States: Summary of the Factual Record before the Commission* (Chicago: ABA, 1994), 18–19; Alexandra A. Ashbrook, "The Unauthorized Practice of Law in Immigration: Examining the Propriety of Non-Lawyer Representation," *Georgetown Journal of Legal Ethics* 5 (1991): 237, 249–51.

53. Reuben, "The Lawyer Turns Peacemaker," 60. See Nader and Smith, *No Contest,* 299–301; Carrie Menkel-Meadow, "Ethics in Alternative Dispute Resolution: New Issues, No Answers from the Adversary Conception of Lawyers' Responsibilities," *South Texas Law Review* 38 (1997): 407; Resnik, "Many Doors," 228.

54. For examples of such proposals, see sources cited in Rhode, "Professionalism," 715; *California Commission on Legal Technicians' Report;* Menkel-Meadow, "Ethics in Alternative Dispute Resolution," 448.

55. See Steven Brint, *In an Age of Experts: The Changing Role of Professionalism in Politics and Public Life* (Princeton: Princeton University Press, 1994), 76 (discussing the unwarranted price increases due to restricting competition); Simon Domberger and Avrom Sherr, "The Impact of Competition on Pricing and Quality of Legal Services," *International Review of Law and Economy* 9 (1989): 41, 55 (discussing Great Britain); George C. Leef, "Lawyer Fees Too High: The Case for Repealing Unauthorized Practice of Law Statutes," *Regulation* (winter 1997): 33, 34–35 (discussing Great Britain and Canada); Rhode, "Professionalism," 712–13; ABA Commission on Multidisciplinary Practice, Report to the ABA House of Delegates, reprinted in *Professional Lawyer* 10 (1999): 1; and ABA Commission on Multidisciplinary Practice, Background Paper on Multidisciplinary Practice: Issues and Developments, reprinted in *Professional Lawyer* 10 (1998): 1; Mark E. Doremus,

"Wisconsin Elderlinks Initiative: Using Technology to Provide Legal Services to Older Persons," *Wake Forest Law Review* 32 (1997): 545.

56. See, for example, Model Rules of Professional Conduct, Rules 5.4 and 5.7; ABA Model Code of Professional Responsibility, DR 3-102, DR 3-103, EC 3-8; Philadelphia Bar Association Professional Guidance Committee, Opinion 97-11 (October 1997), 13; David Kaplan, "Want to Invest in a Law Firm?" *National Law Journal,* January 19, 1987, 28; Roger Cramton, "Delivery of Legal Services to Ordinary Americans," *Case Western Law Review* 44 (1994): 531, 575–77. The ABA Committee on Professional Ethics, *Formal Opinion* 355 (1987) sets forth guidelines.

57. John Gibeaut, "Squeeze Play," *ABA Journal,* February 1998, 42, 43; Cindy K. Goodman, "Line Between Accounting, Law Professions May Soon Blur," *Miami Herald,* March 1, 1999; Boon and Levin, *Ethics and Conduct,* 84; Geoffrey Hazard, "Accountants vs. Lawyers: Let's Consider Facts," *National Law Journal,* November 9, 1998, A24.

58. See Stephen Gillers, "The Anxiety of Influence," *Florida State University Law Review* 27 (1999): 123; Robert Gordon, written remarks to the Multidisciplinary Practice Commission, May 1999.

59. ABA Commission on Multidisciplinary Practice, Report to the House of Delegates; Mary C. Daly, "Choosing Wise Men Wisely: The Risks and Rewards of Purchasing Legal Services from Lawyers in Multidisciplinary Partnerships," *Georgetown Journal of Legal Ethics* 13 (2000): 217.

60. Alan Houseman, "Civil Assistance for the Twenty-first Century: Achieving Equal Justice for All," *Yale Journal of Law and Policy Review* 17 (1998): 369; Fred Rodell, *Woe unto You Lawyers,* 2d ed. (New York: Pageant Press, 1957), 123–36; Galanter, "Predators," 635. Cramton, "Delivery of Legal Services," 562–63; Franklin Strier, *Reconstructing Justice* (Chicago: University of Chicago Press, 1996), 233.

61. Dianne Molvig, "Growing Solutions to Unmet Legal Needs: Commission Issues Key Recommendations," 70 *Wisconsin Lawyer* (1996): 10, 12; State Bar of California, *And Justice for All,* 33–34 (1996); ABA Standing Committee, *Self-Representation,* 21, 37–39; Cantril, *Agenda for Access;* ABA, *Just Solutions: A Program Guide to Innovative Justice System Improvements* (Chicago: ABA, 1995).

62. For examples, see Cantril, *Agenda for Access;* ABA, *Just Solutions;* Houseman, "Civil Legal Assistance." For bar opposition, see Kagan, "Do Lawyers Cause Adversarial Legalism," 56. For image, see chapter 1. For unbundling, see Forrest S. Mosten, "Unbundling of Legal Services and the Family Lawyer," *Family Law Quarterly* 28 (1994): 421, 428; Jean Guccione, "'Unbundling' Legal Services," *San Francisco Daily Journal,* October 31, 1997, 1, 9.

6. REGULATION OF THE PROFESSION

1. Roscoe Pound, *The Lawyer from Antiquity to Modern Times* (St. Paul: West, 1953), 7.

2. Barbara A. Curran, *The Legal Needs of the Public: The Final Report of a National Survey* (Chicago: ABA, 1977), 190; George A. Akerloff, "The Market for Lemons: Qualitative Uncertainty and the Market Mechanism," *Quarterly Journal of Economics* 84 (1970): 488.

3. See Roger Cramton, "Delivery of Legal Services to Ordinary Americans," *Case Western Law Review* 44 (1994): 531, 541–46.

4. Charles Wolfram, *Modern Legal Ethics* (St. Paul, Minn.: West, 1986), 24–33; ABA, Model Rules of Professional Conduct, preamble (Chicago: ABA, 1983).

5. For other countries, see Carl M. Sellinger, "The Public's Interest in Protecting the Dignity and Unity of the Legal Profession," *Wake Forest Law Review* 32 (1997): 863; Andrew Boon and Jennifer Levin, *The Ethics and Conduct of Lawyers in England and Wales* (Oxford: Hart, 1999), 61, 141; Christine Parker, *Just Lawyers* (Oxford: Oxford University Press, 1999), 8–17. For other regulation, see Wolfram, *Modern Legal Ethics,* 26.

6. Deborah L. Rhode and David Luban, *Legal Ethics* (Westbury, N.Y.: Foundation Press, 1998), 124; "ABA Commission Examining Model Rules," *ABA/BNA Manual on Professional Conduct* 14 (1998): 125; Chief Justices Committee on Professionalism and Lawyer Competence, *A National Action Plan on Lawyer Conduct and Professionalism* (Williamsburg, Va.: National Center for State Courts, 1998), 43.

7. Boon and Levin, *Ethics and Conduct,* 112, 141, 142; Parker, *Just Lawyers,* 8, 17–19; Michael Bayles, *Professional Ethics* (Belmont, Calif.: Wadsworth, 1981), 131–38; Bayless Manning, "If Lawyers Were Angels: A Sermon in One Canon," *ABA Journal,* July 1974, 821, 824; "Self-Regulation: Some Lay Participation Still Are Favored," *ABA Journal,* February 1983, 154; Deborah Hensler and Marisa E. Reddy, *California Lawyers View the Future* (Santa Monica, Calif.: RAND Institute for Social Justice, 1994), 23.

8. See the symposium on "Institutional Choices in the Regulation of Lawyers," *Fordham Law Review* 65 (1996), and Charles H. Koch Jr., *Administrative Law and Practice,* sec. 7.12, 2d ed. (St. Paul, Minn.: West, 1997).

9. Rhode and Luban, *Legal Ethics,* 622–23.

10. In re R.M.J., 455 U.S. 191, 203 (1982); Rhode and Luban, *Legal Ethics,* 624–25.

11. ABA Model Rules of Professional Conduct, Rules 7.1, 7.3 (1999); ABA Model Code of Professional Conduct, DR 2-101. Compare *Edenfeld v. Fane,* 507 U.S. 761, 774 (1993) with *Florida Bar v. Went For It,* 515 U.S. 618, 624–25 (1998).

12. Rhode and Luban, *Legal Ethics,* 625; Peter A. Bell and Jeffrey O'Connell, *Accidental Justice: The Dilemma of Tort Law* (New Haven: Yale University Press, 1997), 165–66; Richard Zitrin and Carol M. Langford, *The Moral Compass of the American Lawyer* (New York: Ballantine, 1999), 129, 135.

13. Rhode and Luban, *Legal Ethics* (paraphrasing Chief Justice Burger), 630; Kathleen Sullivan, "Intersection," *Fordham Law Review* 67 (1998): 583; ABA Commission on Advertising, *Report on the Survey on the Image of Lawyers in Advertising* (Chicago: ABA, 1990); Richard J. Cebula, "Does Lawyer Advertising Adversely Influence the Image of Lawyers in the United States?" *Journal of Legal Studies* 27 (1998): 503; "Anti-Lawyer Attitude Up, but NLJ/West Poll Also Shows More People Are Using Attorneys," *National Law Journal,* August 9, 1993, 1; Wiese Research Associates, "Attorney Advertising Perception Study" (Chicago: ABA, 1994), 10–11.

14. Rhode and Luban, *Legal Ethics,* 627; Christine Biederman, "Families of Crash Victims Say Lawyers Ignore Solicitation Ban," *New York Times,* June 4, 1996, A9; Ruth A. Woodruff, "Investigating Lawyer Solicitation in the Aftermath of Tragedy," *Professional Lawyer,* November 1996, 1, 4.

15. Federal Trade Commission, *Improving Consumer Access to Legal Services* (Washington, D.C.: Federal Trade Commission, 1984), 151.

16. Len Tang Smith, "Abraham Lincoln as a Bar Examiner," *Bar Examiner* 51 (1982): 37.

17. See James Willard Hurst, *The Growth of American Law* (Boston: Little, Brown, 1950), 292–93; Rhode, *Professional Responsibility,* 59–60.

18. Chief Justices, *A National Action Plan,* 15; Letter to the Editor, *New York Times,* December 16, 1994, A7.

19. Association of the Bar of the City of New York, Special Committee on the Constitutional Convention, *Final Report* (New York: Association of the Bar of the City of New York, 1988), 5–6 [discussed in Task Force on Mandatory Continuing Legal Education, Report to the Board of Governors of the District of Columbia Bar (Washington, D.C.: District of Columbia Bar, 1995)].

20. Rhode and Luban, *Legal Ethics,* 818–21.

21. *Richardson v. McFadden,* 540 F.2d 744 (4th Cir.1976); sources cited in Rhode and Luban, *Legal Ethics,* 818–21; National Law School Admission Council, *National Longitudinal Bar Passage Study* (Newtown, Pa.: National Law School Admission Council, 1998).

22. Cornish F. Hitchock, quoted in Michael Wines, "At the Bar," *New York Times,* April 15, 1994, B12; Armando Menocal, "Comments," *Bar Examiner,* November 1998, 10; Steve Klein, quoted in Rhode and Luban, *Legal Ethics,* 821.

23. Deborah L. Rhode, "Moral Character as a Professional Credential," *Yale Law Journal* 94 (1985): 491; Mike Allen, "Beyond the Bar Exam," *New York Times,* July 11, 1999, E3; Abdon M. Pollasch, "Screening Process May Become Screaming Process for Bar Applicants," *Chicago Lawyer,* September 1997, 4; M. A. Cunningham, "The Professional Image Standard: An Untold Standard of Admission to the Bar," *Tulane Law Review* 66 (1992): 1015, 1037–39.

24. Rhode, "Moral Character," 537–42, 574; Pam Bellick, "Avowed Racist Barred from Practicing Law," *New York Times,* February 10, 1999, A12.

25. Rhode, "Moral Character," 556–62; Walter Mischel and Yuiche Shada, "A Cognitive Affective Theory of Personality: Reconceptualizing Situations, Dispositions, Dynamics, and Invariances," *Psychological Review* 10 (1995): 246.

26. Stanley S. Herr, "Questioning the Questionnaires: Bar Admissions and Candidates with Disabilities," *Villanova Law Review* 42 (1997): 635, 669–74, 721; Hilary Duke, "The Narrowing of State Bar Examiner Inquiries into the Mental Health of Bar Applicants: Bar Examiner Objectives Are Met Better Through Attorney Education, Rehabilitation, and Discipline," *Georgetown Journal of Legal Ethics* 11 (1998): 101, 105–7; *Clark v. Virginia Board of Bar Examiners,* 880 F. Supp. 430, 436 (E.D. Va. 1995).

27. West Virginia Board of Law Examiners, 408 S.E.2d 675 (W. Va. 1991) (finding higher standard of conduct for bar applicants than admitted attorneys is permissible); Rhode, "Moral Character," 546–51 (discussing double standard).

28. Debra Baker, "Lawyer Go Home," *ABA Journal,* May 1998, 22–23; Lawrence A. Salibra II, "Counsel Seek Changes in Admission System," *National Law Journal,* May 20, 1991, S17; Rhode and Luban, *Legal Ethics,* 845–46; "Moving Toward Interstate Advocacy: Ethical Concerns Facing Multi-State Practitioners," *Journal of the Legal Profession* 22 (1998): 289, 292–93. See Charles W. Wolfram, "Sneaking Around in the Legal Profession: Interjurisdictional Unauthorized Practice by Transactional Lawyers," *South Texas Law Review* 36 (1995): 657.

29. Paul Reidinger, "Bar Exam Blues," *ABA Journal,* July 1987, 84; Charles B. Colvin, "'Yes, There Are Too Many Lawyers.': Now What Do We Do about It?" *Louisiana Bar Journal* 42 (1994): 246–48.

30. Lawrence A. Salibra II, "Counsel Seek Changes in Admission System," *National Law Journal,* May 20, 1991, S17; ABA, Model Rules of Professional Conduct, Rule 8.5;

American Law Institute, *Restatement of the Law Governing Lawyers,* sec. 3, proposed final draft (Philadelphia: American Law Institute, 1998).

31. Carrie Dolan, "California Lawyers, Required to Study, Study at Club Med," *Wall Street Journal,* May 21, 1992, A1; George M. Kraw, "Classroom Capers," *San Francisco Daily Journal,* January 7, 1997, 4.

32. ABA, *The McCrate Report: Building the Educational Continuum,* Conference Proceedings (Chicago: ABA, 1993), 99–100; Task Force on Mandatory Continuing Legal Education, *Report to the Board of Governors of the District of Columbia Bar* (Washington: District of Columbia Bar Association, 1995), 26–28.

33. Carrie Dolan, "California Lawyers," A6; Maura Dolan, "High Court Backs Legal Education," *California Bar Journal,* August 27, 1999, A8.

34. Task Force on Mandatory Continuing Legal Education, *Report,* 33; Victor J. Rubino, "MCLE: The Downside," *CLE Journal* 38 (1992): 14, 17; Joel F. Henning, *Maximizing Law Firm Profitability: Hiring, Training, and Developing Productive Lawyers* (New York: Law Journal Seminars-Press, 1997), §5-4.

35. "A Little Advice on How to Behave at the Firm Retreat," *Illinois Legal Times,* March 1996, 5; William Stevens, "Ethics and CLE," *Philadelphia Lawyer,* winter 1993, 25.

36. Nancy McCarthy, "Poll Shows 2 to 1 Objection to MCLE," *California Bar Journal,* July 1999, A1.

37. Jeremy Perlin, "Special Recognition," *ABA Journal,* May 1998, 76.

38. ABA, Commission on Evaluation of Disciplinary Enforcement, *Lawyer Regulation for a New Century* (Chicago: ABA, 1992), xx; ABA, *Perceptions of the U.S. Justice System* (Chicago: ABA, 1999), 77; Hensler and Reddy, *California Lawyers',* 18; Paula Hannaford, "What Complainants *Really* Expect of Lawyers, Disciplinary Agencies," *Professional Lawyer* 7 (May 1996): 4 (finding majority of complainants rated Virginia's system as poor or very poor).

39. Commission on the Future of the Legal Profession and the State Bar of California, *The Future of the California Bar* (San Francisco: State Bar of California, 1995), 103; Darryl Van Duch, "Best Snitches: Illinois Lawyers," *National Law Journal,* January 26, 1997, A1; John P. Sahl, "The Public Hazard of Lawyer Self-Regulation: Learning from Ohio's Struggle to Reform Its Disciplinary System," *University of Cincinnati Law Review* 68 (1999): 65, 75; Laura Gatland, "The Himmel Effect," *ABA Journal,* April 1997, 24–28. See DR 1-103, which requires reporting by lawyers who have "unprivileged knowledge of a violation of the [Disciplinary Rules]," and Model Rule 8.3, which requires reporting of violations that "raise a substantial question as to [another] lawyer's honesty, trustworthiness, or fitness" unless the knowledge of the violation was received through a privileged communication.

40. Geoffrey Hazard Jr., quoted in David O. Weber, "Still in Good Standing: The Crises in Attorney Discipline," *ABA Journal,* November 1986, 61; Gerald Lynch, "The Lawyer as Informer," *Duke Law Journal* (1986): 491.

41. New York Bar Committee on the Profession and the Courts, *Final Report to the Chief Judge* (November 1995), 44; ABA Commission, *Lawyer Regulation,* xv; Geoffrey C. Hazard Jr., Susan P. Koniak, and Roger Cramton, *The Law and Ethics of Lawyering,* 2d ed. (Westbury, N.Y.: Foundation Press, 1994), 172; "ABA Committee Proposes Rules for Lawyer Client Mediation," *ABA/BNA Lawyers Manual on Professional Conduct* 13 (December 24, 1997):

398; ABA Commission, *Lawyer Regulation*, 129; Dick Goldberg, "Arbitration for Success," *San Francisco Daily Journal*, November 18, 1997, 1; Sahl, "Public Hazard," 86; Ken Armstrong and Maurice Possley, "The Verdict," *Chicago Tribune*, January 10, 1999, A1.

42. Nancy McCarthy, "Bar Starts to Rebuild Discipline," *California Bar Journal*, March 1999, 1; Beth M. Daley, "Is the Illinois Disciplinary System Working?" *Legal Reformer*, spring 1998, 3; Leslie Levin, "The Emperor's Clothes and Other Tales about the Standards for Imposing Lawyer Discipline Sanctions," *American University Law Review* 48 (1998): 1, 39–46; Sahl, "Public Hazard," 69, 82–87; Mike McKee, "Disbarment OK'd for San Francisco Practitioner," *Recorder*, August 7, 1997, 3; Ralph Nader and Wesley J. Smith, *No Contest: Corporate Lawyers and the Perversion of Justice in America* (New York: Random House, 1996), 132.

43. *In re Holloway*, 452 N.E.2d 934, 935 (Ind. 1983); *In re Moore*, 453 N.E.2d 971, 974 (Ind. 1983).

44. Don J. DeBenedictis, "ABA Adopts Most Discipline Proposals," *ABA Journal*, April 1992, 28; Rhode and Luban, *Legal Ethics*, 859n. 2; ABA Commission, *Lawyer Regulation*, 35–39; Sandra L. DeGraw and Bruce W. Burton, "Lawyer Discipline and 'Disclosure Advertising': Towards a New Ethos," *North Carolina Law Review* 72 (1994): 351, 358; Levin, "Emperor's Clothes," 73; Sahl, "Public Hazard," 105–11.

45. Ann Davis, "Bar Readmission Cloaked in Secrecy," *National Law Journal*, August 12, 1996, A17; Ann Davis, "The Myth of Disbarment," *National Law Journal*, August 5, 1996, A1; Wendy Davis, "Advice for the Disbarred: Go West," *New Jersey Law Journal*, July 19, 1999, 1; Susan Adams, "Sleaze Control," *Forbes*, October 21, 1996, 134.

46. ABA Commission, *Lawyer Regulation*, 4; Wilkins, "Who Should Regulate Lawyers?" 17; Kitty Calavita, "Beyond Regulatory Reform: The State, Power, and 'Trouble,'" in *Everyday Practices and Trouble Cases*, ed. Austin Sarat et al. (Chicago: Northwestern University Press, 1998), 126.

47. George M. Kraw, "California's Bad News Bar," *American Lawyer*, June 1998, 110.

48. See Parker, *Just Lawyers*, 17–21; Boon and Levin, *Ethics and Conduct*, 64; Donald Nicolson and Julian Webb, *Professional Legal Ethics: Critical Interrogations* (New York: Oxford University Press, 1999), 87; Rhode and Luban, *Legal Ethics*, 953–54. For a similar proposal, see Robert Fellmeth, "Lessons of the Dues Debacle," *California Bar Journal*, June 1998, 8.

49. ABA Commission, *Lawyer Regulation*, 48; "Lawyer Discipline," *Legal Reformer*, January–March 1996, 3.

50. *In re Himmel*, 533 N.E.2d 790 (Ill. 1988); Gatland, "The Himmel Effect," 24.

51. Michael Higgins, "Getting Out the Word," *ABA Journal*, September 1998, 22. Davis, "Toughening Readmission Procedures," A15; Levin, "Emperor's Clothes," 73. For a modest fee, the ABA National Lawyer Regulatory Data Bank will respond to written inquiries about a lawyer, but will provide only information about public bar disciplinary sanctions, which are imposed in only a small fraction of cases.

52. Hannaford, "What Complainants *Really* Expect," 1, 5–7; Sahl, "Public Hazard," 105–11; Levin, "Emperor's Clothes," 33; Mary Devlin, "The Development of Lawyer Disciplinary Proceedings in the United States," *Georgetown Journal of Legal Ethics* 7 (1994): 921, 931–32.

53. Stuart Auerbach, "Consumer Group Lists 'Questionable Doctors,'" *Washington Post*, April 9, 1996, 7; Robert C. Fellmeth, *Final Report of the California State Bar Discipline Monitor* (San Diego: California State Bar, 1991), 61; Nicolson and Webb, *Professional Legal Ethics*, 90.

54. The Committee on Professional Responsibility, "Discipline of Law Firms," *Record of the Association of the Bar of the City of New York* 48 (1993): 628, 631; Ted Schneyer, "Professional Discipline for Law Firms," *Cornell Law Review* 77 (1991): 1; Steven G. Bene, "Why Not Fine Attorneys? An Economic Approach to Lawyer Disciplinary Sanctions," *Stanford Law Review* 77 (1991): 907.

55. "Figuratively Speaking," *ABA Journal*, October 1996, 12; Manuel R. Ramos, "Legal Malpractice: No Lawyer or Client Is Safe," *Florida Law Review* 47 (1995): 1, 5.

56. ABA Standing Committee on Lawyers' Professional Liability, *Legal Malpractice Claims in the 1990s* (Chicago: ABA, 1996), 12, 16; John Gibeaut, "Good News, Bad News in Malpractice," *ABA Journal*, March 1997, 101; Manuel R. Ramos, "Legal Malpractice: Reforming Lawyers and Law Professors," *Tulane Law Review* 70 (1996): 2582, 2603, 2612; ABA Model Rules, Scope; Model Code, Prefatory Note; Wolfram, *Modern Legal Ethics*, 207–15; Gary A. Munneke and Anthony E. Davis, "The Standard of Care in Legal Malpractice: Do the Model Rules of Professional Conduct Define It?" *Journal of the Legal Profession*, 22 (1998): 33, 62–25; John Leubsdorf, "Legal Malpractice and Professional Responsibility," *Rutgers Law Review* 48 (1995): 101, 111–19; *Wiley v. San Diego County*, 966 P.2d 983 (Cal. 1998).

57. Wolfram, *Modern Legal Ethics*, 218–22; *Baily v. Tucker*, 621 A.2d 108 (Pa. 1993); *Carmel v. Lunney*, 511 N.E. 2d 1126 (N.Y. 1987); *Shaw v. State*, 861 P.2d 566 (Alaska 1993).

58. *Goodman v. Kennedy*, 556 P.2d 737 (Cal. 1976); *Shatz v. Rosenberg*, 943 F.2d 485 (4th Cir. 1991), cert. denied, 503 U.S. 936 (1992); Leubsdorf, "Legal Malpractice," 111, 130–35; Geoffrey C. Hazard Jr., "The Privity Requirement Reconsidered," *South Texas Law Review* 37 (1996): 967; Forest Bowman, "Lawyer Liability to Non-Clients," *Dickinson Law Review* 97 (1993): 267–76.

59. Leubsdorf, "Malpractice," 149.

60. Ramos, "Malpractice: Reforming Lawyers," 2601–4; Daniel Golden, "Elderly Beneficiaries Are Often Ripe for Fraud," *Boston Globe*, December 15, 1997, A1.

61. Ramos, "Malpractice: Reforming Lawyers," 2601–4.

62. ABA Commission, *Lawyer Regulation*, 81–82; Harry H. Scheider, "At Issue: Mandatory Insurance," *ABA Journal*, November 1993, 45. Ramos, "Malpractice: Reforming Lawyers," 2610; Sahl, "Public Hazard," 101–7; Franklin Strier, *Reconstructing Justice* (Chicago: University of Chicago Press, 1996), 218.

63. Ramos, "Malpractice: Reforming Lawyers," 2602; HALT, "Toothless Discipline System Puts Illinois Legal Consumers at Risk," *Legal Reform*, May 7, 1998, 1.

64. Marc Galanter, "Anyone Can Fall Down a Manhole: The Contingency Fee and Its Discontents," *DePaul Law Review* 42 (1994): 457, 459; Lisa Lerman, "Gross Profits: Questions about Lawyer Billing Practices," *Hofstra Law Review* 22 (1994): 645, 649; William G. Ross, *The Honest Hour: The Ethics of Time-Based Billing by Attorneys* (Durham, N.C.: Carolina Academic Press, 1996), 65; John J. Marquess, "Legal Audits and Dishonest Legal Bills," *Hofstra Law Review* 22 (1994): 637, 643–44; Darlene Richter, "Greed, Ignorance, and Overbilling," *ABA Journal*, August 1994, 64–66; Gary Hengstler, "Vox Populi: The Public Perception of Lawyers," *ABA Journal*, September 1993, 63; "The Money Doris Duke Meant for Humanity," *New York Times*, January 24, 1997, A11; Paul Lieberman and John J. Goldman, "Doris Duke's Will Evolves into Ultimate Probate Fight," *Los Angeles Times*, January 1, 1996, 1; "Duke Rebuke," *American Lawyer*, June 2000, 22.

65. Nader and Smith, *No Contest,* 233–42; Ross, *The Honest Hour,* 27–30; James P. Schatz, "Why Attorneys Overbill," *Rutgers Law Review* 50 (1998): 2211, 2214.

66. ABA Committee on Professional Ethics, *Formal Opinion* 302 (1961); Philip M. Stern, *Lawyers on Trial* (New York: Times Books, 1980), 55.

67. *Goldfarb v. Virginia State Bar,* 421 U.S. 773 (1975); Ross, *The Honest Hour,* 16–21; Herbert Kritzer, "Lawyers' Fees and the Holy Grail: Where Should Clients Search for Value?" *Judicature* 77 (1994): 186, 187.

68. ABA Model Rule 1.5. See also Model Code DR 2-106.

69. Ross, *The Honest Hour,* 3, 27; Carl T. Bogus, "The Death of an Honorable Profession," *Indiana Law Review* 71 (1996): 911, 925–26; William H. Rehnquist, "The Legal Profession Today," *Indiana Law Journal* 62 (1987): 151, 153; Harry Maute, "Problem of Overbilling by Many Large Firms Is Confirmed in Surveys," *Wall Street Journal,* September 17, 1993, B7; "Around the Nation," *Chicago Daily Law Bulletin,* January 7, 1998, 3; Nancy D. Holt, "Are Longer Hours Here to Stay?" *ABA Journal,* February 1993, 62, 64.

70. Lisa Lerman, "Blue Chip Bilking: Regulation of Billing and Expense Fraud by Lawyers," *Georgetown Journal of Legal Ethics* 12 (1999): 205, 259–62; Wade Dann, quoted in Barbara B. Serrano, "Lawyer Who Flouted Ethics Rules Escapes Reprimand," *Seattle Times,* March 31, 1996, A1; Webster Hubbell, quoted in Susan Koniak, "When Did Overbilling Become a Habit?" *New York Times,* May 2, 1998, 15.

71. Michael Trotter, *Profit and the Practice of Law* (Athens: University of Georgia Press, 1997), 181; Macklin Fleming, *Lawyers, Money, and Success* (Westport, Conn.: Quorum Books, 1997), 36; "Talk Ain't Cheap," *National Law Journal,* November 16, 1992, A2; Kirsch, "How Do I Bill This?" *California Lawyer* 5 (1985): 15, 17.

72. Geoffrey Hazard Jr., "Ethics," *National Law Journal,* February 17, 1992, A19.

73. Nader and Smith, *No Contest,* 243.

74. For overqualified lawyers, see Elena S. Boisvert, "Is the Legal Profession Violating State and Federal Consumer Protection Laws?" *Professional Lawyer* 9 (November 1997): 1, 6; Ross, *The Honest Hour,* 138–45; Ann Davis, "Lug a Box, Scan Mail: Is It All Billable Time?" *Wall Street Journal,* January 6, 1998, B1; Wes Hansen, "Lawyers, Lawyers, Lawyers," *Ethics: Easier Said than Done,* 1993, 71. For underqualified lawyers, see *In the Matter of Fordham,* 668 N.E.2d 816 (Mass. 1995); Gail Diane Cox, "Excessive Fees Are Attacked Across the Board," *National Law Journal,* November 4, 1996, A1.

75. Nader and Smith, *No Contest,* 233–34.

76. Ross, *The Honest Hour,* 34–38, 83; ABA Committee on Ethics, *Formal Opinion,* 93–379.

77. Susan Beck and Michael Orey, "Skaddenomics," *American Lawyer,* September 1991, 3; Fleming, *Lawyers, Money, and Success,* 38; Sharon Walsh, "Lawyers' Clients Get a Little Cross-Examining," *Washington Post,* June 8, 1992, F1; Marquess, "Legal Audits," 641–44; ABA Committee on Ethics, *Formal Opinion* 93–379.

78. ABA Model Rules of Professional Conduct, Rule 1.5e; Model Code of Professional Responsibility, DR 2-107(A); Jeffrey O'Connell, "Early Offers as Contingent Fee Reform," *DePaul Law Review* 47 (1998), 413, 416; Larry Bodine, "Forwarding Fees: Ethical?" *National Law Journal,* February 5, 1979, 1 (quoting Hazard).

79. Lester A. Brickman, "Contingency Fee Abuses, Ethical Mandates, and the Disciplinary System: The Case Against Case-by-Case Enforcement," *Washington and Lee Law Review* 53

(1996): 1339, 1345n. 22; Margaret Cronin Fisk, "Two Texas Lawyers Hit with $6.3M Overcharging Verdict," *National Law Journal,* December 6, 1999, A11.

80. Rhode and Luban, *Legal Ethics,* 699.

81. Federal Rules of Civil Procedure, Rule 23; John C. Coffee Jr., "The Corruption of the Class Action: The New Technology of Collusion," *Cornell Law Review* 80 (1995): 851, 855; Samuel Issacharoff, "Class Action Conflicts," *University of California at Davis Law Review* 30 (1998): 805, 829.

82. In *re General Motors Pick-up Truck,* 55 F.3d 768 (3d Cir. 1995); Brian Wolfman and Alan B. Morrison, "Representing the Unrepresented in Class Actions Seeking Monetary Relief," *New York University Law Review* 71 (1996): 439, 502–7; Nader and Smith, *No Contest,* 195; Barry Meier, "Fist Full of Coupons," *New York Times,* May 26, 1995, C1.

83. Dave Barry, "Lawyers Put the Bite on Denture-Adhesive Maker," *Orlando Sentinel,* November 23, 1993, 22; E. Paul Warner, "Cottage Industry, *California Law Business,* November 10, 1997; *Mace v. VanRu Credit Corporation,* 109 F.3d 338 (7th Cir.1997); Edward Felsenthal, "Lawyers Rebuked for Pursuing Class Case," *Wall Street Journal,* August 12, 1994, B5; *Kamilewicz v. Bank of Boston Corp.,* 92 F.3d 506, 508 (7th Cir.1996), rehearing denied en banc, 100 F.3d 1348 (7th Cir. 1996).

84. Herbert Kritzer, "The Wages of Risk: The Returns of Contingency Fee Legal Practice," *DePaul Law Review* 47 (1998): 267, 302; Alison Frankel, "Greedy, Greedy, Greedy," *American Lawyer,* November 1996, 71.

85. *Anchem Products v. Windsor,* 521 U.S. 591 (1998); Susan Koniak, "Feasting While the Law Weeps," *Cornell Law Review* 80 (1995): 104; John C. Coffee Jr., "Class Wars: The Dilemma of the Mass Tort Class Action," *Columbia Law Review* 95 (1995): 1343.

86. Neila Lewis, "First Thing We Do, Let's Pay All the Lawyers," *New York Times,* October 11, 1997, A8; Krysten Crawford, "[Tobacco] Defense Firms: No Need to Kick the Habit," *American Lawyer,* May 1998, 59; Lester Brickman, "Will Legal Ethics Go Up in Smoke?" *New York Times,* June 16, 1998, A18; David E. Rosenbaun, "Senate Approves Limiting Fees in Tobacco Cases," *New York Times,* June 17, 1998, A1.

87. Carrie Menkel-Meadow, "Ethics and the Settlement of Mass Torts: When the Rules Meet the Road," *Cornell Law Review* 80 (1995): 1159, 1164; Fleming, *Lawyers, Money, and Success,* 45.

88. See Lester Brickman, "Contingent Fees Without Contingencies: *Hamlet* Without the Prince of Denmark?" *University of California at Los Angeles Law Review* 37 (1989): 29, 49–53; Congress has also debated such proposed disclosure requirements. See "Lawyers Fees Are Subject of Proposed Federal Laws," *ABA/BNA Manual on Professional Conduct* 11 (February 8, 1995): 12.

89. Judith Resnik, Dennis Curtis, and Deborah R. Hensler, "Individuals Within the Aggregate: Relations, Representation, and Fees," *New York University Law Review* 71 (1996): 296, 396; Brickman, "Contingency Fee Abuses," 1349; Lester Brickman, "ABA Regulation of Contingency Fees: Money Talks, Ethics Walks," *Fordham Law Review* 65 (1996): 247, 305–8.

90. Lester Brickman, Michael J. Horowitz, and Jeffrey O'Connell, *Rethinking Contingent Fees* (New York: Manhattan Institute, 1994); Peter Passell, "Contingency Fees in Injury Cases under Attack by Legal Scholars," *New York Times,* February 11, 1994, B1; Lawrence Fox, "Contingent Fees," *ABA Journal,* July 1995, 44; Kritzer, "The Wages of Risk."

91. Robert E. Litan and Steven C. Salop, "Reforming the Lawyer-Client Relationship Through Alternative Billing Methods," *Judicature* 77 (January/February 1994): 191; Richard C. Reed, ed., *Beyond the Billable Hour* (Chicago: ABA, 1989).

92. John A. Beach, "The Rise and Fall of the Billable Hour," *Albany Law Review* 59 (1996): 941, 943; Margaret A. Jacobs, "Problem of Overbilling by Many Large Firms Is Confirmed in Surveys," *Wall Street Journal*, September 18, 1993, B7; Charles Silver and Lynn A. Baker, "Mass Lawsuits and the Aggregate Settlement Rule," *Wake Forest Law Review* 32 (1997): 733, 777.

93. Menkel-Meadow, "Ethics and the Settlement of Mass Torts," 1214–15; Resnik, Curtis, and Hensler, "Representing Individuals Within Aggregates," 396; Coffee, "Corruption," 856.

94. Scott Slavick, "Illinois and the McKay Commission: A Match Made in Heaven?" *Georgetown Journal of Legal Ethics* 11 (1997): 129, 142; Rhode and Luban, *Legal Ethics*, 695; James E. Towery and Linda L. Harrington, "California Fee Arbitration Program," *Professional Lawyer* (February 1997): 18.

95. Lerman, "Blue Chip Bilking," 278–80; Jacobs, "Overbilling," B7; Ross, *The Honest Hour*, 199–219; *Bohatch v. Butler and Binion*, 977 S.W. 2d 543 (Tex. 1998).

96. Lerman, "Blue Chip Bilking," 279, 297–366; Erin White, "More Firms Are Auditing Themselves to Catch Billing Errors," *Wall Street Journal*, July 14, 1998, B5; Joanne Pitulla, "Excessive Fees Bite Back," *ABA Journal*, April 1997, 82; "24th Conference on Professional Responsibility," *ABA/BNA Manual on Professional Conduct* 14 (June 1998), 272.

97. *In re Struthers*, 877 P.2d 789 (Ariz. 1994); Lerman, "Blue Chip Bilking"; Sonia S. Chan, "Double Billing and Padding," *Georgetown Journal of Legal Ethics* 9 (1996): 611, 632; Schratz, "Why Attorneys Overbill," 221. For consumer protection remedies, see Richard B. Schmitt, "Widow's Fight Tests New Way to Sue Lawyers," *Wall Street Journal*, April 21, 1998, B1.

98. Lawrence J. Fox, "Money Didn't Buy Happiness," *Dickenson Law Review* 100 (1996): 531, 539; Lerman, "Blue Chip Bilking," 251.

99. Amitai Etzioni, "What Lawyers Didn't Learn in Kindergarten," *Baltimore Sun*, February 16, 1994, A11.

7. LEGAL EDUCATION

1. For discussion of the issues raised in this chapter, see Deborah L. Rhode, "The Professional Responsibility of Professional Schools," *Journal of Legal Education* 49 (1999): 24; Deborah L. Rhode, "Missing Questions: Feminist Perspectives on Legal Education," *Stanford Law Review* 45 (1993): 1547. See Thomas Jefferson, *Selected Writings*, ed. Merrill P. Peterson (New York: Viking, 1984), 966; Robert Bucking Stevens, *Law School: Legal Education in America from the 1850s to the 1980s* (Chapel Hill: University of North Carolina Press, 1983).

2. William Twining, "Pericles and the Plumber," *Law Quarterly Review* 83 (1967): 396.

3. Thorstein Veblen, *The Higher Learning in America* (New York: Sentry Press, 1918), 211.

4. Stephen P. Klein and Laura Hamilton, *The Validity of the U.S. News and World Report Rankings of ABA Law Schools* (Washington, D.C.: Association of American Law Schools, 1998).

5. Charles B. Colvin, "'Yes, There Are Too Many Lawyers.' Now What Do We Do about It?" *Louisiana Bar Journal* 42 (1994): 246, 247; Robert F. Potts, "Too Many Lawyers, Too Few Jobs," *Chronicle of Higher Education*, February 2, 1996, B1.

6. David Margolick, "The Trouble with American Law Schools," *New York Times Magazine,* May 22, 1983, 21, 39; Alison Schneider, "Law and Finance Professors Are Top Earners in Academe, Survey Finds," *Chronicle of Higher Education,* May 28, 1999, A14.

7. 34 CFR sec. 602.23(b)(5)(1995).

8. Manuel R. Ramos, "Legal Malpractice: No Lawyer or Client Is Safe," *Florida Law Review* 47 (1995): 37; Joanne Marlin and Bryant Garth, "Clinical Education as a Bridge Between Law School and Practice: Mitigating the Misery," *Clinical Law Review* 1 (1994): 443, 448.

9. Alfred Reed, *Training for the Public Profession of Law* (New York: Carnegie Foundation, 1921); W. Scott Van Alstyne Jr., Joseph R. Julin, and Larry D. Barnett, *The Goals and Missions of Law Schools* (New York: Peter Lang, 1990), 43, 84–87, 115–23.

10. Ann Davis, "Graduate Debt Burden Grows," *National Law Journal,* May 22, 1995, A1.

11. Gerald F. Hess, "Seven Principles for Good Practice in Legal Education," *Journal of Legal Education* 49 (1999): 367; Ben Gose, "A New Survey of 'Good Practices' Could Be an Alternative to Rankings," *Chronicle of Higher Education,* October 22, 1999, A63.

12. Richard A. White, Summary from the Directory of Law Teachers, unpublished memoranda, Washington, D.C., Association of American Law Schools, 1998; ABA Commission on Women in the Profession, *Elusive Equality: The Experiences of Women in Legal Education* (Chicago: ABA, 1996); Linda F. Wightman, Law School Admission Council Research Report series, *Women in Legal Education: A Comparison of the Law School Performance and Law School Experience of Women and Men* (Newtown, Pa.: Law School Admission Council, 1996), 25, 36, 72–74; Deborah L. Rhode, "Whistling Vivaldi: Legal Education and the Politics of Progress," *New York University Review of Law and Social Change* 23 (1997): 217; Law School Outreach Project of the Chicago Bar Association Alliance for Women, *Women Students' Experience of Gender Bias in Chicago Area Law Schools* (Chicago: Chicago Bar Association, 1995), 24; Lani Guinier, *Becoming Gentlemen: Women, Law School, and Institutional Change* (Cambridge: Harvard University Press, 1997), 28–29, 51–62.

13. ABA Commission on Minorities in the Profession, *Miles to Go: Progress of Minorities in the Legal Profession* (Chicago: ABA, 1998), 16, 17; *Hopwood v. Texas,* 78 F.3d 932 (5th Cir.1996), cert. den., 518 U.S. 1033 (1996).

14. *Regents of the University of California v. Bakke,* 438 U.S. 312 (1978).

15. "On the Importance of Diversity in Higher Education," statement by sixty-seven higher education organizations, included in the Americus Curaie Brief of the Association of American Law Schools et al., in *Grutter v. Bollinger* (E.D. Mich. 1999); Association of American Colleges and Universities, *Diversity Works: The Emerging Picture of How Students Benefit* (Washington, D.C.: AACU, 1997); Expert Report of Patricia Gurin in *Graetz v. Bollinger,* and *Grutter v. Bollinger;* Maureen T. Hallinen, "Diversity Effects on Students: Social Science Evidence," *Ohio State Law Journal* 59 (1998): 733, 746–50; William G. Bowen and Derek Bok, *The Shape of the River* (Princeton: Princeton University Press, 1998), 218–55; Gary Orfield and Dean Whitla, *Diversity and Legal Education: Student Experiences in Leading Law Schools* (Cambridge: Harvard University Civil Rights Project, 1999), 14–16; Association of American Law Schools, *Statement on Diversity* (Washington, D.C.: AALS, 1998).

16. Linda F. Wightman, *Women in Legal Education,* 25–74; Linda Wightman, "The Threat to Diversity in Legal Education: An Empirical Analysis of the Consequences of Abandoning

Race as a Factor in Law School Admission Decision," *New York University Law Review* 72 (1997): 1; Kacy Collons Keys, "Privileged Classes," *Recorder,* May 28, 1997, 4; ABA Commission on Minorities, *Miles to Go,*18; Lani Guinier, "Lessons and Challenges of Becoming Gentlemen," *New York Review of Law and Social Change* 24 (1998): 1, 12; David Chambers, Richard O. Lempert, and Terry K. Adams, "Doing Well and Doing Good: The Careers of Minority and White Graduates of the University of Michigan Law School, 1970–1996," *Law Quadrangle Notes* 42 (1999): 60.

17. Law School Admission Council, *New Models to Assure Diversity, Fairness, and Appropriate Test Use in Law School Admissions* (Newtown, Pa.: Law School Admission Council, 1999).

18. Deborah J. Merritt and Barbara Reskin, "The Double Minority: Empirical Evidence of a Double Standard in Law School Hiring of Minority Women," *Southern California Law Review* 65 (1992): 2299. See also Richard White, *Preliminary Report: The Promotion, Retention, and Tenuring of New Law School Faculty Hired in 1990 and 1991* (Washington, D.C.: Association of American Law Schools, 1999) (finding disparities in promotion without attempting to control for all variables).

19. Law School Outreach Project, "Women Students," vii, 27, 35, 56; Guinier, *Becoming Gentlemen,* 56, 28–29, 68; Rhode, "Whistling Vivaldi," 220; Lorraine Dusky, *Still Unequal: The Shameful Truth about Women and Justice in America* (New York: Crown, 1996), 28, 39; Scot N. Ihrig, "Sexual Orientation in Law School: Experiences of Gay, Lesbian, and Bisexual Law Students," *Law and Inequality* 14 (1996): 555, 568; Janice L. Austin et al., "Results from a Survey of Lesbian, Gay, and Bisexual Student Attitudes about Law School," *Journal of Legal Education* 48 (1998): 157, 166.

20. Law School Outreach Project, "Women Students," 27.

21. Guinier, *Becoming Gentlemen,* 28–29; Elizabeth Mertz with Wamucii Njogu and Susan Gooding, "What Difference Does Difference Make? The Challenge for Legal Education," *Journal of Legal Education* 48 (1998): 1, 6–7, 27; Rhode, "Whistling Vivaldi," 223.

22. ABA Commission on Women in the Profession, *Don't Just Hear It Through the Grapevine: Studying Gender Questions at Your Law School* (Chicago: ABA, 1998).

23. Fred Rodell, "Good-bye to Law Reviews," *Virginia Law Review* 23 (1936): 38; Steven I. Friedland, "How We Teach: A Survey of Teaching Techniques in American Law Schools," *Seattle University Law Review* 20 (1996): 1.

24. Grant Gilmore, "What Is a Law School?" *Connecticut Law Review* 15 (1982): 1; Hess, "Seven Principles," 367–69; Lawrence S. Krieger, "What We're Not Telling Law Students— and Lawyers," *Journal of Law and Health* 13 (1999): 1, 2–11.

25. Ann L. Iijima, "Lessons Learned: Legal Education and Law Student Dysfunction," *Journal of Legal Education* 48 (1998): 524; Deborah L. Rhode and David Luban, *Legal Ethics* (Westbury, N.Y.: Foundation Press, 1995), 910; Krieger, "What We're Not Telling Law Students," 29–32.

26. ABA Section on Legal Education and Admission to the Bar, *Legal Education and Professional Development—An Educational Continuum* (Chicago: ABA, 1992); Paul Brest, "The Responsibility of Law Schools: Educating Lawyers as Counselors and Problem Solvers," *Law and Contemporary Problems* 58 (1995): 5; Cameron Stracher, *Double Billing* (New York: William Morrow, 1998), 50; Lawrence M. Friedman, quoted in Paul Wice, *Judges and Lawyers: The Human Side of Justice* (New York: HarperCollins, 1991).

27. Gerald P. Lopez, "Training Future Lawyers to Work with the Politically and Socially Subordinated: Anti-Generic Legal Education," *West Virginia Law Review* 91 (1988–89): 305, 321–22.

28. Aric Press, "We're All Connected," *American Lawyer*, November 1998, 5; Arthur Austin, "Womanly Approach Harms Future Lawyers," *National Law Journal*, May 11, 1998, A23.

29. See Rhode and Luban, *Legal Ethics*, 928–29; Gary Trudeau, *Doonsbury*, reprinted in Thomas D. Morgan and Ronald D. Rotunda, *Problems and Materials on Professional Responsibility* (Westbury, N.Y.: Foundation Press, 1995), 1.

30. Daniel S. Kleinberger, "Ethics and Conscience–A Rejoinder," *Connecticut Law Review* 21 (1989): 297, 401n. 23.

31. William Reese Smith Jr., "Teaching and Learning Professionalism," *Wake Forest Law Review* 32 (1997): 617; William Simon, "The Trouble with Legal Ethics," *Journal of Legal Education* 41 (1991): 65, 66; ABA, Young Lawyers Division, *Career Satisfaction* (Chicago: ABA, 1995), 11.

32. Ruth Bader Ginsburg, "Supreme Court Pronouncements on the Conduct of Lawyers," *Journal of the Institute for Study of Legal Ethics* 1 (1996): 1; Deborah L. Rhode, "Into the Valley of Ethics: Professional Responsibility and Educational Reform," *Law and Contemporary Problems* 58 (1995): 139.

33. Deborah L. Rhode, *Professional Responsibility: Ethics by the Pervasive Method* (Boston: Aspen, 1998); Deborah L. Rhode, "Annotated Bibliography of Educational Materials on Legal Ethics," *Georgetown Journal of Legal Ethics* 11 (1998): 1029; Eric Schnapper, "The Myth of Legal Ethics," *ABA Journal*, February 1978, 202, 205. For research on moral conduct and influences such as authority, stress, competition, peer pressure, financial incentives, and time constraints, see Rhode, "Into the Valley of Ethics," 148–49.

34. Peter Caw, "On the Teaching of Ethics in a Pluralist Society," *Hastings Center Report*, October 1978, 32. See research summarized in Rhode, "Valley of Ethics," 148; James R. Rest, "Can Ethics Be Taught in Professional Schools? The Psychological Research," *Ethics: Easier Said than Done*, winter 1988, 22, 23–24; Albert Bandura, "Social Cognitive Theory of Moral Thought and Action," in *Handbook of Moral Behavior and Development*, ed. William M. Kurtines and Jacob L. Gewirtz (Hillsdale, N.J.: Lawrence Erlbaum, 1991), 45, 53.

35. For attorneys' views, see Frances Kahn Zemans and Victor G. Rosenblum, *The Making of a Public Profession* (Chicago: ABA, 1981), 176–77.

36. ABA, Section of Legal Education and Admission to the Bar, Standards for Approval of Law Schools and Interpretation, Standards 302(e), August 1996, at 31; William B. Powers, *Report on Law School Pro Bono Activities* 75 (Chicago: ABA, 1994): 2–5; Association of American Law Schools (AALS) Commission on Pro Bono and Public Service Opportunities in Law Schools, *Learning to Serve: A Summary of the Findings and Recommendations of the AALS Commission on Pro Bono and Public Service Opportunities* (Washington, D.C.: AALS, 1999), 4; AALS Commission, focus group interviews, June 1998; Deborah L. Rhode, "Cultures of Commitment: Pro Bono for Lawyers and Law Students," *Fordham Law Review* 67 (1999): 2415.

37. AALS Commission, *Learning to Serve*.

38. John Kramer, quoted in "Mandatory Pro Bono at Tulane Law School," National Association for Public Interest Law, *Connection Closeup Newsletter*, September 30, 1991,

1–2; Committee on Legal Assistance, "Mandatory Law School Pro Bono Programs: Preparing Students to Meet Their Ethical Obligations," *Record* 50 (1995): 170, 176; Rhode, "Cultures of Commitment," 2434; Virginia A. Hodgkinson et al., *Giving and Volunteering in the United States: Findings from a National Survey* (Washington, D.C.: Independent Sector, 1996), 12–13, 87–88.

39. AALS Commission, Focus Group Interviews; Mark S. Sobus, "Mandating Community Service: Psychological Implications of Requiring Community Service," *Law and Psychology Review* 19 (1999): 153, 164, 170.

40. AALS Commission, *Learning to Serve;* Rhode, "Cultures of Commitment," 2429.

41. Stewart Macaulay, "Law School and the World Outside the Doors II: Some Notes on Two Studies of the Chicago Bar," *Journal of Legal Education* 32 (1982): 506, 524; Robert Granfield, *Making Elite Lawyers: Visions of Law at Harvard and Beyond* (New York: Routledge, 1992), 72–93; Rhode and Luban, *Legal Ethics,* 906–8.

INDEX